"Judith Chernaik is one of the [...] of Shelley I have ever come across. . . . Her book is original and mature; she writes serenely and confidently without any of the polemicism that marks so much of the writing about Shelley" — Frederick A. Pottle.

This reading of Shelley's shorter lyrics moves in roughly chronological order from the major philosophical lyrics written in the summer of 1816, "Hymn to Intellectual Beauty" and "Mont Blanc," to the love poems to Jane Williams written during the months before Shelley's death in July, 1822.

The texts, newly edited from manuscript sources, correct long-established errors in some of Shelley's most famous poems; notes to the poems present many draft readings previously unpublished.

Mrs. Chernaik examines in succession Shelley's literary self-portraits and his conception of poetry; his attempts in meditative poems like "Lines Written Among the Euganean Hills" to relate nature, thought, and power to one another, and to human suffering; his use of poetry as political prophecy and as an instrument of revolution in "Ode to the West Wind" and "Ode to Liberty"; his creation of a new mythology in nature poems like "To a Skylark" and "The Cloud"; and his analysis of love and desire in the famous short lyrics written for Jane Williams.

In her discussion of the qualities of individual lyrics, Mrs. Chernaik has constantly in view the major Shelleyan themes: recognition of the necessity both to strive for social and political change and to affirm the very possibility of such change, and celebration of the regenerative power of love and the human imagination. She analyzes

Continued on back flap

The Lyrics of
SHELLEY

JUDITH CHERNAIK

THE PRESS OF
CASE WESTERN RESERVE UNIVERSITY
CLEVELAND & LONDON
1972

For My Parents

CONTENTS

APPENDIXES

LIST OF ILLUSTRATIONS

ACKNOWLEDGMENTS

To a large degree this book was made possible by a two-year scholarship from the Radcliffe Institute, held from 1966 to 1968. I should like to register my gratitude for the many kindnesses of the late Dean, Constance E. Smith, whose support was instrumental to all those who were associated with the Institute. I should also like to thank the American Council of Learned Societies for a summer grant-in-aid for research in England; the Carl and Lily Pforzheimer Foundation for a grant for study in Italy; and the American Philosophical Society for a grant from the Johnson Fund in support of further study of the Bodleian Shelley collection.

My greatest personal debt is to Frederick A. Pottle, whose encouragement and scrupulous counsel have been extended during all stages of this study from its inception as a doctoral thesis presented to the Yale Graduate School. I am grateful to Stuart Curran for his careful and sympathetic reading of the completed manuscript. Donald H. Reiman read the textual portion and provided invaluable advice on textual problems and procedures, as well as on the location of Shelley holographs. Geoffrey M. Matthews generously shared with me his wide knowledge of Shelley materials; I must thank him in particular for directing me to the holograph of "The Indian Girl's Song," better known as "The Indian Serenade." For advice on grammatical points I thank Eugene Green; for help in deciphering the Italian holograph of "Ode to Liberty," I am indebted to Kristen Murtaugh. I must thank as well Barbara Miranda for typing a difficult text.

Manuscripts are quoted by permission of the Bodleian Library; the British Museum; the Glasgow University Library; the Harvard

College Library; the Huntington Library, San Marino, California; the Pierpont Morgan Library; the University Library, Cambridge; the University Library, King's College, Aberdeen; and the University of Manchester Library. I am particularly grateful to the Bodleian Library, the Harvard College Library, and the Huntington Library for supplying complete microfilms of their extensive Shelley holdings; and to W. H. Bond, Librarian of the Houghton Library, Harvard University, and Rodney G. Dennis, Curator of Manuscripts, for advice and encouragement.

Portions of this book appeared in an earlier form in the following publications, and are reprinted by permission of their respective editors: "The Figure of the Poet in Shelley," *ELH, A Journal of English Literary History,* 35 (1968), 566–90, Copyright The Johns Hopkins Press; "Shelley's 'To Constantia,' A Contemporary Printing Examined," *Times Literary Supplement* (1969), 140; "Textual Emendations for Three Poems by Shelley," *Keats-Shelley Journal,* 19 (1970), 41–48. The Macmillan Company, New York, kindly granted permission to quote from "The Second Coming" and "A Prayer for my Daughter" from *Collected Poems,* by William Butler Yeats (Copyright 1924 by The Macmillan Company, renewed 1952 by Bertha Georgie Yeats). Extracts from *The Letters of Percy Bysshe Shelley,* ed. Frederick L. Jones, are quoted by permission of the Clarendon Press, Oxford; Shelley's poems are quoted from *The Complete Poetical Works,* ed. Thomas Hutchinson, by permission of Oxford University Press.

I must acknowledge, finally, a peculiar debt for a scholarly enterprise—to my children, Laura, David, and Sara, who sorted, clipped, and filed, and became Shelleyans despite themselves. My husband, Warren, my severest and best critic, has read the manuscript in more stages than I care to remember; without his advice and forbearance, I could not have completed it.

NOTE ON THE TEXT

TWENTY-SIX OF THE LYRICS discussed in the following pages are newly edited from the holographs, first printings, and early editions of Shelley's poems. The critical apparatus identifies textual sources, lists significant variants and canceled readings, and offers justification for editorial decisions. The texts of the nine poems published during Shelley's lifetime correct misprints and transcriber's errors in the first printings, and include in textual notes several holograph readings hitherto unprinted (including the complete drafts of "Hymn to Intellectual Beauty" and "Mont Blanc"); the seventeen posthumously printed poems are edited directly from Shelley's holographs. I have tried in editing the poems to take into account all variables: the degree of control Shelley might have exercised over first or later printings; the probable relation of surviving holographs to printed texts and to Mary Shelley's transcripts; Shelley's habits of composition as they can be traced in the holographs. But the more closely one studies the variables, the more one's confidence tends to erode, and I offer these texts in a spirit of humility, with an acute sense of the difficulties borne by past editors, Mary Shelley in particular.

Shelley's nineteenth and early twentieth-century editors were compelled by circumstance and by their own editorial principles to rely primarily on the first editions of Shelley's poems, supplemented by Mary Shelley's editions of the collected *Poetical Works* (1839 and 1840), and in some cases by reference to holographs, usually reported at second hand. But most of the manuscript drafts and copies of Shelley's poems, carefully collected and preserved by Mary after his death, have been available to scholars at least since 1946, the largest number in the collection of notebooks presented to the Bodleian Library, over a period of sixty years, by Shelley's descendants. Some manuscript materials, including most printer's copy and proof sheets, must have been destroyed; some may yet turn up in private hands. But for most of Shelley's poems some holograph evidence survives—a first draft, partial or complete, or a fair copy. For some poems ("Stanzas written in Dejection," "Ode to Naples," "The Indian Girl's Song"), there survive a first draft and two or more fair copies. In view of the questions that must be attached to printed texts of many of Shelley's poems, these holographs assume major significance.

Of the lyrics presented here, three ("Hymn to Intellectual Beauty," "To Constantia," "Ode to Naples") were published first in contemporary periodicals. "Mont Blanc" was published with *History of a Six Weeks' Tour* (1817). Five of the most celebrated lyrics ("Ode to the West Wind," "The Cloud," "To a Sky-Lark," "Ode to Liberty," "Ode to Heaven") were published with *Prometheus Unbound* (1820). The remainder were published posthumously, in periodicals and in Mary Shelley's editions of *Posthumous Poems* (1824) and *Poetical Works* (1839 and 1840). These several forms of publication illustrate the range of editorial problems presented by the printed texts of Shelley's poems.

We can be fairly certain that Shelley sent the texts of "Hymn to Intellectual Beauty" and "To Constantia" directly to the editors of the *Examiner,* in one case, and the *Oxford Herald,* in the other; printer's copy has not survived, but presumably if the poems were not written out by Shelley, they were at least corrected or approved by him. It is unlikely that he had the opportunity to revise proof, however. Indeed, a clipping of the *Examiner* "Hymn to Intellectual Beauty" in one of Shelley's notebooks bears three autograph insertions, one correcting a probable compositor's error ("birds" for "buds"), the other restoring the original version of a phrase perhaps changed at the editor's request ("the name of God & ghosts" replaces "the names of Demon, Ghost"). "Hymn to Intellectual Beauty" was reprinted in *Rosalind and Helen* (1819), when Shelley was living in Italy, but the text supplied was from the *Examiner,* and did not include Shelley's corrections; indeed, additional editorial changes were made, clearly without Shelley's authorization. The

Oxford Herald "To Constantia," which was unknown to Mary Shelley and subsequent editors, appears to be a very good text, but it is likely that Claire Clairmont wrote out at least part of the printer's copy for Shelley, and it is certainly possible that some accidentals which differ from those in Shelley's fair copy were provided by transcriber or compositor. As for the printed text of "Ode to Naples" in the *Military Register,* Shelley was evidently unaware of its publication, though he may well have written out or corrected the copy given to the newspaper. But the text is an earlier version than that of the extant holographic fair copies and includes several readings later changed by Shelley.

I have collated the printed texts of these poems, then, with the holographs: for "Hymn to Intellectual Beauty," a draft of six of the seven stanzas, and the autograph corrections to the *Examiner* clipping; for "To Constantia," a complete draft and an imperfect fair copy; for "Ode to Naples," a partial draft and two fair copies. The "Ode to Naples" has also been collated with the text printed in *Posthumous Poems* (1824). My emendations in "Hymn to Intellectual Beauty" have been limited to Shelley's autograph corrections and in "To Constantia" to accidentals confirmed by both draft and fair copy; but the text of "Ode to Naples" has been drawn from the two holographs, rather than either printed text, on the ground that the holographs appear to represent Shelley's final revisions.

Unlike the poems published first in periodicals, the first edition of "Mont Blanc" appears to be authoritative, since Shelley directly supervised its printing and undoubtedly read proofs. But the poems printed with *Prometheus Unbound* are more obviously susceptible to textual corruption, first because transcription was entrusted to Mary ("Mrs. Shelley is now transcribing for me the little poems to be printed at the end of *Prometheus*"—Shelley to Ollier, May 14, 1820, in *Letters of P.B.S.,* II, 197), and second because Shelley was unable to persuade Ollier to send proofs of the volume to Italy, and revision (that is, correction of proof) had to be left to Peacock. Peacock himself, according to H. B. Forman, spoke of removing Shelley's "frequent dashes" when revising for the press (*The Shelley Library: An Essay in Bibliography,* London, 1886, p. 88); and an examination of the texts in *Prometheus Unbound* and in *Rosalind and Helen,* which Peacock also revised in Shelley's absence, suggests a consistent regularization of Shelley's text, in which capitals and dashes are removed and, in some cases, forms altered ("are" for "art," "among" for "amongst" in "Hymn to Intellectual Beauty"). We know that Shelley was dissatisfied with the text of *Prometheus* as printed; he sent Ollier an errata sheet, a "formidable list" (*Letters of P.B.S.*, II, 257), which probably served as the basis for the dozen or so corrections made in a presentation copy to Leigh Hunt (Huntington Library cat. no. 22460) and for the errata sent by Mary Shelley to Cyrus Redding for use in *The Poetical Works of Coleridge, Shelley, and Keats* (1829) (*Letters of M.W.S.*, II, 10). These corrections were adopted in *Poetical Works* (1839), where Mary's "Note to Prometheus Unbound" mentions that the verbal alterations were made "from a list of errata written by Shelley himself;" later editors have followed some but not all of her corrections. Of the poems presented here, "The Cloud" and "Ode to Liberty" include corrections made presumably from Shelley's errata list; and comparison of the printed texts with the holographs of both these poems suggests additional errors. It is likely that some discrepancies between printed texts and holographs were caused by transcription errors, which Shelley may have missed in overlooking the transcripts; others may have been his own corrections; still others, including the substantial changes in punctuation and capitalization, are probably attributable to Peacock's revision. Since three of the *1820* poems exist in holograph fair copies, evidently the source of Mary's transcripts, I have in these cases used the holographs as copy text, adapting missing punctuation from *1820*. For the poems for which only imperfect drafts survive, I have perforce used *1820* as copy text, emending from the holograph drafts only where the printed text is demonstrably faulty or inconsistent and could have been composed by a hand other than Shelley's (i.e. transcriber or compositor). Variants are recorded in the notes, in all cases.

For the poems printed posthumously, holographs must take precedence over printed texts. Some of the poems edited in the following pages were transcribed by Mary Shelley from drafts in Shelley's notebooks, and subsequently edited for publication in *Posthumous Poems* (1824) and *Poetical Works* (1839). These poems —"The Two Spirits," "My dearest M. wherefore hast thou gone," "When passion's trance is overpast," "Song of Apollo" and "Song of

Pan"—have all been edited directly from the holographs. Numerous
textual corrections have been made (in particular, for "Song of
Apollo" and "Song of Pan," and "The Two Spirits"), and an additional line deciphered for "My dearest M." A number of the posthumously printed poems were written out for printing or presented
to friends during Shelley's lifetime, and survive in one or more fair
copies and drafts. The printed texts of these poems, in turn, include
numerous changes, the result of careless transcription (as in Mary's
two transcripts and all printed versions of the second line of "The
Indian Girl's Song"); or of editorial emendation. I have edited these
poems from the holographs, choosing as copy text the version that
appears to represent Shelley's final intentions, and recording all holograph variants and deletions.

My assumption in editing these poems is that Shelley intended his
poems to be published with conventional punctuation and orthography, given the rather generous options of contemporary printers.
His own preferences are suggested by printed texts of the poems he
supervised through the press, like *Laon and Cythna* and *Adonais,*
and by holograph fair copies. There is some variation in the punctuation of the fair copies, however, and even the most conservative of
Shelley's editors have concluded either that Shelley was careless
about punctuation or that he customarily left pointing to the printer.
There is evidence that some punctuation was originally left to the
printer, at least for certain texts; for instance, Mary Shelley's transcript of part of "Lines written among the Euganean Hills," originally among the Ollier papers and presumably the direct source of
the text printed in *Rosalind and Helen* (1819), omits some pointing
at the ends of lines. But there are other texts that Shelley punctuated
with great care (notably the "Julian and Maddalo" holograph in the
Pierpont Morgan Library, originally among Leigh Hunt's papers,
and the Trelawny manuscripts of the poems to Jane Williams—
though these were intended as gifts rather than printer's copy).
Shelley's comment on the text of *Epipsychidion* sent to Ollier ("I
have written it so as to give very little trouble, I hope, to the printer,
or to the person who revises"—*Letters of P.B.S.,* II, 263) suggests
that he feared the obvious dangers entailed by leaving pointing to
others. Indeed, the best argument against either normalization or
modernization of punctuation is the history of texts thus emended

by successive editors and the resulting changes in sense—for instance, in "Stanzas written in Dejection," lines 8 and 42, and
"The Magnetic Lady to her Patient," lines 20, 22, and 44. I have
therefore followed Shelley's holograph punctuation and the punctuation of printed texts he supervised, even when modern usage has reversed nineteenth-century practice (as in Shelley's occasional use of
the comma to separate compound subject and verb). I have, however, added pointing to the ends of lines, where Shelley often allows
the break itself to signify a pause; and have in a very few cases
emended punctuation where both modern and nineteenth-century
conventions require it. Where it has been necessary to supply more
than minimal additional punctuation, as for poems edited from first
drafts, I have been guided by holograph hints and by rules of intel-
ligibility, and occasionally by Mary Shelley's precedent. I have used
the following guidelines for textual annotation of punctuation.
When a printed text is used as copy text, all emendations are individually noted. When a holograph is used as copy text, all instances in
which a holograph mark of punctuation is removed or altered are
individually noted, as are all additions that involve a possible ambiguity or change of meaning. I have, however, silently added pointing at the ends of lines, and commas between series; the extent of
silent emendation of this kind is indicated in the headnote to each
text. Punctuation variants for texts collated with the copy text are
not noted unless a change of meaning is involved.

In matters of orthography, a better case can probably be made
for modernization, since the danger is not usually a change of
meaning but at most a possible loss of poetic suggestiveness. But it
seems to me that the barriers interposed by older forms are negligible
when compared to the loss incurred by consistent modernization.
Unlike Keats, Shelley usually conforms in his spelling to contemporary usage; where there is a choice of forms, he tends to be conservative, preferring the spelling of Milton and Spenser to the forms that
were replacing them in late eighteenth and early nineteenth-century
usage. On the assumption that Shelley intended his printed texts to
conform to contemporary standards, I have emended his holograph
thier to *their*, *it's* to *its*, *to morrow* to *tomorrow*, *oer* to *o'er* (nor are
these changes noted among the variants). But I have retained holo-
graph spelling which has or had at the time an archaic or poetic fla-

vor or which affects pronunciation, and which is retained in the printed texts Shelley saw through the press: for instance, *thro',* *extacy, chrystal, foizon, shewn, aery, sate.* I have usually followed Shelley's holograph spelling of these words when a holograph and printed text he did not supervise are in conflict. Similarly, Shelley's capitalization, often lowercased by contemporary and modern editors, is retained in the printed texts he supervised, and I have therefore followed the capitalization of the holographs. I have written out all ampersands in the texts, but retain them in the textual notes, which transcribe the holographs literally.

My aim in the textual notes is to recover from the holographs what Shelley wrote. With some exceptions, I do not record variants from Mary Shelley's transcripts unless these seem likely to have independent authority (that is, from a holograph now lost, or from verbal instructions), nor do I provide historical collation, which can be found, more or less accurately, in Hutchinson or *Works.* I have tried to provide full collation of verbal variants from the primary sources; and I include all canceled readings of interest where I can decipher them. I have not tried to approximate the actual appearance of a manuscript, however, or to register every stage in composition—for example, when a revised draft agrees with the final text, only the deleted or first reading is noted. When I cannot decipher a word or line, I do not usually record the fact, though a few conjectural readings are given. A number of holograph readings will be found in the editions and textual studies listed in the Bibliography; editions of particular interest are cited in the notes to individual texts.

SHORT TITLES

Hutchinson

The Complete Poetical Works of Percy Bysshe Shelley, ed. Thomas Hutchinson. London: Oxford University Press, 1934.

Journals of Claire Clairmont

The Journals of Claire Clairmont, ed. Marion Kingston Stocking. Cambridge, Mass.: Harvard University Press, 1968.

Letters of M.W.S.

The Letters of Mary W. Shelley, ed. Frederick L. Jones. 2 vols. Norman: University of Oklahoma Press, 1944.

Letters of P.B.S.

The Letters of Percy Bysshe Shelley, ed. Frederick L. Jones. 2 vols. Oxford: Clarendon Press, 1964.

Mary Shelley's Journal

Mary Shelley's Journal, ed. Frederick L. Jones. Norman: University of Oklahoma Press, 1947.

White

White, Newman Ivey. *Shelley.* 2 vols. New York: Alfred A. Knopf, 1940.

Works

The Complete Works of Percy Bysshe Shelley, ed. Roger Ingpen and Walter E. Peck. 10 vols. London: Ernest Benn, 1926–30 (Julian Edition).

First editions of Shelley's poems, listed in full in the Bibliography, are cited by short title and date. With the exceptions of "Lines written among the Euganean Hills," *Laon and Cythna,* and the poems edited herein, Shelley's poems are quoted from Hutchinson; occasionally I have silently emended Hutchinson's text from the first editions. "Lines written among the Euganean Hills" is quoted from the first edition in *Rosalind and Helen* (1819). *Laon and Cythna* is quoted from *Works,* which follows the first printing, and includes notes on the alterations Shelley made, at his publisher's request, for *The Revolt of Islam.* Shelley's prose, with the exception of his letters, is quoted from *Works.* Unless otherwise noted, English poets are quoted from the Oxford Standard Authors editions; Greek and Latin writers from the editions of the Loeb Classical Library, Harvard University Press; the Bible from the Authorized (King James) Version.

~Commentary~

INTRODUCTION

THESE PAGES offer a reading of Shelley's shorter lyrics, newly edited from manuscript sources, proceeding in chronological order from the major philosophical lyrics written in the summer of 1816, "Hymn to Intellectual Beauty" and "Mont Blanc," to the love poems to Jane Williams written during the months before Shelley's death in July, 1822. "Lyrics" I define simply as poems written in the first person, as opposed to dramatic or epic works. Shelley's lyrics, despite his originality and his tendency to break away from conventional patterns, mainly have their origins in the familiar lyric categories of ode, elegy and sonnet, song, epistle, and meditation, and this is the range of lyrics included. By limiting intensive discussion to the shorter lyrics I necessarily exclude major poems like *Adonais* and *Epipsychidion,* as well as *Alastor* and "The Triumph of Life," which have been considered at length in the critical studies of Shelley's poetry. Other fine and singular poems, usually neglected by critics, like "Letter to Maria Gisborne" and "Julian and Maddalo," have been omitted in the attempt to give the readings thematic unity. My aim has been to trace in Shelley's least fictive, most personal poetry, his distinctive artistic signature and the character of his vision of human life.

While Wordsworth, Coleridge, and Keats have gained in stature from the modern revaluation of Romantic poetry, Shelley's position remains uncertain. Recent criticism has explored the mythopoeic power of Shelley's imagination and its philosophical complexity; I have tried to stress the political and human center of his poetry. The true character of Shelley's poetry was never obscure. He wrote in "A Defence of Poetry" that "poets are the unacknowledged legislators of the world" (Para. 48), and he tried in his own poetry to dramatize the "else unfelt oppressions of this earth" ("Julian and

Maddalo," 450) in such a way as to hasten their end. His poetry is centrally political, as Milton's poetry is political and Shakespeare's is not; it is dominated by Shelley's sense of his mission, and the mission of poetry: to awaken a sleeping earth.

Modern hostility to Shelley's doctrine rests upon a false notion of his millennial optimism, his apparent conviction that the spring of human happiness is destined to follow close upon winter. There is no question that Shelley was moved directly by the political crises of his time, especially in *Prometheus Unbound* and the poems published with it—those "dead thoughts" which were to be driven abroad, like withered leaves, to quicken a new birth. The poems that accompany the drama, "Ode to the West Wind," "Ode to Liberty," "An Ode written October, 1819,"[1] like the drama itself, prophesy a new world to follow upon the revolutionary overthrow of existing tyrannies. They assert faith in the possibility of the better human impulses conquering the worse; they celebrate the power of human love and wisdom and resistance. In these poems Christian and classical myths of good triumphing through suffering over evil are assimilated to a rational, secular faith. The role of intercessor is shifted to the human heart, of divine wisdom to the human mind; for the all-creative word, human liberty is substituted; for the arch-enemy Satan, life itself. And it is in this last displacement that the complexities lie. The analysis of modern life with which the Furies torment Prometheus is as acute today as it was 150 years ago.

> The good want power, but to weep barren tears.
> The powerful goodness want: worse need for them.
> The wise want love; and those who love want wisdom;
> And all best things are thus confused to ill.
>   (*Prometheus Unbound,* I, 625–28)

Like any perceptive student of history, Shelley was aware that liberty was unlikely to triumph or love to enfold the world. His political education tended to confirm his latent skepticism and to dampen the passionate idealism of his first essays at liberation, public and private. His early hatred of church and state was theoretical; through bitter experience he came to understand the strength of social institutions and the roots of their power in human nature. He celebrated the regenerative power of love in his poetry, but he had no illusions about the inevitability or even the likelihood of positive change. He did recognize as a binding ethical imperative the need to work for the good and to affirm its possibility.

Nor did he accept religious consolation for the existence of evil. Browning was certain that Shelley, had he lived, would have moved toward Christianity, and that acceptance of the divinity of Christ and the regeneration of life was implicit in his symbolism. But Shelley's use of terms consistent with religious faith, especially in his last poems, was the product of a loss of interest in theology, not a turning toward it. The apprehensions of divinity which he felt in the world, his sense of "That Beauty in which all things work and move" (*Adonais,* 479), had their origin and end in the human imagination. It is as misleading to insist that Shelley was an embryonic Christian as it is to see in him a believing Platonist. He did not feel the contradictory allegiances that drove Coleridge and Wordsworth to affirm the Christian truths of revelation as against the hypotheses of myth, or the intuitions of the imagination; to Shelley all myths, like art itself, were symbolic ways of understanding and structuring reality.

Shelley's assumptions about the nature of reality should be understood in terms of the epistemological puzzle he explores in "Mont Blanc." In that first major attempt to relate nature, thought, and power one to another and to human suffering, he locates the source of knowledge in sense perception but escapes the deterministic implications of Lockean psychology by making perception active as well as passive, free and self-generating as well as responsive to stimuli. Thus he recovers in perception itself the outlawed intuition, that faculty of vision which bypasses the senses and has access to nonperceptible truth, and which is capable of receiving revelations, of prophecy. His motive is the desire to salvage from discredited orthodoxies, both scientific and religious, those values, images, and myths which answer common human need. His poetry can be read as an attempt to discover new authority in human powers for the divinity of the world and the immortality of the soul. The divine afflatus formerly guaranteed by Scriptural revelation is located in human psychology, and the forms of the created world are discovered in language, especially poetry. The obvious danger of this characteristic Romantic compromise is its circularity, which the old myths, being exclusive and dogmatic, manage to avoid; its great attraction is its openness, its ethical bias, and its conformity both to common experience and to the imaginative life.

The most meaningful recent criticism of the Romantic poets is autobiographical, as perhaps all major criticism is; its insights arise out of the despair of our times, intellectual, moral, political. Shelley's poetry is not a healing or restorative poetry, like Wordsworth's; it is an extremely intelligent poetry, and that intelligence may yet be useful to us. Ideas die slowly, and we are still suffering not only from Victorian myths of progress but from the conservative reaction to their failure, embodied in literature in the poetry and criticism of T. S. Eliot. Shelley renounced the security of Christian faith but substituted a humanistic faith that the creative imagination is commensurate to the world of experience, even when the full dimensions of evil, human and natural, are understood. He did not abandon that early faith, in spite of a gradual erosion of confidence in the power of men to change their circumstances. In our very different times, when optimism seems to be allowed only to the very young or the very old, we can still recognize our options in Shelley's analysis of the powers of will and imagination.

If we are to recover what the Romantic poet has to say to our age, we must return to the idea of poetry as comprehensive in scope, proposing a whole view of life, of society as well as the self, political and philosophical as well as psychological. The Romantic poets took private experience, individual consciousness, to be the proper subject for literature, and insisted upon its primacy as a test not only of knowledge but of wisdom and moral truth. In their judgment they were not abandoning the poet's commitment to a social vision but rather enlarging and deepening it, giving it new vitality and new authority. Shelley explicitly disclaimed didactic purpose in his most purposeful poems, *Laon and Cythna* and *Prometheus Unbound;* the lyrics are surely not intended to preach. But he defined didacticism in a narrow sense as the use of poetry to effect change directly. In a wider sense, his poetry is didactic, as all major poetry is when it attempts to interpret human experience and to assign value to life. I hope in the following discussions to trace the progress of that attempt.

NOTES

1. Entitled in *Prometheus Unbound* (1820) "An Ode [written October, 1819, before the Spaniards had recovered their liberty]." The poem is about the Peterloo massacre; the title may have been altered for political reasons. The draft of the poem is untitled (Bodleian MS Shelley adds. e. 12, pp. 130–32). Mary Shelley retitled it, in *Poetical Works* (1839), "An Ode to the Assertors of Liberty."

CHAPTER ONE

THE FIGURE OF THE POET

As SHELLEY describes the nature and function of poetry in "A Defence of Poetry" and the prefaces to his major poems, its motive is "to comprehend the meaning of the visible and invisible world;" its formulations mediate between "beautiful idealisms of moral excellence"—beauty, love, freedom, justice—and the real experience of world, life, and time. Poetry has no utility in the narrow sense, but useful disciplines—politics, science—have no value apart from the poetic faculty which gives them meaning:

> We have more moral, political and historical wisdom, than we know how to reduce into practice; we have more scientific and economical knowledge than can be accommodated to the just distribution of the produce which it multiplies. The poetry in these systems of thought, is concealed by the accumulation of facts and calculating processes. There is no want of knowledge respecting what is wisest and best in morals, government, and political economy, or at least, what is wiser and better than what men now practise and endure. But . . . we want the creative faculty to imagine that which we know; we want the generous impulse to act that which we imagine; we want the poetry of life: our calculations have outrun conception; we have eaten more than we can digest. The cultivation of those sciences which have enlarged the limits of the empire of man over the external world, has, for want of the poetical faculty, proportionally circumscribed those of the internal world; and man, having enslaved the elements, remains himself a slave.
>
> ("A Defence of Poetry," Para. 37)

The prefaces to Shelley's poems suggest that he was driven by the same motives he ascribes to the greatest poets, Dante and Milton; he disclaims didactic purpose, but his larger purpose is moral and humane: to "awaken and enlarge" the minds of his readers to the understanding of man's condition as it is, and as it might be. The metaphor that dominates his poetry is suggested in the last lines above: his poetry analyzes the "dark slavery" of man, and prophesies his liberation from the chains that bind him. That dark slavery is mental as well as physical, psychological as well as political; it includes man's enslavement to time and to the senses, as well as his oppression by kings and priests. Liberation, which must envisage the overthrow of king and priest, the breaking of political and social chains, is in the first instance psychological, a freeing of the imagination and the feelings.

If we move from Shelley's clear and essentially conventional theory to his poetry, we find at its human center the autobiographical figure of "Ode to the West Wind," who, bowed and enfeebled by the chains of life, struggles with his angel on behalf of an unawakened earth:

> Oh! lift me as a wave, a leaf, a cloud!
> I fall upon the thorns of life! I bleed!   (53–54)

Readers have been right to sense in these lines what is most extreme and insistent in Shelley's vision of human life. If we are to see Shelley clear, we should place the figure of the poet in the context of the poetry as a whole, and in relationship to Shelley's view of the nature and function of poetry.

The figure of the failing poet appears repeatedly in Shelley's poetry; pale of hue and weak of limb, he is consecrated to his youthful vision of beauty, love, or perfection but incapable of realizing or recreating it, and is driven to death by his unassuageable desire. His literary associations vary from poem to poem, but the resemblances between the fictional heroes of *Alastor* and *Laon and Cythna* and the idealized self-portraits of *Adonais* and *Epipsychidion* suggest a large element of self-dramatization. The critical events of Shelley's life furnish the substance not only of the self-portraits but of the fictional narratives. His abortive attempts to liberate the surprised peasantry of Ireland are reconstituted in the heroic struggles of Laon and Lionel; his unhappy marriage to Harriet and his difficult relationship with Mary provide the outlines of the self-portrait in *Epipsychidion*. His physical suffering, his persecution by the law, his exile abroad, his lack of audience—all are traced in several of the portraits, most dramatically in the figure of the "herd-abandoned deer" in *Adonais*. It is tempting to read autobiography not only in the poet's commitment to social justice but in the persistent theme of yearning for the unattainable, the irresistible pull of Eros or Thanatos:

> The desire of the moth for the star,
>   Of the night for the morrow,
> The devotion to something afar
>   From the sphere of our sorrow . . .
>   ("One word is too often profaned," 13–16)

Yet the figure of the poet is literary and traditional as well as auto-biographical. Shelley took his precedent for allegorizing personal experience from Dante and Milton; the peculiar authority he attributed to his own thought and its history and process suggests the example of those he considered the "extraordinary intellects of the new age," especially Wordsworth. The self-portraits exemplify that complex relationship between the personal and the traditional at the heart of his poetry, the recasting of subjective experience in terms suggested by the great poetic and philosophical formulations of man's condition. The figure of the poet participates as well in the ambitious symbolism that characterizes all of Shelley's poetry; it is part of his grand design, meant to be read as serious in the sense in which not only Shelley but Henry James and Matthew Arnold apply that term to art, and to the artist's rendering of human life as a significant choice between good and evil. If the artist, like Shelley, rejects the received dogmas and moral systems of his time, then poetry becomes a surrogate for religion, an independent and self-sustaining means of asserting or discovering value. When dogma and morality are no longer viable, the center of interest shifts to the seeking mind. It is a commonplace that a central figure for late

Romantic writers is the image of the artist, or the novice at life, the youthful hero or heroine whose impressions of the surface are his only means of penetrating the mystery at the heart of things. For Shelley the central figure is the poet, whose education is similarly rendered in terms of his own naive motive, and the world that resists his vision.

The unpromising plot of *Alastor,* an amalgam of Platonic myth and biographical fact, with gleanings from Scott, Wordsworth, and Mrs. Radcliffe, haunted Shelley's imagination and became a vehicle for his repeated attempts to define the poet's relationship to the world he lives in and the vision he serves. The Poet of *Alastor* is idealized as a lovely youth gifted with the traditional virtues of the prince: "Gentle, and brave, and generous" (58). Each later portrait suggests a heroic ideal. Prince Athanase, like the Poet of *Alastor,* has a Spenserian cast:

> He had a gentle yet aspiring mind;
> Just, innocent, with varied learning fed . . .
> Fearless he was, and scorning all disguise . . .
> Liberal he was of soul, and frank of heart . . .
> ("Prince Athanase," 22–23, 43, 46)

In "Ode to the West Wind," the poet describes himself in his youth as "tameless, and swift, and proud" (56)—terms that suggest the strength and freedom of a natural force; in *Adonais* the frail Form, who represents Shelley, is described in similar terms as a "pardlike Spirit beautiful and swift" (280).

The young Poet of *Alastor* is educated by "solemn vision, and bright silver dream" (67), by nature, philosophy, and the "sacred past" (73). Education, the growth of the poet's mind, includes both passive and active processes, not only the receiving of impressions and the study of books but the active seeking of experience; thus Shelley describes his studies and travels, in the preface to *Laon and Cythna,* as "an education peculiarly fitted for a Poet" (Para. 6). The Poet of *Alastor,* like the poet-author, wanders abroad in search of "Nature's most secret steps" (*Alastor,* 81); the poet's travels reappear in *Epipsychidion* as "visioned wanderings" undertaken "In the clear golden prime of my youth's dawn" (*Epipsychidion,* 191–92).

Suddenly a vision appears, which forms a turning point in the youth's spiritual history; his earlier education is a preparation for it, his adult life is determined by its appearance and its loss. The vision is variously defined in the poems as truth, intellectual beauty, or, more obscurely, a thirst for love, a vacancy of spirit, an awakening to absence. In *Alastor* the vision comes upon the Poet as he sleeps, in the form of a veiled maiden, sent by the "spirit of sweet human love" (203); her voice is "like the voice of his own soul" (153); her theme is "Knowledge and truth and virtue" (158). The vision of "Hymn to Intellectual Beauty" descends upon the poet "like the truth / Of nature" (78–79); the Being who appears to the poet in *Epipsychidion* is like Dante's Beatrice, "robed in such exceeding glory, / That I beheld her not . . . Her Spirit was the harmony of truth" (*Epipsychidion*, 199–200, 216).[1]

The reality of a vision is attested by the ecstasy that admits it. The poet of "Hymn to Intellectual Beauty" describes his visionary seizure thus: "I shrieked, and clasped my hands in extacy!" (60). The Poet of *Alastor* experiences in dream the ecstasy of sexual union with the veiled maiden (*Alastor*, 182–87). But the vision dissolves; the spirit vanishes, and the moment of ecstasy is followed by a trial of despair, as the poet, awakened to a cold reality, pursues in vain his lost vision of perfection. In *Alastor* the Poet flees back through time and civilization to the primeval source of being, where he discovers not life or love but death. Prince Athanase, blasted in his promise by a mysterious ailment, wanders from land to land, weakened by grief. In several of the more personal lyrics, as in these two allegories, the poet's despair identifies the vision as love, and its betrayal as the cause of the poet's loss of vital powers and his physical decline.

The dedicatory stanzas of *Laon and Cythna* form Shelley's first full-length self-portrait, an expansion of the history briefly sketched in "Hymn to Intellectual Beauty." Shelley describes his youthful study of nature and of the past, his preparation for a heroic task; he recounts the visionary hour in which his poetic mission is revealed to him:

> I do remember well the hour which burst
> My spirit's sleep: a fresh May-dawn it was,

When I walked forth upon the glittering grass,
And wept, I knew not why . . .
("To Mary ———— ————," 21–24)

But he suffers a sudden deflection of purpose with the appearance of love or, more specifically, with the desire for love, a "sense of loneliness, a thirst" (45), which comes upon his mind, even as the vision of the veiled maiden descends upon the Poet of *Alastor*. Thereafter he seeks in vain, until his meeting with Mary, for one who answers the thirst of his soul:

Alas, that love should be a blight and snare
To those who seek all sympathies in one!—
Such once I sought in vain; then black despair,
The shadow of a starless night, was thrown
Over the world in which I moved alone:—
Yet never found I one not false to me,
Hard hearts, and cold, like weights of icy stone
Which crushed and withered mine, that could not be
Aught but a lifeless clod, until revived by thee.
("To Mary ———— ————," 46–54)

The poet's despair is analogous to the death of winter, the hardening and freezing of the land; as the land dies when its source of life is removed, so the spirit dies when it is not nourished by love. The suggestion is that the spirit, once it has been awakened (or given life) by a vision of truth, requires continuing relationship with a human embodiment of that truth.

Shelley's last extended self-portrait, in *Epipsychidion,* is modified by the discovery that the revival of love which Mary brings is delusive; her light illumines but does not warm. The sequence of events follows the pattern of the dedicatory stanzas of *Laon and Cythna:* a vision appears, creation and creator of the poet's thought; it is withdrawn; a black night of despair follows. The poet seeks for a human shape of his ideal; he is betrayed by false lovers and subsequently suffers a spiritual "death;" at last he is revived by true love. The poet's pursuit of his lost vision imitates Dante's pursuit of Beatrice, once glimpsed and ever afterward sought, and the vision itself has the multiple forms of Dante's love. It is a star toward which

the spirit soars, a God who can only be reached by crossing the
grave, a veiled Divinity of thought and poetry, a "soul out of my
soul," as well as a love in human form:

> I questioned every tongueless wind that flew
> Over my tower of mourning, if it knew
> Whither 'twas fled, this soul out of my soul . . .
> But neither prayer nor verse could dissipate
> The night which closed on her; nor uncreate
> That world within this Chaos, mine and me,
> Of which she was the veiled Divinity,
> The world I say of thoughts that worshipped her:
> And therefore I went forth, with hope and fear
> And every gentle passion sick to death,
> Feeding my course with expectation's breath,
> Into the wintry forest of our life;
> And struggling through its error with vain strife,
> And stumbling in my weakness and my haste,
> And half bewildered by new forms, I past
> Seeking among those untaught foresters
> If I could find one form resembling hers,
> In which she might have masked herself from me.
>   (*Epipsychidion*, 236–38, 241–55)

The wilderness image of the earlier poems becomes in *Epipsychidion*
the Dantesque "obscure Forest" (321), the "wintry forest of our
life," the "wintry wilderness of thorns" (323). And the images of
struggle and "vain strife" suggest that this time is not only a quest
but a trial of the soul in its pilgrimage through life. There is a temporary relief of pain as Mary appears, a mirror image of the poet's
lost visionary love. But Mary's love, cold and chaste at best, is withdrawn, and the poet succumbs to despair. Conventional metaphor
is abandoned, and the poet is portrayed not as a wanderer in the
wilderness or a mariner on a storm-tossed sea (as in "Lines written
among the Euganean Hills"), but as that storm-tossed sea itself, as
an earth, a world, shaken by natural catastrophe:

> What storms then shook the ocean of my sleep,
> Blotting that Moon, whose pale and waning lips
> Then shrank as in the sickness of eclipse;—

And how my soul was as a lampless sea,
And who was then its Tempest; and when She,
The Planet of that hour, was quenched, what frost
Crept o'er those waters, till from coast to coast
The moving billows of my being fell
Into a death of ice, immovable;—
And then—what earthquakes made it gape and split,
The white Moon smiling all the while on it,
These words conceal:—If not, each word would be
The key of staunchless tears. Weep not for me!
                              (*Epipsychidion,* 308–20)

The "death of ice" recalls the imagery of a withered earth in the
dedication to *Laon and Cythna;* as in the earlier passage, the physical analogy asserts the dependence of the poet's creative powers
upon love, as the natural creation is dependent upon heat and light.
But the suffering expressed has a new intensity, suggestive of the
cosmic suffering of a Lear and justified by the tragic perception
which in Shelley's last poems seems to suffuse and darken his
idealism, his awareness that life is indeed at the mercy of death, love
at the mercy of life.

The final turn of the allegory restores the natural order; Emily
appears, the poet's "long night" ends, and life is miraculously reborn
with love. The poet prays to Mary and Emily—Moon and Sun to
the poet's "passive Earth"—to govern his "sphere of being" in
harmony and love:

Twin Spheres of light who rule this passive Earth,
This world of love, this *me;* and into birth
Awaken all its fruits and flowers, and dart
Magnetic might into its central heart;
And lift its billows and its mists, and guide
By everlasting laws, each wind and tide
To its fit cloud, and its appointed cave . . .
So ye, bright regents, with alternate sway
Govern my sphere of being, night and day!
                              (*Epipsychidion,* 345–51, 360–61)

The prayer to the "bright regents" for governance is similar to the
poet's prayer in "Ode to the West Wind" for strength. The creative

powers of the failing prophet require extraordinary inspiration, for which the violence of storm provides a metaphor. The solitary human being, a "world of love," can exist creatively only as part of a harmonious social order; his "fruits and flowers" are awakened by the power of love exercised through social relationship.

In his despair the poet is represented as physically powerless. But his failing power must be seen against the initial portrayal of the youthful poet as fearless, strong, capable of "visioned wanderings." It is only after the vision seizes his imagination that he loses his strength and becomes "a Power / Girt round with weakness" (*Adonais*, 281–82). Images of a physical wearing away occur in each version of the time of despair. In *Alastor* the Poet's embrace of Death is anticipated in his physical decline:

> And now his limbs were lean; his scattered hair
> Sered by the autumn of strange suffering
> Sung dirges in the wind; his listless hand
> Hung like dead bone within its withered skin . . .
>   (*Alastor*, 248–51)

The Poet is a "spectral form" (259); his eyes are "wild" with a "strange light" (264–65). In the dedicatory stanzas to *Laon and Cythna*, the poet laments his weakness, in a reference to actual physical illness, even as he prays for strength to serve as a prophet:

> . . . I would fain
> Reply in hope—but I am worn away,
> And Death and Love are yet contending for their prey.
>   ("To Mary ———— ————," 88–90)

The most dramatic representation of the poet's physical weakness is the description of the mourning poet in *Adonais*. The sequence of images, similar to those in "Ode to the West Wind," suggests original or potential strength even as it asserts actual failure:

> A Love in desolation masked;—a Power
> Girt round with weakness;—it can scarce uplift
> The weight of the superincumbent hour;
> It is a dying lamp, a falling shower,

A breaking billow;—even whilst we speak
Is it not broken?

(*Adonais*, 281–86)

The phrases suggest the exhausted final movement of a process that
began in strength but has run the course of its given or self-generated
power.

The poet's loss of strength, though it is imaged in physical terms,
is clearly mental and spiritual, like the torments of Prometheus. In
both *Adonais* and *Epipsychidion* the image of the hunted deer
describes the weakness and extremity of the poet. But the "raging
hounds" that pursue him are his own thoughts:

. . . now he fled astray
With feeble steps o'er the world's wilderness,
And his own thoughts, along that rugged way,
Pursued, like raging hounds, their father and their prey.

(*Adonais*, 276–79)

Then, as a hunted deer that could not flee,
I turned upon my thoughts, and stood at bay,
Wounded and weak and panting . . .

(*Epipsychidion*, 272–74)

The image in both poems dramatizes the compulsive nature of the
poet's flight; he is not only drawn in pursuit of his vision but is
himself pursued, and the furies that pursue him are internal as well
as external. The vision, also self-generated—a "soul out of my soul"
—is not only a blessing but a curse, a high transgression, as the
myth of Actaeon suggests. The poet's own thoughts are the cause of
his misery, yet his powerlessness is reinforced by the double impetus
given his flight; he is not only led by his vision, beckoned on, but
driven from behind.

The poet's spiritual history reaches its climax in a sudden reversal,
a triumph over despair; the dying youth undergoes an apotheosis.
In *Alastor* the Poet discovers a "little shallop floating near the
shore" (299), in which he is inspired to embark. Beckoned on by
"the light / That shone within his soul" (492–93), he voyages
through a symbolic topography of tempest-torn sea and wintry river,
through a dark cavern and over a raging whirlpool, to a calm dell

deep in the forest, where he at last submits to Death. Each of the
major poems ends with some version of this voyage, this true ending
and consummation, whether of love or death. The effect in *Adonais*
and *Epipsychidion* is of a sudden widening and lifting, an imaginative transcendence of life. In *Epipsychidion,* as in *Alastor,* a boat
materializes, and the poet in imagination embarks:

> A ship is floating in the harbour now,
> A wind is hovering o'er the mountain's brow;
> There is a path on the sea's azure floor,
> No keel has ever ploughed that path before . . .
> The merry mariners are bold and free:
> Say, my heart's sister, wilt thou sail with me?
> Our bark is as an albatross, whose nest
> Is a far Eden of the purple East;
> And we between her wings will sit, while Night
> And Day, and Storm, and Calm, pursue their flight,
> Our ministers, along the boundless Sea,
> Treading each other's heels, unheededly.
> (*Epipsychidion,* 408–11; 414–21)

The voyage in *Epipsychidion* reads like an inspired transfiguration
of the voyagings of the "little shallop" of *Alastor,* mediated through
several other flights, the "divine canoe" that transports Laon and
Cythna to the "Temple of the Spirit," (XII, xxxii–xli), the departure
of Prometheus and Asia "beyond the peak / Of Bacchic Nysa,
Maenad-haunted mountain" to the "simple dwelling" where they
may live restored to love and happiness (III, iii, 22, 154–55).

Adonais also ends with an imagined voyage:

> The breath whose might I have invoked in song
> Descends on me; my spirit's bark is driven,
> Far from the shore, far from the trembling throng
> Whose sails were never to the tempest given;
> The massy earth and spherèd skies are riven!
> I am borne darkly, fearfully, afar;
> Whilst, burning through the inmost veil of Heaven,
> The soul of Adonais, like a star,
> Beacons from the abode where the Eternal are.   (487–95)

The elements of the more extensively developed voyages are all present in these lines: the "spirit's bark," the sails given to the tempest, the spirits that beckon the poet on, the setting apart of the poet from all other men, his triumph over physical impossibility, his far goal beyond the limits of the known world. The voyage is always a voyage of the spirit, a return to the source.

The resemblances among the major poems suggest, then, that there is but a single figure of the poet with several variations. How are we to understand its dramatic and symbolic character and its relationship to Shelley's theory of poetry?

It may be useful to note first the care with which the several portraits are rendered dramatic and given an objective form that discourages simple autobiographical reading. *Alastor* introduces its subject in the manner of Wordsworthian story-telling: "There was a Poet . . ." (50). The preface presents the Poet as an example of a willful isolation which the author, presumably, deplores. *Epipsychidion* is presented in the elaborate "Advertisement" as the work of an "unfortunate" young man who died at Florence while preparing for the voyage described at the end of the poem. The fiction suggests a second voice, a second view of the hero, which both frames and distances the subject. In both *Alastor* and *Adonais* the martyred poet, singular both in his extraordinary gifts and in the severity of his fate, is described through the eyes of another poet, who speaks in his own person and appears to be more representative than the poet he mourns. The dedicatory stanzas of *Laon and Cythna* serve a similar function: the idealized account of Shelley's history and his love for Mary frames the poem of Laon and Cythna, the two young martyrs to political idealism, who stand in relation to each other and to the world very much as Shelley and Mary do. As in *Alastor* and *Adonais,* there is a double perspective, that of the romantic fable, heroic, tragic, and exemplary, and of the poet, human and of the world, who meditates upon it. Similarly, despite the inevitable identification of Shelley with the mourning poet in *Adonais,* the language suggests that he is distinct from the elegist of the poem, who applies the same impersonal description to him as to the other mourners:

> . . . he, as I guess,
> Had gazed on Nature's naked loveliness . . .   (274–75)

It is not until the final line of his presentation—"oh! that it should be so!" (306) that the sudden breaking through of emotion suggests that the elegist is lamenting his own fate.

The framing devices, then, even when they are false clues, are plain obstacles to a simple autobiographical reading. But even where there is a single voice, as in the shorter lyrics, the tone is heightened to suggest that the poet is assuming a literary role as elegist or bard, prophet or dreamer. The effect is to generalize his spiritual history, making it subservient to his function as a vessel for divine inspiration, intermediary between the corrupt world and its source. The propriety of tone is part of a general stylization of the portraits; the elements of the poet's history and the metaphors that describe it are peculiarly appropriate to the context, determined by the mission of the poet or by the occasion that summons him forth. The visionary ecstasy of the poet in "Hymn to Intellectual Beauty," the "beating heart and streaming eyes" (63) which signify his commitment, are metaphors for the initiation of a novice to the service of his divinity, or the Spirit which represents it; they are part of the poem's attempt to substitute "Intellectual Beauty"—the "truth / Of nature" (78–79)—for the "poisonous names" (53) of orthodox religion, the "frail spells" (29) of traditional worship. The poet prays not for salvation but for "calm" for his "onward life" (80–81); his vow is not to fear God and obey his commandments, but to "fear himself, and love all human kind" (84). The controlling effect of metaphor —in this case a metaphor inseparable from the natural and symbolic occasion of the poem—is most striking in "Ode to the West Wind," where the self-portrait is a matter of only a few lines:

> . . . If even
> I were as in my boyhood, and could be
>
> The comrade of thy wanderings over Heaven,
> As then, when to outstrip thy skiey speed
> Scarce seemed a vision; I would ne'er have striven

As thus with thee in prayer in my sore need.
Oh! lift me as a wave, a leaf, a cloud!
I fall upon the thorns of life! I bleed!

A heavy weight of hours has chained and bowed
One too like thee: tameless, and swift, and proud.   (47–56)

The characterization of the poet in youth is drawn from analogy with the wind, which is free, swift, and tameless; his "strife" is a striving with the wind, as with an angel of God, and the central line, suggestive of the wilderness imagery in all the portraits ("I fall upon the thorns of life! I bleed!") is a direct metaphorical response to the prayer that immediately precedes it and that summarizes the natural action of the wind upon all of nature except man. Thus the verb in "I fall" is suggested by the prayer "Oh! lift me," as the "thorns of life" is suggested by the image of leaf and seed.

The portrait of the "frail Form" in *Adonais* is similarly governed by its context and occasion. The example of earlier pastoral elegies, especially Milton's *Lycidas,* suggests the procession of a "gentle band" of mountain shepherds come to mourn their fallen comrade, "Their garlands sere, their magic mantles rent." Shelley's expansive use of tradition suggests the additional figures of the Pilgrim, the sweet lyrist from the "wilds of Ierne," and the "frail Form," a dying singer of songs, whose description incorporates the related images of a solitary wanderer, a poet-priest, a swift hunter transformed into the hunter's prey, a "Stranger" identifiable only by the ensanguined mark that links him to the hunter Cain, most grievous of sinners, or to the greatest of shepherds and poet-teachers, Christ. As the "Stranger" weeps his own fate in that of the martyred poet, so the facts of Keats's life suggest other details: physical illness, the neglect and hostility of the world, and the fact that Keats died abroad, as Shelley himself lived in exile (*Adonais,* xxx–xxxiv).

Each self-portrait, then, has its special rationale. But the persistence of a single pattern—the account of the idealized youth, the vision that comes upon him, his search to recover it, his final voyage to an imagined Elysium—suggests a larger meaning. The narrative presents itself inescapably as a myth or allegory dramatizing the nature of the creative imagination, both its inherent power to change and recreate the world, and its mortal dependence upon love, or relationship with that which lies outside itself. As Shelley rewrote Aeschylus and Dante, so he incorporated in his history of the Poet earlier myths of power and dependency, vision and its loss. The vision of "Hymn to Intellectual Beauty" and the awakening described in *Laon and Cythna* suggest the vision of supreme beauty described by Diotima in the *Symposium*.[2] And the loss of the golden strength of youth, the conception of mature life as a progress toward death, a blind stumbling and search, suggest Platonic myths of an earlier golden world and its loss. But the broad outlines of the poet's history, from his early innocent happiness and strength, his free communion with nature and divinity, to his wandering in the world's wilderness, and his final transcendence of despair, suggest most directly the analogy of the myth of Genesis and parallel classical myths of the Golden Age. Youth's "golden prime" is a time prior to knowledge, love, experience. The mind is described as sleeping, "passive;" it has not yet been created. And the black night of the soul which follows the vision suggests the loss of Eden following upon some necessary but fatal knowledge, and exile to a "wilderness of thorns," a fallen world of time and death. As the spirit is awakened to knowledge, so the "mortal passions" of the human being are released, and he becomes as a deer hunted by the "raging hounds" of his own thought. There is no temptation in Shelley's narrative; he consistently attacked the doctrine that man's fall results from his disobedience.[3] But there are repeated suggestions of an error, whether it is defined as (in the preface to *Alastor*) the attempt to exist without human sympathy or as the mistake of seeking to find in mortal form that which is immortal. And there are repeated hints of a curse, lying either upon the youth who has dared too much or upon the life which it is the lot of all men to endure.

The fallen state, after all, is indisputable; mortality, time, passion are facts of reality. Poetry, like religion, gives meaning to reality by conjecturing a before and after, by naming the present a "fall" from the past. The myth Shelley substitutes for the orthodox fall reflects his sense that the condition of human life must be conceived in terms of loss if it is to be tolerable. It is the nature of the human being to err, he suggests, in seeking to remedy its loss. Yet the single imperative for the imagination is recovery of that absolute—whether knowledge, love, or beauty—which human desire asserts to be the necessary source and sustaining power of life. He uses related imagery in *Epipsychidion* when he speaks of those

> . . . to whom this world of life
> Is as a garden ravaged, and whose strife
> Tills for the promise of a later birth
> The wilderness of this Elysian earth.   (186–89)

The poet is one of these—not the poet who goes astray, like the hero of *Alastor,* but the poet who laments him, and whose "strife" is the poem he utters. The "promise of a later birth" insists on the primacy of hope and the significance of poetry, the power of the imagination to recover what it divines of the original or potential beauty of the world. And this is the motive behind the spiritual autobiographies in the poems, as it is the informing principle of "Ode to the West Wind." A similar figure is used in "A Defence of Poetry" to describe the function of poetry as mediator between the human and divine: "Poetry redeems from decay the visitations of the divinity in Man . . . Poetry defeats the curse which binds us to be subjected to the accident of surrounding impressions" (Para. 40, 42).[4] In the context of Shelley's general discussion of poetry, the religious metaphor is unobtrusive. But it confirms what we read in the poems: that redemptive power is displaced from an omnipotent deity to the human imagination, which unfortunately has limited powers. The perspective is not that of the divinely inspired prophet but that of the faltering human being whose visionary glimpses are fleeting and evanescent, who looks "before and after," whose most precious faculty (and only hope of redemption), his poetic imagination, like the "sensitive plant," requires love if it is not to wither and die. The sojourn in the wilderness, the time of strife, of pain and suffering, is the image for life in the world, for man's condition as a state of longing for what he does not possess and can scarcely apprehend. The central human interest is not the "fearless youth" in his "golden prime" but the lost soul struggling in the wilderness, the "frail Form," the weakest of hearts, identified in *Epipsychidion* with the poet-lover who alone of men is granted a vision of the eternal, and in *Adonais* both with the suffering Christ and with Cain, the greatest of sinners, a "fugitive and a vagabond in the earth," whose punishment is "greater than [he] can bear."[5]

The form the poet's strife takes, his restless flight and pursuit, and his final apotheosis—the precipitate flight out of his own nature and toward a transcendent vision—should be understood in relation to Shelley's conception of the imagination as the sole hope of defeating the curse that binds us to ourselves. The poet's struggle can be considered a dramatic representation of the familiar doctrine of the "Defence":

> The great secret of morals is love; or a going out of our own nature, and an identification of ourselves with the beautiful which exists in thought, action, or person, not our own. A man, to be greatly good, must imagine intensely and comprehensively; he must put himself in the place of another and of many others; the pains and pleasures of his species must become his own. The great instrument of moral good is the imagination . . .   (Para. 13)

As Laon and Prometheus, Shelley's heroes, represent the conscious effort of the human spirit "to be greatly good," so the figure of the poet in flight from himself, in restless pursuit of his lost vision, dramatizes the extreme effort of the imagination, imprisoned in its own nature, to identify "with the beautiful which exists in thought, action, or person, not our own." It is in this light that we should read the impulse toward identification with the ideal; in "Ode to the West Wind" the poet praying to be one with that "Spirit fierce;" in *Epipsychidion* the poet seeking union with the beloved; in *Adonais* the elegist putting himself "in the place of another and of many others," as he bears in his own person the "pains . . . of his species," even to Cain's and Christ's, laments in another's fate his own and at last seeks identification with the departed poet he mourns. The portrait of the poet, so often regarded as self-indulgence on Shelley's part, is actually an attempt to render dramatically the imaginative process that is the only escape from self. The great defense Shelley makes of poetry is that it counters egoism, the surrender to ourselves and our time; for both creator and reader it involves an identification with the "other," hence self-forgetfulness.[6] For a nonbeliever, one who cannot see beyond the language of the poem itself to the sacred or absolute truth it claims to embody, this stretching of the imagination must still serve as the definitive value of art.

The relationship between imaginative sympathy and moral good is most explicit in "Ode to the West Wind," where the prayer of the poet for identification with the wind—"Be thou, Spirit fierce, / My spirit! Be thou me, impetuous one!" (61–62)—is the condition for his social mission, to "quicken a new birth" (64), to prophesy a spring to follow the winter of destruction and desolation. But in what sense can we relate the spiritual travail of the poet in *Adonais* or *Epipsychidion* to a "moral good?" The two poems are not even implicitly revolutionary or political; neither asserts the possibility of hope in the world. One hesitates to take as exemplary the poet's lucid and terrible axiom in *Adonais:* "Die, / If thou wouldst be with that which thou dost seek!" (464–65). This paradox is very different from the poet's prophecy in "Ode to the West Wind," which insists that the living world itself can be reborn. The "moral good," if it is to be found in the poem, lies in the act of imagination itself. The poet demonstrates in the last stanzas of *Adonais* the step-by-step process Shelley describes in the "Defence" as an awakening and enlarging of the "circumference" of the imagination to possibilities that the familiar world resists, that "going out of our own nature" which is the converse of egoism. The pessimism of the ending is secondary to its imaginative transcendence of physical reality, of time and decay and cold mortality, all that Shelley means by "the shadow of our night" (352), which is not death but life, as death is not sleep but an awakening. The mourning poet, addressed earlier in the poem as "Fond wretch" (416) for not understanding this paradox, is bid to exercise his imagination, his "spirit's light," in preparation for a final revelation.

> Clasp with thy panting soul the pendulous Earth;
> As from a centre, dart thy spirit's light
> Beyond all worlds, until its spacious might
> Satiate the void circumference: then shrink
> Even to a point within our day and night . . .   (417–21)

These difficult lines affirm the power of spirit over space and time, its independence from the laws of mass and motion. They anticipate the consolation of the elegy, that poetry alone is immortal; they prepare the poet for the actual exercise of his power to move "Be-

yond all worlds." For in the final stanza of the poem the imagination
effects in the physical world the miracle envisaged here.

The familiar rhetoric of despair and ecstasy should also be read
in its dramatic context. Why is the poet in his despair identified with
such extreme suffering? Alternately he is identified with Christ—
one who suffers for all men—or with figures like Cain, Actaeon, a
"Stranger"—one whose suffering is a mark of his exile from human
community, one cursed by God. He is not merely weak but the
weakest of hearts. These references are not primarily autobiographical but symbolic; they suggest the suffering of such figures as Byron's
Manfred and Cain or Shelley's Prometheus, who stand apart from
the "trembling throng" because they have dared all, and have re-
fused obedience to whatever reigns. Dramatically the extreme suffering of the poet must precede the final triumph of the spirit's light,
the imagination freed by love, as earlier it is fettered by hate. Liberation thus appears not only willed but miraculous. But what the
reader may miss in the drama is the act of willed rebellion, comparable to man's eating of the apple, or Faust's bargain with the
devil, or Prometheus' cursing of Jupiter. The poet, unlike Prometheus, seems to be essentially passive. The vision, whether blessing
or curse, comes upon him unsought; his quest consists of drifting
and wandering, being laid asleep. Redemption appears miraculously
on his path; his final act is of submission to his destiny. He is compared to a stricken deer, a bleeding God; he is a "passive Earth"
who prays to be governed by Sun and Moon (*Epipsychidion,* 345).
The most memorable lines in the poems dramatically render his sub-
jection and weakness: "I fall upon the thorns of life! I bleed!" ("Ode
to the West Wind," 54); "I pant, I sink, I tremble, I expire!" (*Epipsychidion,* 591).

The poet's passivity is paired inextricably to a doctrine it appears
to contradict—that it lies in man's will, and only in his will, to be
what he envisions. It is this doctrine that Julian propounds against
Maddalo's dark fatalism. Julian speaks for Shelley, Maddalo for
Byron:

> '. . . it is our will
> That thus enchains us to permitted ill—
> We might be otherwise—we might be all

We dream of happy, high, majestical.
Where is the love, beauty, and truth we seek
But in our mind? and if we were not weak
Should we be less in deed than in desire?'
                                    ("Julian and Maddalo," 170–76)

And it is the doctrine that *Prometheus Unbound* exemplifies: both
good and evil lie in man's will; guilt and pain exist because man's
will "made or suffered them" (III, iv, 199). We are weak, as Julian
asserts; it is his sense of human infirmity that Shelley renders in the
history of the poet. But the ethical imperatives remain the same for
weak or strong:

To suffer woes which Hope thinks infinite;
To forgive wrongs darker than death or night;
   To defy Power, which seems omnipotent;
To love, and bear; to hope till Hope creates
From its own wreck the thing it contemplates . . .
                                    (*Prometheus Unbound,* IV, 570–74)

In the self-portraits the ethical imperatives are embodied most
clearly in the proud flights of the youth, the vows he makes to be
"wise / And just, and free, and mild" ("To Mary ——— ———,"
31–32). But they can be discerned as well in his seeking after his
vision, his blind stumbling. His "black night" is terrible because it
is a removal from the possibility of ethical action, a freezing of the
will and the imagination. Yet his struggle and strife represent the
effort of his imagination against the impediments of life and the
weak self, and his final flight, whether a giving of himself to Death
or an imagined flight with Love and the beloved to a "sinless Eden,"
is a triumph of his imagination to be what it dreams, if not in the
real then in the imagined world.

Correspondences between Shelley's prose and his poetry have
often been demonstrated. But the differences between a prose statement of an idea and its poetic rendering are especially significant in
Shelley's work, and indeed mark him off radically from a poet like
Blake. Ideas that are presented tentatively, with qualifications, in the
prose, are rendered absolute and categorical in the poetry; negatives

are rendered positively; logic and analogy, proposing relationship, yield to metaphor or myth, asserting identity. Shelley's notes to *Hellas* demonstrate his sophisticated awareness of the nature of poetic truth, and they suggest why it is possible for one reader to consider him a religious poet, another reader to consider him a rationalist. In his poetry Shelley adopts the prophetic convention in which truth is revealed to one singled out as mediator between the divine and the human; the convention assumes the absolute nature of the truth so revealed, and the independent existence of divinity. But in his prose Shelley consistently recognizes the subjective limitations on knowledge, and truth is relative. The faculty of prophecy is one that bards "possess or feign;" the visions of Isaiah and Virgil were a product not of divine visitation but of their "ardent spirits overleaping the actual reign of evil;" the desire for immortality is the "strongest and the only presumption" for its existence. With regard to ultimate questions, apart from our desire, apart from the imaginative projections of human desire in myth and legend, "all men are equally ignorant" (*Hellas,* notes 2 and 7). Or, in the positive, poetic, and religious statement of a prose agnosticism: "The deep truth is imageless" (*Prometheus Unbound,* II, iv, 116).

The expressions in the poems, both of prophetic hope and of prophetic despair, have their rational, qualified, prose counterparts. Shelley wrote to Mrs. Gisborne: "Let us believe in a kind of optimism in which we are our own gods . . . because Hope, as Coleridge says is a solemn duty which we owe alike to ourselves & to the world" (*Letters of P.B.S.,* II, 125).[7] But the pragmatic counsel of a good friend is irrelevant to a prophetic poetry in which faith is granted from above, and its object is not intuited but revealed.

The poetic rendering of the figure of the poet may be similarly understood in terms of the difference between prose and poetry. Shelley consistently defines the imagination as a combination of active and passive faculties, in both his prose and his poetry. The mind receives data from the external world, but colors what it receives with its own light. Man is, like the lyre, an instrument responsive to impressions. "But there is a principle within the human being . . which acts otherwise than in the lyre, and produces not melody alone, but harmony, by an internal adjustment of the sounds or motions thus excited to the impressions which excite them" ("A Defence of Poetry," Para. 2). For Shelley, as for Wordsworth and Keats, passivity of mind suggests not merely the origin of mental experience in passive sensation but the poetic faculty of profound and unconscious receptiveness to reality—Wordsworth's "wise passiveness" which receives more of truth than sensory perception can admit to consciousness. The faculty depends, as it does for Wordsworth, on a prior intuition of "influences," which can be felt if the poet is attuned to them, and it includes the possibility of visionary experience, trance, visitations of divinity. But the passivity of the poet merely prepares him for the creative act. Shelley insists as strongly as Coleridge and Wordsworth do that the imagination is essentially active; it "creates anew the universe;" it raises the poet above other men to the level of a god.[8]

How shall we relate a theory of the imagination that insists upon its creativity, its power to inform and give value to life, with a symbolic rendering of the poet as passive, dependent, subject to a vision that can neither be summoned nor recalled, submissive to the powers that call him to his destiny? If the history of the poet is allegorical of the poetic imagination, then the narrative is a paradoxical dramatization of the prose doctrine it seems to contradict, for in fact the powers to whom the poet submits, and upon whom he depends, are originally extensions of his own active powers of mind. The vision is a "soul out of my soul;" the voyage is imagined, a function of the "spirit's light" darting "Beyond all worlds." The difference between saying "the poet images to himself the being whom he loves" and "the Being whom he loves appears to him" is not substantive but rhetorical. But the second statement implicitly substitutes passive receptivity for active creation on the part of the poet, and attributes to the vision an independent reality that the first statement leaves questionable. The prose version is unarguable. The poetic version depends for its truth on its emotional conviction and rhetorical persuasiveness; it substitutes myth for doctrine.

Shelley's poetic genius lay in his openness to experience and to ideas, his restless, educated eclecticism; his poetry, while it is consistent in its themes, is unsystematic and cannot be reduced to formulas. But there is always a double perception in the poetry, though the emphasis changes and the formulations vary. As he enters into the limitless aspiration of the spirit, so he recognizes and laments the frailty of the body to which the spirit is bound. His rhetoric may be that of the mystic or visionary with eyes turned to the other world, but his perspective is essentially that of the rational artist pondering the human condition. The emotional power of his poetry lies in his recognition of the imperatives binding upon the human being powerless to fulfill them, and dependent for what power he has on others of similar frailty. Yet his poetry consistently asserts the power of the imagination to transcend the limitations of sense and language; it is an effort to assert hope, even against his own full knowledge of the grounds for despair.

NOTES

1. Cf. also Lionel's awakening to his political calling: "And as the meteor's midnight flame / Startles the dreamer, sun-like truth / Flashed on his visionary youth" (*Rosalind and Helen*, 617–19). Cythna's history also resembles that of the Poet; she has a vision of a shape of speechless beauty, a dream-lover, who calls her to political action (*Laon and Cythna*, I, xxxix–xliii).

2. "On a sudden [he] beholds a beauty wonderful in its nature" (Shelley's translation, "The Banquet of Plato," *Works*, VII, 206). Cf. Dante's vision of beatitude in *Paradiso*, Canto 33, esp. lines 55–63.

3. In notes 2 and 8 to *Hellas*, Shelley attacks the "received hypothesis" of "a power, who tempted, betrayed, and punished the innocent beings who were called into existence by his sole will."

4. Cf. the preface to *The Cenci:* "Imagination is as the immortal God which should assume flesh for the redemption of mortal passion" (Para. 7).

5. Genesis 4:9–15. Cain serves, like Christ, as an example of the greatest human suffering imaginable. Shelley had the likenesses in mind rather than the differences: both are forsaken by God and hunted by men, and marked out from all others, like the Poet, "a herd-abandoned deer struck by the hunter's dart" (*Adonais*, 297).

6. "Poetry and the principle of Self . . . are the God and Mammon of the world;" while the effects of poetry last, "self appears as what it is, an atom to a Universe" ("A Defence of Poetry," *Para.* 37, 40). See also the discussion of selfishness and the imagination in "Speculations on Morals:" "The only distinction between the selfish man, and the virtuous man, is that the imagination of the former is confined within a narrow limit, whilst that of the latter embraces a comprehensive circumference" (*Works*, VII, 75).

7. Shelley wrote to Peacock (September 9, 1819) of the Manchester riots: "These are, as it were, the distant thunders of the terrible storm which is approaching," using the same metaphor he used in "Ode to the West Wind," a month later, to welcome the impending revolution. But he

continues pragmatically: "I still think there will be no coming to close quarters until financial affairs decidedly bring the oppressors and the oppressed together" (*Letters of P.B.S.*, II, 119).

8. Shelley quotes Tasso: "Non merita nome di creatore, se non Iddio ed il Poeta" ("A Defence of Poetry," *Para.* 42). Cf. the analysis of poetic creation in *Prometheus Unbound*, I, 737–51: "He will watch from dawn to gloom / The lake-reflected sun illume / The yellow bees in the ivy-bloom, / Nor heed nor see, what things they be; / But from these create he can / Forms more real than living man, / Nurslings of immortality!" (743–49). The poet "receives" the reflected and illuminated reality; the creative process that builds upon this is independent of ordinary sensation, which registers only material reality.

CHAPTER TWO

THE MIND'S IMAGININGS
& THE WORLD OF THINGS

In the two major lyrics of the summer of 1816, "Hymn to Intellectual Beauty" and "Mont Blanc," Shelley presents himself publicly as a poet and announces his claim to recognition. Having allegorized the figure of a poet in *Alastor*—one nurtured, like Shelley himself, "By solemn vision, and bright silver dream" (67), by nature, philosophy, and history, only to be seized by a vision he must forever pursue—he now formulates for the first time in his own voice the themes that are to dominate his major work.

These lyrics have at their center the poet's social and political commitment, characteristically expressed in his vow to "fear himself, and love all human kind" ("Hymn to Intellectual Beauty," 84). Shelley's revision of the Biblical injunction to fear God and keep his commandments substitutes the human for the divine as the poet's source of authority and power. Yet the poet's spiritual experience can never be merely personal but must be directed outward, into the world, despite his severe doubts of his adequacy to the task. The lyrics attempt to establish the poet's relation to primary forces of life and death; they assert his commitment to interpret his singular vision to an enslaved world. The poet must not only feel but interpret and create, and in creating must serve—or so these essentially hopeful lyrics affirm.

Both poems open with flat statements about the nature of reality, unprovable hypotheses that the poem supports through metaphor and analogy. "Hymn to Intellectual Beauty" defines an unseen power that makes beautiful the world of things. "Mont Blanc" proposes a relationship between the "everlasting universe of things" and the world of mind. Both poems analyze the relationship of the temporal to the fixed, of man to nature or to a generative, informing power manifested in nature. The confident opening generalizations are followed in each poem by a dramatic presentation of the poet, who, driven by intense desire, seeks vainly among shadows for the ideal and absolute. Suddenly a vision of that ideal descends on him or appears before him; he then becomes an intermediary between two worlds, a prophet and interpreter. His vision commits him to believe in the power of the ideal to transform the real. In "Hymn to Intellectual Beauty" the poet affirms his hope that the Spirit of Beauty can free the world from its "dark slavery" (69–70); in "Mont Blanc" the poet declares that the "great Mountain," as its lesson is understood by the "wise, and great, and good," has "a voice . . . to repeal / Large codes of fraud and woe" (80–82). The two poems thus initiate Shelley's major theme of apocalyptic hope, his vision of future good to come out of present evil.

The differences between the two poems in their treatment of the power that moves, illuminates, or gives meaning to "This various world" ("Hymn to Intellectual Beauty," 3), suggest two alternative ways of conceptualizing reality and the relation of the mind to that which it experiences and to that which it intuits or desires beyond experience. For "Hymn to Intellectual Beauty" is positive, visionary, ecstatic, the record of the poet's intuitive apprehension of truth; "Mont Blanc" is somber, speculative, tentative in its findings, an attempt to discover truth by meditating on a visible reality. The two poems taken together present the young Shelley as a religious and philosophical poet who passionately questions the traditional formulations of religion and philosophy, and who will accept no authority for belief other than that of his own mind, his own senses, his own powers of intuition.

For Shelley, Wordsworth was the great teacher, one whose wisdom remained a source and inspiration well after his own betrayal of principle, as Shelley conceived of it. Shelley's "Hymn to Intellectual Beauty" consciously recalls Wordsworth's "Ode: Intimations of Immortality" and attempts to extend and modify its central theme. As Wordsworth's great "Ode" laments a radiance gone from the world, Shelley's "Hymn" describes the poet's perception of a beauty that is inconstant, that leaves the world "vacant and desolate," and

that is yet the chief source of meaning in a world otherwise accidental, formless, purposeless. Like the "Ode," "Hymn to Intellectual
Beauty" ends with a contrast between the youth, who is graced with
a moment of ecstatic communion with the absolute, and the man,
who prays for a steadier, surer source of strength. Both poems signify a new stage in the life of the poet, his coming to manhood,
marked by two related experiences, a recognition of the unreliabil-
ity of consciousness, and a renewal of faith that incorporates adult
knowledge of evil. Shelley, like Wordsworth, attempts to affirm the
continuity of experience, through memory, imagination, and love,
despite his subjective conviction that each moment is discrete and
its loss irremediable.

In his insistence on the human mind as the final referent of value,
Shelley departs significantly from Wordsworth. He follows Wordsworth in proposing a central image of an illuminating power, the
source of beauty, life, grace, in the visible world. But Wordsworth
presents the failure of beauty, the loss of meaning which is the real
subject of his "Ode," as a failure of the imagination; he passionately
affirms the objective beauty of the real world. The poet's despair
comes from his sense that the natural and the human, the human
and the divine, are essentially in harmony, and his own failure is a
falling away from the natural order of things, a blot upon a stainless
world. Wordsworth affirms the sacredness of life, the beneficent
providence of a God known through his creatures and through revelation. He accepts the suffering that is a sign of man's alienation
from God as necessary and as a source of wisdom; he embraces the
Christian virtues of humility and obedience to God, which depend
upon recognizing the limitations of both human knowledge and human action:

> . . . "One adequate support
> For the calamities of mortal life
> Exists—one only; an assured belief
> That the procession of our fate, howe'er
> Sad or disturbed, is ordered by a Being
> Of infinite benevolence and power;
> Whose everlasting purposes embrace
> All accidents, converting them to good."
>
> (*The Excursion,* IV, 10–17)

Shelley, on the other hand, having denied the authority of Scriptural revelation, draws his conception of deity from the workings of nature alone. These suggest to him that Power is not wise and providential but indifferent to human life, or at best capricious. He accepts the logical consequences of his denial of providence; the virtue of humility is replaced by pride or "Self-esteem," and obedience is redefined as obedience to one's own instinct for good. His sense of the random, purposeless quality of life, his conviction that the Absolute is at a far remove from the world of experience, dominate his earliest poetry and remain constant throughout his work. "Hymn to Intellectual Beauty" and "Mont Blanc" both constitute attempts to counter the pessimistic strain in his thought with a secular substitute for faith in God and immortality.

As its title suggests, "Hymn to Intellectual Beauty" is an assertion of faith and a prayer. The poet addresses a Spirit who is glimpsed only fleetingly, the object not of knowledge but of visionary revelation. "Intellectual Beauty"[1] is presented as a distinctly pagan deity, capricious, touched with human willfulness and partiality, susceptible to the flattery of worship. The deity, addressed as "SPIRIT fair" (83), "awful LOVELINESS" (71), is feminine both in its fickleness and in its effect on the world, which is to transfigure reality (like a light, a breath, a shadow) rather than to change it. The poet stands in relation to the Spirit as a neophyte to a divinity, and his language throughout suggests traditional religious ecstasy. But the doctrine of the poem is explicitly secular. The poet states categorically that "the name of God and ghosts and Heaven," the "frail spells" offered by traditional religion, cannot explain or justify the actual, observable conditions of life, its "Doubt, chance, and mutability." The Spirit of Beauty alone "Gives grace and truth to life's unquiet dream" (27–36). Her "glorious train" consists of the secular virtues of "Love" (human rather than divine love, the context suggests), "Hope," and the curiously modern "Self-esteem," a virtue honored by Rousseau, whom Shelley had just been reading—the contrary to that self-contempt which appears often in Shelley's poetry as a major evil (37–41). The "spells" of his deity, finally (unlike the "frail spells" of religion), bind the poet to Shelley's version of "the whole duty of man," not "to fear God and keep his commandments," but "To fear himself, and love all human kind" (83–84).[2]

Shelley's readers have repeatedly tried to assimilate the Spirit of Beauty either to Platonic categories or to the Christian categories that are explicitly denied; but Shelley is deliberately eclectic and personal in his formulations. The idea of "Intellectual Beauty" closely resembles the idea of the good in Platonic thought:

> In the intelligible place, the idea of *the good* is the last object of vision, and is scarcely to be seen; but if it be seen, we must collect by reasoning that it is the cause to all of every thing right and beautiful, generating in the visible place, light, and its lord the sun; and in the intelligible place, it is itself the lord, producing truth and intellect; and this must be beheld by him who is to act wisely, either privately or in public.[3]

Here are Shelley's thoughts in order: that the absolute is difficult to perceive, and functions at a double remove ("The awful shadow of some unseen Power / Floats tho' unseen amongst us"); it is the cause of all that is right and beautiful in all things ("Thy light alone . . . Gives grace and truth to life's unquiet dream"); it is the giver of truth and intellect ("Thou—that to human thought art nourishment . . ."); perception of the absolute leads to right action, public and private. The poet's knowledge of "Intellectual Beauty" is achieved not by intellectual discipline (as by the ascending rungs of the Platonic ladder), but by prayer, petition, vision—the traditional methods of apprehending the Christian God. Yet intellectual discipline is implied in the youth's hours of "studious zeal," and in his effort to pursue right, his vows to hold fast to truth. And in fact Shelley follows Plato in his attempt to balance the need for active effort, training and discipline, with the mystery of divine visitation— the perception that the gifts of the gods come rarely and unsolicited. The poem is one of Shelley's first attempts to create a personal and secular myth, to deny the authority of dogma or Scriptural revelation ("the false name with which our youth is fed," in the original version of line 53), while implicitly granting the validity of the irrational yet profound human needs that traditional religion claims to satisfy.

"Hymn to Intellectual Beauty" has at its center one of the first of Shelley's self-portraits. The personal experience dramatized in lines 49–72 is almost painfully authentic. Shelley was subject to visions

and hallucinations, which both he and Mary made a point of recording;[4] he haunted graveyards as a youth (as "A Summer Evening
Churchyard" records); he read voluminously and fell in love often.
But the personal details in the portrait, like the bardic ecstasy, the
"beating heart and streaming eyes," serve the symbolic rendering of
the poet's nature and function. The studies and travels of youth are
represented as an active seeking after experience, an active questioning of the meaning of life. The knowledge that is sought appears
of its own accord, in the literary guise of a dream-vision, in which
the poet on a spring morning is "awakened" out of his winter sleep.
The vision represents an absolute commitment; the poet's vows are
permanently binding, his ecstasy is the appropriate human response
to a divine visitation. Shelley is providing a religious metaphor for
rational experience, substituting images of divine and external authority for his own mind and conscience. His Spirit of Beauty is
purely hypothetical; the grave and life and fear indeed constitute a
dark reality—one that is unacceptable to the ardent imagination of
the poet. His great desire is to discover, to experience, to prove the
reality of that power whose presence he asserts so confidently; and
it is as if his desire worked in one direction against the combined
weight of his rational knowledge, his sensory experience, and his
ordinary skepticism. The fiction of the visionary seizure is a way of
reinforcing the frail hypothesis, ultimately of removing it from hypothesis to the kind of reality that can sustain faith. The love, hope,
and self-esteem that Shelley consistently invokes against the forces
of life are active virtues. They are immensely difficult to sustain,
given human frailty, and they require external nourishment—in
secular terms, relationship with the external world, or with the
beauty that moves in it. The inconstancy of the spirit is really a
metaphor for human frailty. Deity cannot be seen; its effects can
only be felt intermittently, or intuited in occasional natural presences. The poet chooses to say that deity is capricious rather than to
deny its existence.

The art of the "Hymn" is evident in its ingenious stanza form, a
prosodic imitation of the grace and inconstancy of the Spirit of
Beauty, and in its structure, in the lyric movement from the general
to the personal, from statement and reflection to confession, prayer,
and prophecy. Thus much Shelley learned from the odes of Words-

worth and Coleridge; but more distinctively, the "Hymn" shows him
working toward analogy as the basic technique of poetry, the definition of the unknown through its analogy with the known, the discovery in related observable phenomena of their invisible cause,
the isolation and identification of the missing term of an equation
for which only three parts are verifiable.

The action of beauty in the world is first described (lines 5–12)
in a series of similes comparing its inconstant visitations to fleeting
natural phenomena: moonbeams, clouds, music. These similes are
echoed in lines 32–36, with some variation, to suggest the transfig-
uring effect of the fleeting visitation on the unquiet world. Specific
phrases may seem merely pretty, wanting in the strength and ten-
sion that one finds in the comparable nature imagery of Coleridge
or Wordsworth: "moonbeams that behind some piny mountain
shower" (5); "clouds in starlight widely spread" (9); "mist o'er
mountains driven" (32); "moonlight on a midnight stream" (35).
But this web of references to observable phenomena sustains the
poet's assertion of a power that is unseen, hence indefinable except
through its effects. The similes are all natural instances of "grace,"
or loveliness, and "mystery," or inconstancy, impalpability. They
illustrate very precisely the double remove of beauty from its source,
the hiatus between the lovely, transient effect, as it can be perceived
by the senses, and its stable cause in nature. Thus moonbeams are
flickering, though the moon is fixed; clouds and mist are visible momentarily through reflected light; the rainbow is a chance effect of
sunlight in mist; music is caused by wind passing over strings; moonlight on a stream is a wavering reflection of a real astronomical
body. In each case the effect may be perceptible while the cause is
hidden, yet we know that the effect is a consequence of its cause in
nature. Just so, from the effects of beauty in the world, and upon
the "human heart and countenance," may we infer the existence
both of the "shadow" which can barely be felt or can only be perceived in vision, and of the unseen spirit that is its source.

The poem is unified by a dominant pattern of imagery, a recurring contrast of light and dark. Beauty is imaged as a light that con-
secrates with its own hues all that it shines upon; its effect is compared to various forms of natural light (that of sun, moon, stars),
and to light seen through substance or reflected or refracted by it

(clouds, mist, rainbow, hues and harmonies of evening). The world of "Doubt, chance, and mutability" is imaged in terms of darkness. Our state, in the absence of beauty, is a "dim vast vale of tears" (17); "fear and dream and death and birth" cast a "gloom" on the "daylight" of this earth (21–23); human thought is like a "dying flame" (45); life is a "dark reality" (48); this world is imprisoned in a "dark slavery" (70). Yet the associations of light and dark are not fixed; it is the "shadow" of Beauty that visits the world and falls upon the poet; Beauty nourishes human thought as darkness nourishes a dying flame.[5] What governs the imagery is not a pattern of symbolic association but the logic of relationship, explored freshly in each new simile. Shelley's subject is not a definition of "Intellectual Beauty" but an analysis of its relationship to human life, and to the poet who is its hierophant.

Despite the apparent explicitness of the "Hymn," there is a surprising shift in meaning in its closing lines. The imagery of the opening stanzas emphasizes the accidental character of change, the flickering inconstancy of Beauty's appearances, the supremacy in this world of "Doubt, chance, and mutability," the uncertain appearances of the moral and social impulses. The sense of change as random, purposeless, without cause or consequence, is conveyed in the statement that all that is shown must fail and fade, and in images of accidental and unpredictable phenomena—clouds, mist, winds, moonbeams, memory and dream, as well as the verbs "float," "visit," "depart and come." At the end of the poem there is a shift from images of change as accident to images of change as growth, ripening. The two natural cycles—day and night, the seasonal cycle— suggest the ripening of youth into maturity. The heat of noon yields to the serenity of afternoon; the brilliance of summer yields to the harmony of autumn; the ecstatic vision of the youth is replaced by the calm wisdom of the man. In each case something intense and brief yields naturally to something steadier, more enduring. Yet the images seem to be a natural summation of those used in the opening stanzas to suggest that the passage of beauty means nothing more than loss, vacancy: "hues and harmonies of evening" (8); "summer winds that creep from flower to flower" (4); images of light shining briefly and then disappearing, change that is a matter of atmosphere rather than substance. The metaphor raises the possibility that the capricious Spirit can be compelled to stay, that hope is warranted, even imperative, against all contrary evidence.

> . . . there is a harmony
>   In autumn, and a lustre in its sky,
> Which thro' the summer is not heard or seen,
> As if it could not be, as if it had not been!   (74–77)

The evidence of the senses is limited to present time. What cannot be seen or heard, does not exist; memory denies that it ever has existed. And yet change occurs, the seasons repeat the miracle, and the senses report on a new reality. Again the analogy between the known and the unknown urges belief in the hidden term—the Spirit whose presence, when it is not felt, can neither be remembered nor predicted. Once the divine revelation of Scripture is denied, as it is explicitly by Shelley, the fact that knowledge depends upon sense perception alone, and hence is by definition limited, becomes the best, perhaps the only, justification for faith—even though the gods of such faith must be invented and faith itself be an act of will.

Shelley wrote of "Mont Blanc" that "it was composed under the immediate impression of the deep and powerful feelings excited by the objects which it attempts to describe; and . . . rests its claim to approbation on an attempt to imitate the untameable wildness and inaccessible solemnity from which those feelings sprang" (preface to *History of a Six Weeks' Tour,* in *Works,* VI, 88). In its difficulty and scope the poem is certainly more than an imitation of scene. Shelley wrote that "if we would arrive at any knowledge which should be serviceable . . . we ought to consider the mind of man and the universe as the great whole on which to exercise our speculations" ("Speculations on Metaphysics," *Works,* VII, 65). His poetry from *Alastor* through "The Triumph of Life" could be considered a series of such speculations; "Mont Blanc" is his first fully realized attempt to give poetic expression to the "great whole."

The scene itself, in its "untameable wildness and inaccessible solemnity," is the source of speculation about "the mind of man and the universe." However, it is with mind in its relation to "things" that Shelley begins. The opening section analyzes this relationship in terms of an extended metaphor of landscape, which has something of the vibrancy and suggestiveness of the landscape of Coleridge's "Kubla Khan." The "unremitting interchange" (39) between things and thought is pictured first on the ideal or "intellectual" level. The "universe of things"—physical reality—flows in a rapid current through the mind,[6] where it meets and mingles with the waters of human thought. In lines 7–11 the opening metaphor—the meeting of waters—is compared to another more violent interchange, between a "feeble brook" and a "vast river." The feeble brook assumes a character beyond its own in its wild and tumultuous environs; so the waters of human thought, it is implied, take on splendor from the "rapid waves" of the universe of things. The simile suggests the immense force of the universe of things, and the relative weakness of human thought confronting experience. A sense of his own limited powers is one of the chief elements of the poet's reaction to the scene; he is stunned, awed by it, profoundly challenged to comprehend its immensity.

The opening metaphor, not very different from conventional metaphors of the "flow" of impressions, the "current" of ideas, the "river" of thought,[7] is elaborated in lines 7–11 into a landscape image which in its details (the "wild woods," the "mountains lone," the "vast river") graphically anticipates the scene before the poet, the subject of Section II. Here the poet moves from the ideal or mental world to another kind of reality, multiple and ever-changing, but with its own kind of permanence. As the "universe of things" flows through the mind, so the "many-coloured, many-voiced vale" (13) is invaded by the ceaseless motion, the "unresting sound" (33) of clouds, winds, and river. Although the passage is primarily a detailed, evocative description of the scene, it also continues to illustrate point for point the metaphor of Section I. For each detail is a full realization of the hypothetical scene sketched earlier, the contending woods and winds, the leaping waterfalls, the ceaseless commotion of the river, the interchange of light and gloom, the mingling of sounds.

The poet next returns to his original subject—mind and its workings—in terms of the description he has just given of the ravine. He seems (as in a trance) to see in the ravine an emblem of the workings of his own, his "human mind" (thus distinguished from "the

mind" of Section I). As the ravine receives the Arve, is at once its
"couch and [its] creation" (*Letters of P.B.S.,* I, 496), so his mind
passively receives and renders back external "influencings" (38) or
impressions; as the winds cause the movements of the pines, but also
"drink their odours" and listen to "their mighty swinging" (23), so
his mind holds an "unremitting interchange / With the clear universe of things around" (39–40).[8] The lines offer a specific instance
of the poet's opening generalization, as his own mind receives the
scene before it, and muses on it both in its own reality and as an
emblem of thought. Now the mind appears to be active as well as
passive, for the poet's thoughts, freed by his trancelike state to wander above the ravine or in the cave of Poesy, seek "among the shadows that pass by, / Ghosts of all things that are"[9] in quest of "Some
phantom, some faint image" of the scene, until the poet, his strange
trance broken, suddenly recalls them to his breast—"thou art there!"
(45–48). The last line represents a return to the self and its powers
for the mind driven to seek among shadows for reality.

As the sight of the ravine is introduced by a generalization about
the relation of the world of things to mind, so the sight of the mountain, towering far above the ravine, is introduced by another generalization, on the relation of human thought to "a remoter world,"
accessible only in sleep or death. This second generalization is hypothetical, as if to emphasize that in this region all is uncertain, impossible to verify. As nature includes more than one order of experience, so thought includes not only perception of the "clear universe
of things," not only images of the witch Poesy, but the mysterious
shapes that visit sleep or death, "gleams of a remoter world" (49).
And as the mountain is more awesome, more incomprehensible than
the vale, so the complex interchange of human thought with experience appears to be but a portion of something infinitely larger,
grander, the "mightier world" (55) of sleep and death, whose shapes
outnumber "the busy thoughts . . . / Of those who wake and live"
(51–52). While the human mind is relatively at ease in its relation
with the world of things, as it "floats" above the darkness of the ravine, or rests in the cave of Poesy, it is at a loss to comprehend the
unearthly, inaccessible forms of Mont Blanc: "For the very spirit
fails, / Driven like a homeless cloud from steep to steep / That
vanishes among the viewless gales!" (57–59). Mont Blanc itself is

When musing deeply on the lot
Of life—at that sweet time when winds are wooing
All vital things to wake & bring
News of buds & blossoming
Sudden thy shadow fell on me
I shrieked & clasped my hands in ecstasy

The day becomes more solemn & serene
When noon is past— there is a harmony
In autumn & a lustre in its sky
Which thro the summer is not heard or seen
As if it could not be—as if it had not been

like the truth
Of nature on my passive youth
Descended to my onward life supply
Thy calm, to one that worships thee
And every form containing thee

I. Draft of "Hymn to Intellectual Beauty," lines 55–60, 73–82
(Bodleian MS Shelley adds. e. 16, p. 60). Approximate size. By
permission of the Bodleian Library.

II. Draft of "Mont Blanc," lines 63–90 (Bodleian MS Shelley adds. e. 16, pp. 7–8). Approximate size. By permission of the Bodleian Library.

~~...~~

~~...~~

Mountains, ye have ~~...~~

~~By all~~ but which the wise & great & good

~~...~~ Interpret or make felt or deeply feel

In such a faith with Nature reconciled ———

Ye have a voice great Mountains — to repeal

Large codes of ~~...~~

~~...~~ fraud & woe — not understood

By all — but which the wise & great & good

Interpret, or make felt or deeply feel.

~~dreamless sleep~~
~~when feeble dreams~~

Or visit the hidden beds, or dreamless sleep

~~...~~ every fading leaf or flower

Ye ~~have subdued~~

~~Ye have awakened~~ ~~...~~ the forest & the stream.

~~Ye The power that ... the wood themselves~~
~~... the forest the ... & the woods~~
~~... the green meadow ... the stream~~

An ocean & all the living things that dwell

Within the dædal earth, lightning & ~~...~~

Earthquake ~~...~~ & hurricane

~~The ... of the hurricane ... when sleep~~

~~... winter ...~~

~~... death ... the~~ stream

III. "Song of Pan," lines 1–17 (Bodleian MS Shelley adds. e. 6, p. 27). Approximate size. By permission of the Bodleian Library.

described in terms of a reign of death antedating and outlasting the brief moments of human history. The Ravine, the world of the living, is "many-coloured, many-voiced," echoing to the Arve's "commotion;" the mountain towering above is "still, snowy, and serene" (61). The deathlike stillness of its "subject mountains" with their "unearthly forms" (62) of ice and rock contrasts with the "giant brood of pines" that cling around the ravine (20); the frozen floods contrast with the rushing waters below. The ravine suggests a natural religion: the pines are "Children of elder time, in whose devotion" (21) the winds come and go; the waterfall veils some "unsculptured image" (27). The mountain, hideous and magnificent, suggests primitive myth, "the scene / Where the old Earthquake-daemon taught her young / Ruin" (71–73).

The section ends with the poet's first attempt to define the meaning of the scene for the human being gazing on it. The natural scene has a lesson to teach the "adverting mind," but as the tongue of the wilderness is mysterious, its voice silent, the lesson must be discovered and interpreted by the poet. In its aspect of terror and inhumanity, the scene teaches "awful doubt," which one may take as a synonym for agnosticism, doubt that a creative deity exists. In its aspect of eternity and magnificence, the scene teaches a faith "so mild, / So solemn, so serene" (77–78) that it becomes a means of reconciliation with nature. There is no doubt that the "faith" thus taught is desirable; it is the same faith that Julian avows in "Julian and Maddalo" when he argues against man's passivity and the religious doctrines that enforce and justify evil:

> '. . . if man be
> The passive thing you say, I should not see
> Much harm in the religions and old saws
> (Tho' I may never own such leaden laws)
> Which break a teachless nature to the yoke:
> Mine is another faith'—
>
>   ("Julian and Maddalo," 160–65)

That faith is belief in the power of mind and will. Man can only be "reconciled" with the cruelty and indifference of nature when he refuses to accept the thesis that suffering is fated and deserved.

'. . . it is our will
That thus enchains us to permitted ill— . . .
Where is the love, beauty, and truth wc scck
But in our mind?'
                    ("Julian and Maddalo," 170–71, 174–75)

As it teaches skepticism, and as it teaches "another faith," the lesson
of the scene is opposed to the "large codes of fraud and woe" that
affirm the source of all life to be an omniscient, omnipotent, and
beneficent God, in whose name evil is justified and woe perpetuated.
For the mountain presents emblematically the source of life and
thought as a power destructive as well as creative, indifferent alike
to good and evil. The truth of nature is affirmed against the tyranny
of religious dogma; in the poet's terms it is a wilderness rather than
an Eden that is the primeval birthplace and image of eternity. The
wise, great, and good—Wordsworth, Godwin, Rousseau—who understand the voice of the mountain, through feeling as well as
thought, serve as prophets to the age, in opposition to established
truth, the institutionalized error which perpetuates the rule of tyrannical priest and king. Only by accepting the terror and indifference
of nature, the workings of physical necessity, are they enabled to
accept its corollaries, the importance of freedom and the power of
mind.

The fourth section returns again to the world of the living. The
poet, gazing upon the naked countenance of earth, the tumultuous
ravine, and the frozen peaks above, conceives that there is an absolute separation between the human world, with its natural, recurring
cycles of life and death, its ceaseless motion, its drive toward be-
coming, and that Power which dwells apart, "Remote, serene, and
inaccessible." The poet recapitulates the scene in its entirety, from
the peaks above, the "city of death" with its creeping glaciers, which
send down a "flood of ruin," despoiling the habitation of man, to
the vale below, where power is translated through the "one majestic
River" into "The breath and blood of distant lands." All the forces
of nature, destructive as well as life-giving, repeat their processes
apart from man and his cycles, in an interchange that is complete
and self-perpetuating. Lines 100–26 recall once more the opening
landscape image, as the tempest streams down into the vale and the

rushing torrents below well up from their "secret chasms" to meet in "one majestic River." But now the scene is an image not only for thought but for the elemental exchanges of life itself, the naked force of nature and the civilizing power of man, the powers of creation and destruction, of harmony and strife.

In the final section of the poem, the poet, having meditated on the destruction the mountains send down, the ceaseless motion and clamor of the vale below, turns his eyes again to the single peak towering above—apart from frozen floods and living vale, and yet the source of both. The suggestions of immanent religious power in lines 136–39 prepare for a statement toward which the poem has been building, from the first mention of an "unsculptured image" in the vale, through the poet's speculations on early myth. For the first time the faith anticipated at the end of the third section becomes explicit, that faith so "mild, / So solemn, so serene" that it can reconcile man with the nature from which (in Section IV) he "flies far in dread."

> . . . The secret strength of things
> Which governs thought, and to the infinite dome
> Of heaven is as a law, inhabits thee!
> And what were thou, and earth, and stars, and sea,
> If to the human mind's imaginings
> Silence and solitude were vacancy?   (139–44)

For an explanation of the closing lines, I turn to Shelley's prose account of the scene:

> And remember this was all one scene. It all pressed home to our regard & to our imagination.—Though it embraced a great number of miles the snowy pyramids which shot into the bright blue sky seemed to overhang our path—the ravine, clothed with gigantic pines and black with its depth below.—so deep that the very roaring of the untameable Arve which rolled through it could not be heard above—was close to our very footsteps. All was as much our own as if we had been the creators of such impressions in the minds of others, as now occupied our own.   (*Letters of P.B.S.*, I, 497)

The human mind, which conducts an "unremitting interchange" with the world of things, which seeks among shadows for images of its origins, is at last hesitantly recognized in its aspect of creator. The final lines affirm faith in the human mind, despite its acknowledged feebleness, its dependence both on the world of things and on "the secret strength of things / Which governs thought." Such faith is consistent with all that has gone before, as it is with Shelley's thought throughout his poetry, and, indeed, his prose as well. He writes in "Speculations on Morals:" "Imagination or mind employed in prophetically [imaging forth] its objects is that faculty of human nature on which every gradation of its progress, nay, every, the minutest change depends" (*Works,* VII, 75). It is the highest function of the mind to discover in the face of nature that which is above and apart from all life, the very source of life and thought. At the same time the significance of that "secret strength" depends in some way on the continually searching activities of the mind which appears so powerless in relation to its object.

"Mont Blanc" is indeed as ambitious as recent philosophical readings make it appear,[10] though the truth it defines is poetic rather than philosophical. Shelley maintains a double truth, in fact: there is an absolute division between the world of man and the power that wields all things (not in this poem, with "never-wearied love"—*Adonais,* 377), and despite this gulf, the two realms are interdependent. For if the source of all thought, all life, is ultimately the power that dwells apart from, inaccessible to, thought and life, only human thought can speculate on power and invest its habitations in nature with the mind's imaginings. The poet's function is to experience and to know what cannot be seen or heard, to create in language the forms his imagination craves. The poet, unlike the philosopher, can hold in his mind at once the conviction of absolute distance and the necessity of bridging it, without trying to choose between two incompatible propositions. This double truth is the moral of the poem, set forth consistently from beginning to end. The inescapable lesson of the scene, in both its physical aspect (the solitude and silence of the peak) and its moral aspect (the indifference of nature to human life), is that power dwells apart, "Remote, serene, and inaccessible" (97). That it directly rules the life of man, despite its remoteness, is equally clear. Power descends "in likeness of the Arve" (16); the snows at the peak are the source of the destructive glaciers and the life-giving river. At the same time, the creative power of the mind is affirmed by statement and indirectly by metaphor, and in the unfolding meditation of the poem itself. Human thought is imaged as an interchange; the mind receives but also renders "fast influencings" (38). The poet's thoughts seek actively for images of all things that are; throughout the poem the mind is attempting both to experience and to define or "imagine" the scene before it, not merely that which is open to the senses, but the inaccessible heights beyond. Though Shelley does not say so, it is not far-fetched to see in these last "imaginings" the mind going beyond active contemplation to creation itself, since there are in effect no data given.

In "Mont Blanc" Shelley struggles with the epistemological questions that dominate the poetry of Wordsworth and Coleridge, the meaning of nature, the relation of mind to nature and to the power embodied in nature. He follows Wordsworth and Coleridge in denying that mind is passive, arguing in terms of a compromise, an interchange between the human mind and "the universe of things"— which, if we go beyond epistemology to ethics or metaphysics, is a means of asserting human creativity. Coleridge is probably Shelley's model for the image of the mind as a "legion of wild thoughts," a rendering and receiving of "fast influencings:"

> Full many a thought uncall'd and undetain'd,
> And many idle flitting phantasies,
> Traverse my indolent and passive brain,
> As wild and various as the random gales
> That swell and flutter on this subject Lute!
>   And what if all of animated nature
> Be but organic Harps diversely fram'd,
> That tremble into thought, as o'er them sweeps
> Plastic and vast, one intellectual breeze,
> At once the Soul of each, and God of all?
>   ("The Eolian Harp," 39–48)

But Coleridge's lines imply their own refutation of the dangerous doctrine of passivity of mind. The original paradox of the spiritus breathed into man—the Soul of each, and God of all—transferred to epistemology, asserts both dependence and creative possibility. Coleridge repeatedly attacks materialistic philosophy for reducing the mind to a merely passive agent—"a lazy looker-on on an external World."[11] Ideally the mind of the poet is a meeting

> Of tides obedient to external force,
> And currents self-determined, as might seem,
> Or by some inner Power . . .
>
> ("To William Wordsworth," 14–16)

Similarly, Shelley affirms that the primary source of knowledge is perception ("It is an axiom in mental philosophy, that we can think of nothing which we have not perceived," he writes in "Speculations on Metaphysics," *Works*, VII, 59). Yet he is unwilling to relinquish the possibility of vision and revelation.

With regard to the nature of the power embodied in the mountain, Shelley departs from the more orthodox poetic statements of Coleridge and Wordsworth. The power that is "the secret strength of things / Which governs thought, and to the infinite dome / Of heaven is as a law" is related to the "presence," in "Tintern Abbey," that disturbs the poet "with the joy / Of elevated thoughts:"

> . . . a sense sublime
> Of something far more deeply interfused,
> Whose dwelling is the light of setting suns,
> And the round ocean and the living air,
> And the blue sky, and in the mind of man . . . (94–99)

The resemblance extends to verbal echoes: Shelley's power "inhabits" the mountain, as well as "earth, and stars, and sea;" in Wordsworth's poem power has its "dwelling" in sun, ocean, air, sky. In "Mont Blanc" the "secret strength of things . . . governs thought;" in "Tintern Abbey" a "motion and a spirit . . . impels / All thinking things, all objects of all thought, / And rolls through all things" (100–02). But in "Tintern Abbey" the sense of Deity follows directly from the poet's intimate love for the "beauteous forms" of the scene; in "Mont Blanc" the shapes are "hideous" though magnificent. The dwelling of power is not the life-giving sun, the "living air," but the realm of ice and death, presented above all in its destructive aspect, inspirer not of joy but of terror and awe, not of vision but of an ecstasy akin to madness. And the poet's response is not, as in Wordsworth's poem, to recognize in nature "the guide, the guardian of my heart, and soul / Of all my moral being" (110–11), but to question, to persist in the highest task of the imagination.

The daring suggestion of the final lines of the poem[12]—that the scene is actually a creation by the human mind out of "vacancy"— is supported by the structure of the poem, which is a deliberate reversal of the natural order of thought in a meditation on a scene. In "Tintern Abbey," in most of Coleridge's conversation poems, as well as in "Dejection: An Ode," in Shelley's early "A Summer Evening Churchyard" and in his "Stanzas written in Dejection," the poet moves naturally from the physical scene to the reflection it suggests, its application to human life. In "Mont Blanc" Shelley seems to make the physical scene contingent upon the generalization it has prompted but which precedes it in the poem. Instead of saying: "The Arve flows through the ravine; thus experience flows through the mind," he says: "Experience flows through the mind; thus the Arve flows through the ravine." This curious logical displacement suggests, as against the explicit statement of the poem, that physical reality is a function of the structuring imagination that perceives and orders it, and relates it by analogy to universal patterns of thought and experience.

What, then, are we to say of the poem's truth to nature? To what extent is the description, rather than symbolic or allegorical, an attempt to imitate, in best eighteenth-century fashion, the "untameable wildness and inaccessible solemnity" of the scene? Certain passages from Shelley's prose account of the scene find their way almost literally into the poem, so that one feels Shelley must have used the letter as a source:

> On all sides precipitous mountains the abodes of unrelenting frost surround this vale. Their sides are banked up with ice & snow broken & heaped up & exhibiting terrific chasms . . . They pierce the clouds like things not belonging to this earth. The vale itself is filled with a mass of undulating ice . . . It exhibits an appearance as if frost had suddenly bound up the

> waves & whir[l]pools of a mighty torrent. . . . the waves are
> elevated about 12 or 15 feet from the surface of the mass which
> is intersected with long gaps of unfathomable depth, the ice of
> whose sides is more beautifully azure than the sky.
>
> (*Letters of P.B.S.*, I, 500)

The description in the letter is condensed and intensified in the poem.
Metaphor is substituted for literal fact: the mountains that "surround" the vale become the "subject mountains" of the greater Mont
Blanc. The simple prose word yields to the more poetic phrase: the
"sky" becomes "overhanging heaven;" as if to compensate, prose
periphrasis is replaced by barer, more concise terms: "pile," for
"heaped high;" "blue" for "beautifully azure."

The part of the poem most closely related to the prose account is
the description of the "city of death," the glaciers that descend from
the mountain peaks:

> The glaciers perpetually move onwards at the rate of a foot
> each day with a motion which commences at the spot where,
> on the boundaries of perpetual congelation they are produced
> by the freezing of the waters which arise from the partial melt-
> ing of the eternal snows. They drag with them from the regions
> whence they derive their origin all the ruins of the mountain,
> enormous rocks, & immense accumulations of sand & stones.
> These are driven onwards by the irresistible progress of the
> stream of solid ice & when they arrive at a declivity of the
> mountain sufficiently rapid, roll down scattering ruin. . . .
> The verge of a glacier . . . presents the most vivid image of
> desolation that it is possible to conceive. No one dares to
> approach it, for the enormous pinnacles of ice perpetually fall,
> & are perpetually reproduced.—The pines of the forest which
> bounds it at one extremity are overthrown & shattered;—there
> is something inexpressibly dreadful in the aspect of the few
> branchless trunks which . . . still stand in the uprooted soil.
> The meadows perish overwhelmed with sand & stones.
>
> (*Letters of P.B.S.*, I, 498–99)

Again metaphor is substituted for the scientific precision of the prose
account: "The glaciers creep / Like snakes that watch their prey;"
"A city of death, distinct with many a tower / And wall impregnable

of beaming ice" (100–01; 105–06). The principal change, apart from the tendency noted earlier to condense and intensify, lies in the attribution of will to the elements: "there, many a precipice, / Frost and the Sun in scorn of mortal power / Have piled" (102–04). The physical scene is dramatized as a moral conflict between man and the deified elements. The observation of ruin and desolation in the prose passage is translated in the poem into a vision of a predatory Nature, unfolding its horrors according to the laws of its destiny.

The letter to Peacock speculates on the relationship of the physical scene in its magnificence and terror to conceptions of divinity;

> There is more in all these scenes than mere magnitude of proportion—there is a majesty of outline, there is an awful grace in the very colours which invest these wonderful shapes —a charm which is peculiar to them, quite distinct even from the reality of their unutterable greatness. . . . One would think that Mont Blanc was a living being & that the frozen blood forever circulated slowly thro' his stony veins.
> (*Letters of P.B.S.*, I, 497–98; 500)

And Shelley imagines Mont Blanc as the throne of the terrible Persian god Ahriman, who casts around him, "as the first essays of his final usurpation avalanches, torrents, rocks, & thunders—and above all, these deadly glaciers at once the proofs and the symbols of his reign." But there is nothing in the letter to support the grand affirmative statements in the poem:

> Thou hast a voice, great Mountain, to repeal
> Large codes of fraud and woe . . .   (80–81)

or

> . . . The secret strength of things
> Which governs thought, and to the infinite dome
> Of heaven is as a law, inhabits thee!   (139–41)

That is to say, there is nothing in Shelley's initial reaction to the scene to suggest that the power which the mountain embodies is related either to positive forces for social good or to the human thought that is the agent of social good. Affirmation of hope is the consequence of his ethical commitment. The mountain's voice is silent; and the poet who interprets the voice is responsible not only to the reality he sees and feels, but to his own vision of good. I note the difference between Shelley's prose record of the actual experience and his poetic rendering of it as still another example of the double strand that runs through his work: his clear view of evil, mutability, the facts of human experience, which can lead either to fatalism or to a rejection of life; and his desire to affirm hope, to insist on the possibility of human responsibility and creativity, in spite of a fundamentally indifferent order in the universe.

Unlike "Hymn to Intellectual Beauty" and "Mont Blanc," "To Constantia" has never been accorded weight in the canon of Shelley's poetry, mainly because its text was long known only in a chaotic manuscript draft, transcribed by Mary Shelley for *Posthumous Poems* (1824) and revised in C. D. Locock, *An Examination of the Shelley Manuscripts in the Bodleian Library* (Oxford, 1903). It was correctly assumed by Shelley's editors that the poem was addressed to Claire Clairmont and was written in the summer or fall of 1817, when Claire and her infant Allegra were living with Shelley and Mary at Marlow.

Shortly before Claire Clairmont's death, an American admirer of Shelley's poetry, Edward Silsbee, obtained from her the two Shelley notebooks now in the Harvard College Library. (The peculiar circumstances of this transaction served Henry James as inspiration for *The Aspern Papers*.) One of the notebooks contains a fair copy in Shelley's hand of "To Constantia," with a penciled notation: "written at Marlowe 1817   wd not let Mary see it   sent it to Oxford Gazette or some Oxford or county paper without his name." The poem was published on January 31, 1818, under the pseudonym "Pleyel," in the *Oxford University and City Herald,* which had advertised Shelley's works while he was at Oxford and frequently printed excerpts from his poetry.

"Hymn to Intellectual Beauty" is addressed to a spirit barely glimpsed, yearned after, felt in presences of nature; in "Mont Blanc" the poet broods upon and tries to encompass imaginatively a power manifest in the violent paradoxes of the visible scene. In both lyrics the presence or spirit addressed is hypothesized and created through the effort of the poet's imagination, impelled by his desire to discover meaning in the indifferent activities of nature. In "To Constantia" the poet addresses another human being; the poem is on first reading a periphrastic love poem, its erotic passion displaced from the woman to her song. But as in the two earlier lyrics, reality is mediated, its significance created, through art: in "Mont Blanc" the poet's "imaginings," in "To Constantia" the woman's song. In that process of mediation the self is dissolved, released from the failing body and infused with a power which has its source, or its manifest source, in the "dark eyes," the voice, the "blood and life" of the artist. The poem thus invites comparison with both of the earlier lyrics in its rendering of the relationship between imaginative power and the "secret strength of things." Like the 1816 lyrics, it represents and analyzes the power of the mind, inspired by love or vision, to create images of reality and to transcend both reality and image, to break through the veil.

The occasion of "To Constantia" is social: the poet is paying a compliment to a woman singing and accompanying herself on the piano. The names Shelley uses are part of the literary and social context; "Constantia" is the heroine of Brockden Brown's *Ormond,* an intellectual young woman who entertains her admirers by her accomplished playing and singing; "Pleyel" is the rationalist lover of Clara Wieland in Brown's *Wieland.* The pet names were part of the Shelleys' social games and flirtations during the summer at Marlow; Peacock mentions that they considered building a summer house on the model of the garden house in *Wieland.*[13]

But the poem goes far beyond its social context. Like "Mont Blanc," "To Constantia" gives the impression of a free lyric flight from its occasion, which provides the stimulus, the subject, and also the metaphor for a sustained imaginative drama. The woman's voice rises slowly, hovers with "soft and lulling wings" (2) over the listener's soul, calling it forth. The poet responds with the physical symptoms that precede trance and the vision that follows: quick breathing, wild thoughts, tears, an arrest of the blood. He is dissolved, consumed; his life is absorbed into the spirit of the woman, or the melody that emanates from her. Her song now rises free, flows on, and, like the life-giving air itself, fills all things with melody, changes in its course from tempest to calm, and again to another mode, more mysterious and more powerful, a "deep and breathless awe" (23). (The change is akin to those explored in "Mont Blanc," as the poet contemplates first the tumult of the Ravine, then the frozen steeps above, and the still and silent mountain peak towering beyond sight, and speculates upon the parallel mental phenomena, the wild thoughts of the poet, the images of poesy, and the "gleams of a remoter world.") The liberated spirit of the listener, released from the body and merged with the source of power, rejoices in its freedom from gravity, rides upon the impulse of song (as the cloud rides the tempest), and surveys the far bounds of the earth. Caught up in the "fast ascending numbers" of song (26), it grows wings (like the Platonic soul) and soars beyond the limits of space and time, past all natural experience, until at last the poet, fearful that the loss of consciousness—of the self, the world's walls—is indeed madness or death, implores the singer to cease, to turn, or return. (Again, the recall is comparable to the poet's recall of his wild and wandering thoughts in Section II of "Mont Blanc.") The song ends, but the poet passionately affirms that the power of the vision continues to exist, resides in the woman though her voice has become silent, lingers like odor on her breath and hair.

The strong center of the poem was apparent even in the garbled transcript in the standard editions of Shelley's poems. The lyric is at once an anatomy and an imitation of the experience of romantic inspiration, as Shelley conceived it: the dissolution of self, the spirit's flight into vision, and its terrifying descent. Music charms the senses and releases the soul from their bondage, but it effects that release by an annihilation of the whole self—blood, brain, heart—akin to the religious ecstasy of "Hymn to Intellectual Beauty:" "Sudden, thy shadow fell on me; / I shrieked, and clasped my hands in extacy!" And the release of the spirit, while it is primarily imaginative—a response to song, a visionary journey past the boundaries of sense—follows the patterns of sexual and religious ecstasy, a death that is a consummation, an absorption into a new life:

> As morning dew, that in the sunbeam dies,
> I am dissolved in these consuming extacies.
>
> I have no life, Constantia, but in thee . . .   (10–12)

The patterns of the song are frankly erotic: the "tempest, swift and strong" yielding to the breath of summer's night, the voluptuous flight of the soul followed by its momentary suspension, the fast-ascending numbers that take the soul beyond the world's sphere, the sinking that is akin to death, the lingering effects of ecstasy. The rhythms of sexual passion provide a metaphor for the workings of art, the response of the spirit to the powers of imagination.

The ecstatic swoon rendered in the poem is akin to other moments of erotic passion in Shelley's lyrics, in which the poet embraces dissolution: "I die, I faint, I fail!" in "The Indian Girl's Song" or the fragment beginning:

> I pant for the music which is divine,
> My heart in its thirst is a dying flower.

But the lyric has even stronger affinities with Shelley's major visionary poems. In its rendering of the poet's vision, "To Constantia" anticipates Shelley's mature mythology: the consuming of the self in the "fire for which all thirst" (*Adonais,* 485); the voyage beyond the spheres and the rending of heaven and earth, as in the final stanza of *Adonais;* the ambiguous identification of love with death in an "annihilation;" an abrupt sinking or falling away, which follows ecstasy. The final stanza suggests the rhetoric of *Epipsychidion,* the flight into "love's rare Universe" and the descent: "Ah, woe is me! / What have I dared? where am I lifted? how / Shall I descend, and perish not?" (123–25).

The most immediate parallels, as editors have noted, are Panthea's account of her dream of Prometheus (*Prometheus Unbound,* II, i, 56–92), and the duet of Asia with the "Voice in the Air" (II, v, 48–110). In both of these passages music, "which makes giddy the dim brain" (II, i, 66) is the effective agent of visionary transport, of love, and, through love, of the power to change or transcend nature. Panthea describes Prometheus' voice "falling" on her, bidding her lift her eyes:

> I lifted them: the overpowering light
> Of that immortal shape was shadowed o'er
> By love; which, from his soft and flowing limbs,
> And passion-parted lips, and keen, faint eyes,

Steamed forth like vaporous fire; an atmosphere
Which wrapped me in its all-dissolving power,
As the warm æther of the morning sun
Wraps ere it drinks some cloud of wandering dew.
I saw not, heard not, moved not, only felt
His presence flow and mingle through my blood
Till it became his life, and his grew mine,
And I was thus absorbed . . .
                    (*Prometheus Unbound*, II, i, 71–82)

Prometheus is "shadowed o'er" by love, the same love that "steam[s] forth" like vaporous fire and wraps the loved one. From Panthea's point of view, that of the immortals, the senses are irrelevant, she "saw not, heard not, moved not," but "felt" (the least specific indication of sense) his presence flow through her blood, "Till it became his life, and his grew mine." Both Prometheus and Panthea are subject to the power which infuses and unites them, and bears them on its surge, and which can be known or identified only through analogy with natural powers—sun, fire, wind. Similarly, in "To Constantia," Shelley endows the physical reality—the woman playing her instrument and singing, the lover listening to her voice —with divine and magical possibilities. The "instrumental strings" are taught "witchcraft" by the blood and life within the "snowy fingers" (3–4)—that is, the invisible principle of life within the visible flesh; her voice rises like a spirit, an emanation that leaves the body far behind. The image of one spirit dissolved and consumed by the power emanating from another is more explicit in Panthea's lines than in "To Constantia;" Panthea is recondensed as Prometheus' presence passes from her (as the lover in "To Constantia" returns to earth in the last stanza). The imagery of dissolution and consumption has a peculiar meaning for Shelley: these are basic natural processes, which appear to defy scientific observation and yet demonstrate scientific law. The apparent disappearance of matter, or its change to another state, is mysterious, explicable only in terms of the action of invisible power upon an invisible form or principle; return, or reconstitution, condensation, is similarly mysterious and yet predictable. Applied to human experience, these physical processes urge the possibility of modes of mental experience that appear to contradict the limitations of our present state. They also serve as physical evidence of unity in multiplicity, of eternity in change.

The second parallel passage, Asia's song, describes a journey that echoes the visionary journey of the poet's spirit in "To Constantia:"

> My soul is an enchanted boat,
> Which, like a sleeping swan, doth float
> Upon the silver waves of thy sweet singing . . .
>   It seems to float ever, for ever,
>   Upon that many-winding river,
>   Between mountains, woods, abysses,
>   A paradise of wildernesses!
> Till, like one in slumber bound,
> Borne to the ocean, I float down, around,
> Into a sea profound, of ever-spreading sound . . .
>   (*Prometheus Unbound*, II, v, 72–74, 78–84)

Asia's response to song differs from the poet's in that it is beyond the changes of sexual passion; the course of her enchanted boat has a sublime ease, and her destiny is an elysium of love and harmony. In "To Constantia," as in *Adonais*, the ascent, "Wild, sweet, yet incommunicably strange" (25), is violent; the "cope of Heaven seems rent and cloven" (27) (as the earth and skies are "riven" in *Adonais*), and what lies beyond is fearful, as the breaking of all mortal ties must be. But the two passages from *Prometheus Unbound* suggest that Shelley's subject in "To Constantia" is more intellectual than romantic, has to do less with the experience of erotic response than with its analogy to modes of visionary experience. The "dark reality" that lies unspoken behind the poem is the prison of sense experience, even more, of the solitary self. Although the questioning mind fights against the felt inadequacy of sense experience and the heart rebels against the poverty and incompleteness of the self, the senses and the self remain the point of return; and the poet is quite right to fear that the only escape from sanity—which implies staying within the limits of sense experience—is madness or death.

Like the 1816 lyrics, "To Constantia" hypothesizes a power that can be known or inferred only through its effects, and attempts to derive from sense experience, from the intuitions of dream and poetry, from nonrational experience like vision and sexual ecstasy, a reality other than the common one. That reality is intuited in the woman's transfigured presence, in her song, as in presences of nature; it is actively given form and image by the liberated imagination of the artist, and retained in memory—perhaps as a bar against that collapse and disintegration which always threatens the imprisoned self. The last lines urge the power of the imagination, of music and feeling, to survive their mortal forms; they suggest that the singer herself is but an agent of a greater power, which speaks through her and possesses her, as her voice possesses the poet. Thus the poem expresses Shelley's chief defense against despair: his conviction that the life of objects lies in the spirit that fills and animates them, and in the imagination that endows them with meaning, rather than in their physical identity.

NOTES

1. White, I, 701, suggests Wieland's *Agathon* as a source for the term "intellectual beauty." "Intellectual" is a synonym for "spiritual" or "abstract," beauty as apprehended by the intellect rather than the senses. In the notes "On Life" Shelley explains his rejection of materialism and "the popular philosophy of mind and matter," and his commitment to the "Intellectual Philosophy" as defined in Sir William Drummond's *Academical Questions* (*Works*, VI, 194–95).
2. See Elizabeth Nitchie, "Shelley's 'Hymn to Intellectual Beauty,'" *PMLA*, 63 (1948), 752–53. A similar play on religious doctrine occurs in "Ode to Liberty," 231–33.
3. *Republic* VII.517 in *The Works of Plato*, tr. Floyer Sydenham and Thomas Taylor, 5 vols. (London: printed for Thomas Taylor, 1804), I, 360.
4. White describes Shelley's early experiences with the supernatural: I, esp. chaps. 6, 11.
5. "Thou—that to human thought art nourishment, / Like darkness to a dying flame!" Darkness nourishes a dying flame in the sense that it makes the flame appear brighter than it is. Human thought, like a dying flame in that it is frail, requiring sustenance to keep alive, must be fed by beauty; in the absence of beauty, thought flickers and dies.
6. Some readers have taken "the mind" to mean "Universal Mind;" thus the poet, when in Section II he refers to "My own, my human mind," distinguishes his own mind from "the mind" (Universal Mind) of Section I. Shelley speaks of "the one mind" or "universal mind" in "On Life" (*Works*, VI, 196), "The Daemon of the World," Part II, 539–46, and *Laon and Cythna*, VII, xxxi, 5–6. But "Mont Blanc" refers only to "the mind" and "thought" (140); if Shelley meant to refer to

"the One Mind," a rather esoteric concept then as now, he would have done so specifically.

7. Cf. "Speculations on Metaphysics:" "Thought can with difficulty visit the intricate and winding chambers which it inhabits. It is like a river whose rapid and perpetual stream flows outwards . . . The caverns of the mind are obscure, and shadowy; or pervaded with a lustre, beautifully bright indeed, but shining not beyond their portals" (*Works*, VII, 64). A similar image is used in *Alastor*, 505–08.

8. The emblematic function of the landscape is even clearer in the first draft of "Mont Blanc" (see below, Appendix B, ii), where the movement from the "unremitted interchange" between the mind and the universe to the heights above, and the "still cave of the witch Poesy" (41–45) is parallel to the movement earlier in the section from the "ceaseless motion" and "unresting sound" of the ravine to the "aerial waterfall whose veil / Robes some unsculptured image" and the "sleep" which inhabits the scene (27–33).

9. Cf. Lucretius, *De rerum natura*, IV.26–41, esp. 30–31: "there exist what we call images of things; which, like films drawn from the outermost surface of things, flit about hither and thither through the air." Tr. W. H. D. Rouse, Loeb Classical Library (Cambridge, Mass.: Harvard University Press, 1924).

10. Readings of interest are Earl R. Wasserman, *The Subtler Language: Critical Readings of Neoclassic and Romantic Poems* (Baltimore: Johns Hopkins Press, 1959), pp. 195–250; and Harold Bloom. *Shelley's Mythmaking* (New Haven: Yale University Press, 1959), pp. 11–45. Bloom argues for what seems to me a rather forced reading of lines 76–79. The grammatical heart of the sentence is the same in the draft and the printed text: "which teaches . . . doubt, or faith so mild . . . that man may be . . . with nature reconciled." The draft reading, "In such a faith" (which is the final uncanceled version of several canceled attempts at the same thought, viz. "With such a faith," "In such wise faith"), qualifies by reinforcing; it seems unlikely that the revised version, "But for such faith," should reverse the original meaning through a qualifying clause, as Bloom argues (i.e. a faith so mild "as to prevent us" from being reconciled with nature, p. 32). But it could qualify by intensification, "but" meaning "only." That is, the sense would then be: "which teaches faith so mild, solemn, and serene that man, only to achieve such faith, may be reconciled with nature." Many readers have tackled the phrase; there seems a good case for choosing the reading most consistent with Shelley's other writing.

11. Letter to Thomas Poole, March 23, 1801, in *Collected Letters of Samuel Taylor Coleridge*, ed. Earl Leslie Griggs, 4 vols. (Oxford: Clarendon, 1956), Letter 388.

12. The final lines of "Mont Blanc" suggest the idealism which forms one stage of Shelley's philosophical development, i.e. "nothing exists but as it is perceived," "On Life," *Works*, VI. 194. But Shelley's mature views are more accurately represented by the uncontroversial statement in "A Defence of Poetry:" "All things exist as they are perceived; at least in relation to the percipient" (Para. 42). The "Defence" also in-

cludes a sentence that poses the same question as the last three lines of "Mont Blanc" in the same grammatical form; the passage probably provides the best commentary on the conclusion of the poem: "What were Virtue, Love, Patriotism, Friendship—what were the scenery of this beautiful Universe which we inhabit . . . if Poetry did not ascend to bring light and fire from those eternal regions where the owl-winged faculty of calculation dare not ever soar?" (Para. 39).

13. Peacock, *Memoirs of Shelley,* in *The Life of Percy Bysshe Shelley, as Comprised in "The Life of Shelley" by Thomas Jefferson Hogg, "The Recollections of Shelley & Byron" by Edward John Trelawny, "Memoirs of Shelley" by Thomas Love Peacock,* ed. Humbert Wolfe, 2 vols. (London, 1933), II, 327–28.

CHAPTER THREE

THE HUMAN CONDITION
"The frail bark of this lone being"

In "Lines written among the Euganean Hills" Shelley continues the epistemological and ethical debate argued in "Mont Blanc." The poet, meditating upon a natural scene, weighs against the reality of human misery the power of the imagination to repeal "codes of fraud and woe" in the actual world, or to create a refuge from them. The young radical hopes for change; he prays that tyranny will be brought low, and that freedom will awaken from its long sleep. But Shelley had no illusions about the difficulty of accomplishing revolution or ensuring its happy outcome. He writes in the fragment "Marenghi," also composed in 1818:

> The sweetest flowers are ever frail and rare,
> And love and freedom blossom but to wither;
> And good and ill like vines entangled are,
> So that their grapes may oft be plucked together.
>
> (x, 47–50)

He who would separate the good from the ill needs more than any-one else to recognize their interconnectedness.

"Lines written among the Euganean Hills" is on first reading loose and digressive, in the tradition of the prospect poem from "Grongar Hill" to Wordsworth's "Descriptive Sketches" and Coleridge's "Fears in Solitude." The poet moves easily from the account of his day in the hills to political and social commentary. But as in "Mont Blanc," natural description serves as a basis for allegory, and natural fact and historical reality serve as metaphors for a vision of life as it might be and ought to be.

Throughout the poem the relationship between the scene and the thought it occasions is complex. Nature is a source of inspiration, of *feeling;* thus the dejected poet may find himself miraculously eased by the combined influences of sun and sky and landscape, as the poet of "Mont Blanc" is affected by the sublimity and terror of the physical scene. To the poet who not only feels but observes and interprets, whose imagination seeks in all it sees for analogy and type, nature is also a source of metaphor, hence of meaning. Thus the familiar aphorism of the opening lines—"Many a green isle needs must be / In the deep wide sea of misery"—appears to have been suggested by the appearance of the landscape, the hills in the distance which bear "The likeness of a clump of peaked isles" ("Julian and Maddalo," 79). Yet the order of thought, as in "Mont Blanc," suggests that nature is not the source of the metaphor but rather illustrates universal truths. The effect of putting the generalization before rather than after the description of scene makes nature appear to be contingent upon thought; it liberates the poet from the tyranny of fact. At the same time his reflections take on a hypothetical, tentative, and ultimately arbitrary character. In Wordsworth's meditations, one has the sense of an indubitable reality that stands before the poet; he can refer to the scene with confidence in its existence not only for himself but for his reader. The truth of nature lends substance to the poet's symbolic reading of nature, giving it a kind of prior inevitability, similar to the conviction generated by the mass of detail, the documentation of place and time and character in the Victorian novel. In Shelley's poetry reality is at once a product of artifice and intensely personal, even when, as in "Mont Blanc" and "Lines written among the Euganean Hills," the center of the poem is precise description of an actual scene. It seems that with every poem Shelley starts afresh; he does not identify himself with a constant subject matter, the specific English reality of time and scene which Wordsworth draws upon, nor does he assume a single role as observer or analyst, a consistent poetic voice. His poems appear to invent their argument as they proceed, constantly revising assumptions, moving toward possibility, toward questions, rather than demonstrating or reaffirming doctrine.

The poet's meditation, then, begins with a proposition about life.

> Many a green isle needs must be
> In the deep wide sea of misery,
> Or the mariner, worn and wan,
> Never thus could voyage on . . .   (1–4)[1]

There are green isles, there "needs must be;" if there were no flicker-
ings of hope, who would not, in Hamlet's words, wish to "take arms
against a sea of troubles, / And by opposing, end them?" But having suggested the possibility of hope, Shelley fastens upon the
thought of human distress—betrayed love and friendship, pain, bitter words—imaged as the mariner's endless drifting toward the
"haven of the grave."

> Day and night, and night and day,
> Drifting on his dreary way,
> With the solid darkness black
> Closing round his vessel's track;
> Whilst above the sunless sky,
> Big with clouds, hangs heavily,
> And behind the tempest fleet
> Hurries on with lightning feet . . .   (5–12)

The mariner's wanderings end in a solitary, unlamented death on an
alien shore:

> On the beach of a northern sea
> Which tempests shake eternally,
> As once the wretch there lay to sleep,
> Lies a solitary heap,
> One white skull and seven dry bones,
> On the margin of the stones,
> Where a few grey rushes stand,
> Boundaries of the sea and land . . .
> Those unburied bones around
> There is many a mournful sound;
> There is no lament for him,
> Like a sunless vapour, dim,
> Who once clothed with life and thought
> What now moves nor murmurs not.
>   (45–52, 60–65)

The sea-mews wail over his bones, but no one laments for the extinguished spirit of the human being.[2] The "northern sea" suggests the edge of the world, tempest-shaken, desolate of all life.

Behind Shelley's allegory of life as an uncharted voyage, the human being as a mariner at the mercy of the elements, the unknown and the perilous, stand the great classical examples of wandering and exile.[3] The most immediate contemporary analogue was Coleridge's "The Rime of the Ancient Mariner," with its terrible analysis of a "divided will," a helpless drifting.[4] In the preface to the *Rosalind and Helen* volume, in which "Lines written among the Euganean Hills" appeared, Shelley describes the opening lines of the poem as an "image of deep despondency"—that same dejection he analyzed a few months later in the "Stanzas" written at Naples. The emphasis is upon the impotence of the self and the hostility and treachery of the natural world, the meaninglessness of effort. The nightmare horror of life, the absence of meaning, is reinforced by the likeness of the voyage to "that sleep / When the dreamer seems to be / Weltering through eternity." The only hope—the green isle —appears accidental and unpredictable.

The poet's account of his day, a "flowering isle" surrounded by pain, begins with a description of sunrise in the hills.

> 'Mid the mountains Euganean
> I stood listening to the pæan,
> With which the legioned rooks did hail
> The sun's uprise majestical;
> Gathering round with wings all hoar,
> Thro' the dewy mist they soar
> Like grey shades, till th' eastern heaven
> Bursts, and then, as clouds of even,
> Flecked with fire and azure, lie
> In the unfathomable sky,
> So their plumes of purple grain,
> Starred with drops of golden rain,
> Gleam above the sunlight woods,
> As in silent multitudes
> On the morning's fitful gale
> Thro' the broken mist they sail,
> And the vapours cloven and gleaming

> Follow down the dark steep streaming,
> Till all is bright, and clear, and still,
> Round the solitary hill. (70–89)

The description is so precise as to color, sound, motion, the quality of the atmosphere, the changes that light effects on clouds, birds, hill, that a reader of visual imagination is invited to reconstruct the scene exactly as it must have been. The implication is that the poet's eye is similarly trained on its object, not only to see it as it appears (the shift from past to present tense suggests the effort of exact reconstruction), but to understand what it is, in terms of its likeness to other phenomena, its effect on its surroundings. As an image of the sudden relief of the poet's despondency, the sunrise is the moment of a breaking through. The sudden evaporation of mist and clouds allows the vision beyond to appear; motion and intense activity are followed by sudden calm. The description focuses on the rooks' anticipation of the sunrise rather than the sunrise itself; it is as if the poet, in the peculiar state of receptiveness that precedes prophecy, is granted a sign from the gods. The spontaneous, natural "pæan" of the rooks, their soaring into the sun, contrasts with the "drifting" of the mariner, the downward motion of the opening section: "And sinks down, down, like that sleep" (16)—downward motion being associated with despair and death, upward motion, as in music, with joy, celebration, life, freedom. The image of the rooks in flight not only parallels the poet's sudden joy but anticipates the theme of freedom that is to occupy his thoughts as he mourns the fate of Italy.

The "green isle" is not only a physical refuge but a moment of time, a metaphor for the poet's day:

> Aye, many flowering islands lie
> In the waters of wide Agony:
> To such a one this morn was led,
> My bark by soft winds piloted . . . (66–69)

So the original metaphor of the green isle in the sea of misery suffuses the poet's view of the landscape, which appears to him like a green sea islanded by fair cities:

> Beneath is spread like a green sea
> The waveless plain of Lombardy,
> Bounded by the vaporous air,
> Islanded by cities fair . . .   (90–93)

It appears that the actual scene, in its morning clarity, denies the poet's despair and his subjective fantasy. It presents against his image of the solitary mariner, the populous city; against the image of a dark and perilous natural world, a world sunny and beneficent; against the image of a godless universe, without purpose or boundary, a civilization rich in history and myth:

> Underneath day's azure eyes
> Ocean's nursling, Venice lies,
> A peopled labyrinth of walls,
> Amphitrite's destined halls,
> Which her hoary sire now paves
> With his blue and beaming waves.   (94–99)

But the fair appearance is deceptive, and the poet, though he is tempted by its beauty, shakes off the spell and turns to the political reality that lies behind the vision: the fair cities are, in fact, prisons of misery and corruption. And so the original terms of the poet's allegory are not denied by reality, but prophetically fulfilled. Padua is a "peopled solitude," Venice, "conquest-branded," shall rightly be reduced to her ancient state, claimed by Ocean, depopulated, the haunt of the sea-mew. The cities of Italy are "fair isles" only in the sense that they have sheltered the great poets. In the tribute to Byron, lines 167–205, the image of hope in despair, the "green isle" in the waters of agony, shifts to the image of the single spirit, the voice of the poet, which alone has power to dispel the mists and clouds, the "sins and slaveries" of life:

> As the ghost of Homer clings
> Round Scamander's wasting springs;
> As divinest Shakespeare's might
> Fills Avon and the world with light
> Like omniscient power, which he
> Imaged 'mid mortality;

As the love from Petrarch's urn,
Yet amid yon hills doth burn,
A quenchless lamp, by which the heart
Sees things unearthly; so thou art,
Mighty spirit: so shall be
The city that did refuge thee.   (194–205)

The theme of hope shifts from the image of the green isle in the sea
to the image of the "quenchless lamp" of poetry illuminating the
surrounding dark. So too the opening vision of a solitary, unlamented death yields to a vision of apocalypse: Venice sunk into the
sea, the Italian cities destroyed by revolution:

Sepulchres, where human forms,
Like pollution-nourished worms
To the corpse of greatness cling,
Murdered, and now mouldering . . . (146–49)

Shelley echoes Dante, appropriately, prophesying a great fire from
a little spark,[5] and Tyranny itself groveling before the flames "howl-
ing through the darkened sky." This apocalyptic vision dominates
"Ode to the West Wind," written a year later; the treatment of the
theme in "Lines written among the Euganean Hills" explains, perhaps, Shelley's apparent willingness to sacrifice the beauty of the
past ("old palaces and towers / Quivering within the wave's intenser
day") in the conviction that only the total destruction of the old
tyranny will suffice. But in "Lines written among the Euganean
Hills," destruction is one of several possibilities which the poet entertains as he meditates upon the scene. And the ending of the poem
appears to reject revolution in favor of an ideal image of nonviolent
reform, accomplished through a Shelleyan form of anarchism, in
which a community of kindred spirits has the power, through example, to change the world.

As the body of the poem is framed by an allegory for human life,
so the meditation is organized by the progress of the day from sunrise to sunset. The opening metaphor is repeated and varied like a
musical theme, as it introduces and closes the account of the day:

Many a green isle needs must be
In the deep wide sea of misery . . .   (1–2)

> Aye, many flowering islands lie
> In the waters of wide Agony . . .   (66–67)

> Other flowering isles must be
> In the sea of life and agony . . .   (335–36)

Similarly, Shelley creates a counterpoint, a recurring second theme, with the introduction of each point of time, marked by the position of the sun in relation to the horizon, and the quality of the light:

> Lo! the sun upsprings behind,
> Broad, red, radiant, half reclined
> On the level quivering line
> Of the waters chrystalline . . .   (100–03)

> Lo, the sun floats up the sky
> Like thought-winged Liberty,
> Till the universal light
> Seems to level plain and height . . .   (206–09)

> Noon descends around me now:
> 'Tis the noon of autumn's glow,
> When a soft and purple mist . . .
> Fills the overflowing sky . . .   (285–87, 293)

> Noon descends, and after noon
> Autumn's evening meets me soon,
> Leading the infantine moon,
> And that one star, which to her
> Almost seems to minister
> Half the crimson light she brings
> From the sunset's radiant springs . . . (320–26)

The repeated phrases, like the marked and insistent rhythm of the trochaic tetrameter, give form to an apparently discursive piece, both by framing it and by marking it off into distinct parts. But there is a more intimate connection between the framing metaphor and the marking off of the day. The immediate contrast is between the darkness, the sunless sky, the dim ever-receding shore of the allegory, and the bright sunlight, the clear, sharply-outlined horizon, of the actual scene. Similarly, there is a contrast between the treacherous and hostile sea and the "unfathomable" sky, one "o'er-brimming," the other "overflowing" with light—the sea representing misery, death, an eternity of despair, the sky representing hope and immortality. But the sequence of metaphor also suggests a shift of emphasis of the kind noted in the last stanza of "Hymn to Intellectual Beauty." The poem moves from images of change as accidental and unpredictable (the occasional green isle) or as meaningless (the succession of "Day and night, and night and day,") to images of change as the rhythm of life itself, a ripening in harmony from morning to noon to evening. The central moment of the poet's day, which stands against the opening image of despondency as an image of total, joyous identification with nature, appears to suggest precisely this kind of immanent meaning in natural process:

> Noon descends around me now:
> 'Tis the noon of autumn's glow,
> When a soft and purple mist
> Like a vaporous amethyst,
> Or an air-dissolved star
> Mingling light and fragrance, far
> From the curved horizon's bound
> To the point of heaven's profound,
> Fills the overflowing sky;
> And the plains that silent lie
> Underneath, the leaves unsodden
> Where the infant frost has trodden
> With his morning-winged feet,
> Whose bright print is gleaming yet;
> And the red and golden vines,
> Piercing with their trellised lines
> The rough, dark-skirted wilderness;
> The dun and bladed grass no less,
> Pointing from this hoary tower
> In the windless air; the flower
> Glimmering at my feet; the line
> Of the olive-sandalled Apennine
> In the south dimly islanded;
> And the Alps, whose snows are spread
> High between the clouds and sun;

And of living things each one;
And my spirit which so long
Darkened this swift stream of song,
Interpenetrated lie
By the glory of the sky:
Be it love, light, harmony,
Odour, or the soul of all
Which from heaven like dew doth fall,
Or the mind which feeds this verse
Peopling the lone universe.   (285–319)

This is a remarkable and beautiful passage, often cited out of context as an example of Shelley's nature description at its best. But what is less often noted is its correspondence to the despairing images of the opening lines, which describe nature as atomistic and hostile and allegorize life as purposeless misery. The opening allegory implies that there is no relationship between man and man, man and nature. The account of the noon moment answers the opening image not simply by supplying positives for the earlier negatives—light and fragrance for dark, the land and sky and life-giving earth and sun for the treacherous sea—but by interpreting the natural scene as a felt relationship among all the elements of the visible scene, life and mind and spirit. The moment described is a "natural" equivalent of the visionary experience of "Hymn to Intellectual Beauty," in which the poet is seized and penetrated by the "truth of nature"—that spirit which leaves the earth "vacant and desolate" when it passes. The "darkening" spirit of the poet, dark as it conceives of life as agony, as it laments the death of freedom in Italy, is, as by a miracle, penetrated with light. The poet's spirit is released not by a visionary ecstasy, however, as in "Hymn to Intellectual Beauty," but by a response to nature, and to a specific moment in nature, in which all boundary, all limit, is dissolved—and yet all the elements of nature are sharply etched as in the clarity of a dream. The precise observation of detail contributes to the radiance of the whole—the bright gleam of frost, the red and golden vines "piercing" the rough wilderness, as the soft autumnal moment, suggesting at once fulfilment and promise, is held in the imagination. The scene itself—distant mountains, fertile plains, the single flower—suggests the relativity of time in nature and the continuity in change and process. The "interpenetration" of nature, of all "living things," with the poet's spirit represents at once the dissolution of the solitude imaged by the mariner, and a rediscovery of the mind's creative power. Shelley leaves the question of a first cause for the felt harmony open, as he does in "Mont Blanc": be it the "soul of all" or the mind of the poet, the "secret strength of things" or the imagination. The emphasis is upon the subjective intuition of harmony, not its ultimate source.

The moment is but a moment, an interlude; it passes with the day itself, and the poet resumes his original metaphor.

> Noon descends, and after noon
> Autumn's evening meets me soon,
> Leading the infantine moon,
> And that one star, which to her
> Almost seems to minister
> Half the crimson light she brings
> From the sunset's radiant springs:
> And the soft dreams of the morn,
> (Which like winged winds had borne
> To that silent isle, which lies
> 'Mid remembered agonies,
> The frail bark of this lone being,)
> Pass, to other sufferers fleeing,
> And its antient pilot, Pain,
> Sits beside the helm again. (320–34)

The evening, which signals the passing of the day and hence of joy, is observed with the same imaginative sympathy that marks the description of noon and the earlier account of the rooks in flight, as if to suggest the continuity of nature's processes with or without the participation of man. The sense of nature's separateness from man is never very far from the perception of its power, for Shelley as for Wordsworth. The poet turns to nature as it is real and indubitable, as it affects his feeling and his thought, as it yields revelations, as it embodies symbolic patterns. But it is intractable to his imagination, separate and distinct from him, indifferent—he is inevitably thrown back upon his own mind. And so the poet returns to his old familiar, Pain.[6] Still the movement of the poem will not permit a closing of the

circle; as in "Hymn to Intellectual Beauty," the vision alters the
poet's life, or his sense of life's possibilities, even though the vision
itself passes. As the green isle lies amid "remembered agonies," so
the noon moment of harmony persists in memory, encouraging the
hope of other "flowering isles." The final section of the poem has a
quality of liberation, as of the fancy set free; hope is resurgent both
for the dejected poet and for the civilization whose corruption he has
witnessed. The poem ends with a vision of love healing all, the earth
grown young again—an island paradise (reminiscent of the *Tempest*) capable of subduing the rage of all who enter there:

> Other flowering isles must be
> In the sea of life and agony:
> Other spirits float and flee
> O'er that gulph: even now, perhaps,
> On some rock the wild wave wraps,
> With folded wings they waiting sit
> For my bark, to pilot it
> To some calm and blooming cove,
> Where for me, and those I love,
> May a windless bower be built,
> Far from passion, pain, and guilt,
> In a dell 'mid lawny hills,
> Which the wild sea-murmur fills,
> And soft sunshine, and the sound
> Of old forests echoing round,
> And the light and smell divine
> Of all flowers that breathe and shine:
> We may live so happy there,
> That the spirits of the air,
> Envying us, may even entice
> To our healing paradise
> The polluting multitude;
> But their rage would be subdued
> By that clime divine and calm . . .   (335–58)

This last section enacts the process Shelley describes as the "inspired
soul" supplying "its own . . . melodies." The poet has experienced
the moment of harmony; it has since passed; his imagination is free
now to recreate it, to take it as far as he can. So all the elements of
the earlier moment recur in generalized form: the landscape reap-

pears as a "dell 'mid lawny hills," filled with "soft sunshine," and light and fragrance, the sound of "old forests." In the actual scene there is a single flower, in the imagined scene "the light and smell divine / Of all flowers that breathe and shine." It is as if the real elements of the scene—not simply the physical landscape, but the poet, his song, even the universals of love, light, harmony, odor— are rendered in their spiritual essence. Such a rendering is appropriate to a vision of a healing paradise, ruled by spirits of the air, circled by "the love which heals all strife" (366) and inhabited by the "uplifted soul" (360).

The poem moves, then, from the opening images of unbreachable solitude and isolation to a final vision of community, rendered first in the poet's experience of oneness with nature and with all "living things," and repeated in the final lines as a prayer for the future.[7] For while the poet appears to be merely returning to his opening theme —"Other flowering isles must be / In the sea of life and agony"— in fact he has qualified his pessimism. If one movement of the poem is toward fatalism, in the image of the sea of misery, the drifting of the mariner, the unlamented death of the exile, the vision of Italy's cities in ruins, there is an equally strong movement against despair, in the poet's response to the beauty of the day, in his sense that the glorious poetry that had birth in Italy was nourished by the same natural presences he feels. It is not surprising that although the moment passes and pain resumes its place, the possibility remains that the good spirits of a beneficent and harmonious natural world, in alliance with the powers of poetry and love, can effect a reversal of historical process, as they may well have the power to rekindle in modern thought the dead spark of antique light. The voice of political experience speaks first, and is ultimately unanswerable:

> Men must reap the things they sow,
> Force from force must ever flow,
> Or worse; but 'tis a bitter woe
> That love or reason cannot change
> The despot's rage, the slave's revenge.   (231–35)

The student of Aeschylus—as well as of the French Revolution— speaks in these lines. The lesson can be read in more than one way: as a counsel of fatalism or a counsel of revolution. If love or reason

cannot change the despot's rage, only force can answer force. Total
destruction of the old tyranny is necessary and inevitable; the slave
will—and should—have his revenge. Yet Shelley has no faith in the
wisdom of an enslaved populace; slavery breeds the same evils in the
slave as in the tyrant. But in the final lines the poet weighs against
his own knowledge the counsel of his heart; love and reason may
after all be empowered to soothe rage and prevent revenge. And so
he prophesies of the "polluting multitude," source and victim of error, that when exposed to the love which heals all strife,

> They, not it would change; and soon
> Every sprite beneath the moon
> Would repent its envy vain,
> And the earth grow young again.   (370–73)

As much chance of one as of the other—but this charming fantasy
can well be read as a lighter tetrameter version of *Prometheus Unbound,* Act III. Shelley was writing the first act of *Prometheus* in the
fall of 1818, and "Lines written among the Euganean Hills" bears
the marks of his central preoccupation. The "sea of agony" is another version of the torments of Prometheus, which represent the
condition of life: "Ah me! alas, pain, pain ever, for ever!" And the
triumph of *Prometheus Unbound* is of precisely the kind envisioned
in "Lines written among the Euganean Hills," the earth grown young
again, nature renewed in harmony, through the radiating effects of
restored love.[8] The resemblances suggest that the constant in Shelley's "visions" is not apocalypse, not rebirth through destruction and
death, but the repeated affirmation of the power of the imagination
and love to renew and recreate.

In "Lines written among the Euganean Hills" Shelley's characteristic idealism asserts itself against his conviction of despair. He
cannot deny the experience of isolation and powerlessness, but he
balances against it an equally authentic experience of harmony, joy,
and imaginative power. "Stanzas written in Dejection—December
1818, near Naples" is an analysis of despair; it returns to the image
of the sea, not as a hostile and treacherous enemy but as a refuge
from "a life of care." For the Romantic poet despair, rather than

disobedience, is the fatal temptation; the danger is that in its weariness the spirit will turn away from struggle, from relationship, from life itself.

"Stanzas written in Dejection," like "Lines written among the Euganean Hills," describes a single "sweet day," a noontide moment of beauty in sea and sky, when the manifold elements of a single nature, "Like many a voice of one delight" are interpenetrated and in harmony. But in "Stanzas written in Dejection" the poet is excluded from the circle of love. The glory of sky, sun, and sea, so potent in "Lines written among the Euganean Hills," cannot release him from despair, it can only soften his pain, so that he is impelled to yield himself to the seductive monotony of the sea. When Coleridge, in the scene described in "Dejection: An Ode," looks upon nature, he sees but cannot feel; the heart fails to respond to the data that the poet's eye receives and normally feeds upon. Shelley's alienation from nature has its origin in his alienation from other human beings; it is his solitude that separates him from the scene and urges the felicity of death.[9]

The clarity and immediacy of the scene described in the opening stanza suggest a heightened sensibility on the poet's part and at the same time a peculiar detachment, a sense of his own separateness from the scene he observes so minutely. Nature is spontaneous, innocent, joyous, quick with life. Its elements are in perpetual harmony; sun, sea, and earth interact and imitate one another in the natural processes of gestation and growth. In a letter to Leigh Hunt, Shelley described Italy as a land "composed of the green earth & transparent sea . . . and aerial mountains, & the warm & radiant atmosphere which is interfused through all things" (*Letters of P.B.S.*, II, 67). This is essentially the quality of the scene described in the poem. But the descriptive terms of the poem suffer a sea-change: "blue isles" as against "green earth" suggests a visual illusion, the islands seen through a faint noonday haze, or taking on the color of the surrounding sea. Transparency is attributed not to the sea, as in the letter, but to the source of light and its object: "Blue isles and snowy mountains wear / The purple noon's transparent might"—an image that draws the disparate elements of the landscape into unity and relationship. The hint of animism is reinforced by the image of the "breath of the moist earth" (the continuous slow evaporation of moisture); the choice of the word "unexpanded" to describe the not-yet-open buds suggests promise, the power immanent in nature. The description of the scene suggests not only the harmony of nature but the mediating power of the particular noonday moment: "The City's voice itself is soft like Solitude's"—the City's voice is normally noisy, even strident; Solitude's voice is soft, of course, because there is no one to hear her.[10]

The second stanza moves from the scene to the poet observing the scene and narrows the focus to the sea. The quiet, precise, parallel statements again suggest both the detachment that permits an itemization of the separate elements of the scene and an intense, almost hypersensitive response to the quality of the whole. As in the first stanza, the imagery suggests the joyous plenitude of nature and its self-containment, to which the works and ways of men are irrelevant. Thus the floor of the Deep is "untrampled," in the sense that it cannot be walked upon;[11] the images of the waves "Like light dissolved in star-showers," the "lightning" of the ocean flashing round the poet, suggest purity, spontaneous motion, an excess of energy; both "strown" and "thrown" suggest profusion. The description of one element in terms of another implies both that natural forces are interrelated and that their motions are analogous.

The sorrow of the poet is introduced obliquely, in the contrast between the harmony and delight of the scene and his unhappiness. The emphasis in the last line of Stanza 2 is still on the sweetness of the scene. But the third and central stanza makes a full statement of despair. The orderly summation of the elements of life contrasts the poet's state point for point with the delight, harmony, and promise of nature. The catalog of woe isolates him categorically from human fulfilment, its inner gratifications and external signs. The "sweet day," so calm, so bright, makes more poignant his own distress, which is equivalent to the storm-tossed state of the mariner in "Lines written among the Euganean Hills." Yet if the scene cannot make him happy, it softens his despair, even as the voice of the populous city is softened by the noon atmosphere. The scene before the poet suggests the form his desire takes; as he sits upon the sand, how simple it appears to lie down, to submit himself to the processes of nature, to cease to struggle. The seductive appeal of death is an extension of the qualities of the scene described earlier: "mild" recalls the "soft" voices of nature; the "warm air" is an echo of the opening line of Stanza 1; the sea's "last monotony" recalls the "measured motion" of Stanza 2; the "breathing" of the sea around the poet's dying brain is similar to the breath of the moist earth around its buds—an image of the kind of unity the poet has despaired of. The language of despair is consciously Biblical in line 27: "To me that cup has been dealt in another measure." Less obviously, perhaps, the fourth stanza recalls the language of the Psalms: "By the waters of Babylon I lay down and wept;" "He leadeth me beside the still waters." The effect is to associate the sorrow of the poet with the affliction of the Psalmist. And the scene itself, earth, mountains, sea, is associated with the context of the Psalms, in which the Psalmist both celebrates and laments his isolation from an earth fulfilled and bountiful.

The argument of the fifth stanza confirms the poet's solitude, his disharmony with nature and society; even if he were merged with nature in death, he would preserve his unhappy identity. The stanza makes a double statement of the poet's relation to the day, one contrasting his bitter life and the sweet day, the other comparing his death and the closing of the day. To paraphrase: *Some might lament my death, as I shall lament when this day is ended—this day that I insult with my cry of personal despair, untimely in the sense of inappropriate, because the day should call forth joy rather than despair,*[12] *and untimely in the sense of premature, for my heart is grown old before its time. Some might lament my death—I say "might" rather than "will" because men usually lament the loss of what they love. But I am one whom men love not, and yet are pained by. How unlike my life is this sweet day, a source of joy both in its stainless glory and, once ended, in memory.* The careful logic, the puns, the final turn on "enjoy" and "joy," like the simple description of the opening stanzas, give the poem a precision that fixes its emotion; the poem ends, indeed, with the sweet day, rather than the poet's dejection. Yet the effect of the final argument, once it has been unraveled, is to establish absolutely the poet's unique isolation from the processes of life.

Images of premature age, affliction, and impotence are central to many of the self-portraits in Shelley's major poems.[13] The theme of the unlamented death, the image of the poet as one betrayed by love and exiled from human community—themes that easily merge into self-pity, or the appearance of it—dominate the figure of the mariner in "Lines written among the Euganean Hills." "Stanzas written in Dejection" isolates these images from the major social, political, and philosophical questions of the longer poems. The poem is an expression of the conflict between the need to endure and the desire to escape pain, responsibility, life itself—to be rocked to sleep like a child. The "dejection" of the poem is specifically that of adulthood; the failures of the poet are those of life in the adult world—fame, power, love. The day represents a momentary escape from care; it lulls the poet into a kind of self-forgetfulness that makes it possible to return, in imagination, to the simplicities of childhood. It is this nostalgic lament for a lost innocence that colors the final contrast between the poet's life and the life of the day: the glory of the day is "stainless," its purity suggested by the "unexpanded buds," the "untrampled floor" of the Deep, while the poet's heart is "lost" and he is "too soon grown old." Yet the poet recognizes the necessity of endurance, even though the poem emphasizes the desire to escape:

> I could lie down like a tired child
> And weep away the life of care
> Which I have borne and yet must bear . . .   (30–32)

The fantasy of escape is as much in the nature of an interlude as the day itself; the interlude over, Pain resumes its familiar place.

Other poems of the same period, like "Invocation to Misery," emphasize the theme of endurance:

> Misery! we have known each other,
> Like a sister and a brother
> Living in the same lone home,
> Many years—we must live some
> Hours or ages yet to come.
>
> 'Tis an evil lot, and yet
> Let us make the best of it . . .   (11–17)

The veiled allusion is to Mary, whose unhappiness and coldness condemn the poet to solitude.[14] The theme reappears in the intimate poems of 1821–22 to Edward and Jane Williams, in which Shelley's relationship to Mary is obliquely and despairingly analyzed. The failed elements of life—fame, fortune, health, hope, power—are once again assessed. The single element with the power to make all other losses endurable is love, and the death of love is the subject of all these late lyrics. The impulse to "lie down like a tired child" is analyzed once more in "The Magnetic Lady to her Patient." The seraphic Jane, her cool fingers on the poet's forehead, advises him to banish care by closing his eyes:

> "Sleep, sleep, and with the slumber of
>   The dead and the unborn . . .
>   Forget thy life and love;
> Forget that thou must wake,—forever
>   Forget the world's dull scorn.—
> Forget lost health, and the divine
> Feelings which died in youth's brief morn;
> And forget me, for I can never
>   Be thine—"   (19–27)

But Jane's sympathy cannot touch the center of pain, and the poet replies to her question about a "cure:"

> "What would cure that would kill me, Jane,
> And as I must on earth abide
> Awhile yet, tempt me not to break
>   My chain."   (42–45)

These lyrics of private as opposed to vatic woe have a peculiar poignancy, which has to do with the artistic elaboration of the personal dilemma. In each case the expressive element—which the unsympathetic reader is tempted to call self-pity—is masked or subordinated to the patterns of the poem. The fiction of "Invocation to Misery," the invitation to Misery, the bride, to consummate her dark marriage with the poet, controls the autobiography. In the poems to Edward and Jane Williams personal distress is mediated through the epistolary form, with its implications of social context, relationship, continuity of experience. In "Stanzas written in Dejection," the central statement of the poem is expressive ("Alas! I have nor hope nor health"), but the tone of the whole is so analytic, so measured, so logical in its drawing of consequences, its development of analogies, that the poet's lament is tied by a hundred threads to the scene and occasion that frame the poem and enclose its central experience. The control of form, the balance between observation and feeling, feeling and thought, is reflected in the modified Spenserian stanza. The returning rhymes, the steady beat of the tetrameter, reproduce the monotony of the sea, the "measured motion" of the returning waves; and as the scene softens the poet's despair, the tetrameter softens and subdues its expression. When the regularity of the tetrameter is emphasized by close parallelism of phrase and line, as in the first three stanzas, it has the sound of absolute clarity, and possibly a certain flatness. Yet the final alexandrine gives the hint of emotion suppressed or potential; in each of the first three stanzas it has the effect of a sudden expansion.

Baudelaire, who admired Shelley's poetry, was particularly struck by "Stanzas written in Dejection," singling out for special praise the line "I am one / Whom men love not, and yet regret." The experience the line describes was felt keenly by Baudelaire in his own life —the ironic relationship of the artist to his kind. Shelley lamented that the artist—the "nerve o'er which do creep / The else unfelt oppressions of this earth"—should be vilified, hated, and scorned by those for whom he conceives of himself as speaking. But what Baudelaire admired was not merely the sentiment but that monotony, symmetry, and surprise which characterize the work of art.[15]

NOTES

1. Quotations are from the text of the first printing, in *Rosalind and Helen* (1819). There is a holograph of lines 167–205 in private hands, and a transcript of lines 56–112 in Mary's hand, with holograph corrections, in the Huntington Library (HM 331), but no other drafts or copies appear to have survived.
2. The image of the unlamented death recalls *Alastor*, 50–54, and the "sunless vapour" echoes lines 663–65. Shelley may have been inspired by Wordsworth's prefatory note to "The Forsaken Indian Woman," in *Lyrical Ballads* (1798). Several critics have read this passage as an autobiographical allegory—for instance, White, II, 41; and Donald H. Reiman, "Structure, Symbol, and Theme in 'Lines written among the Euganean Hills,'" *PMLA*, 76 (1962), 404–13.
3. Shelley may have had the choral poem from *Oedipus at Colonus* in

mind: "The endless hours pile up a drift of pain / More unrelieved each day . . . And in the end he comes to strengthless age, / Abhorred by all men, without company, / Unfriended in that uttermost twilight / Where he must live with every bitter thing . . . Think of some shore in the north the / Concussive waves make stream / This way and that in the gales of winter: / It is like that with him: / The wild wrack breaking over him / From head to foot, and coming on forever . . ." (1214–15, 1235–44). Tr. Robert Fitzgerald, in *The Complete Greek Tragedies,* ed. David Grene and Richmond Lattimore, 4 vols. (Chicago: University of Chicago Press, 1959). Cf. also *Aeneid* 5.871: "nudus in ignota, Palinure, iacebis harena." Mary records readings of Aeschylus and Sophocles in August and September, 1818, and mentions that Shelley read *Oedipus Tyrannus* aloud: *Mary Shelley's Journal,* p. 105.

4. See A. C. Bradley, "Coleridge-Echoes in Shelley's Poems," in *A Miscellany* (London, 1929), pp. 171–76. Shelley wrote to Ollier on July 13, 1817, urgently requesting a copy of *Sybilline Leaves,* which included "The Rime of the Ancient Mariner" (*Letters of P.B.S.,* I, 548). Among other resemblances, perhaps the most striking are Shelley's "deep wide sea of misery" and "waters of wide Agony," a condensed version of Coleridge's "Alone on a wide wide sea! / And never a saint took pity on / My soul in agony" ("Ancient Mariner," 233–35); Shelley's description of the sun, lines 100–03, which echoes lines 173–74 of the "Ancient Mariner;" and the dice game of Death and Sin in "Lines written among the Euganean Hills," 238–40, which echoes the dice game in "Ancient Mariner," 195–98.

5. Dante, *Paradiso,* I, 34: "Poca favilla gran fiamma seconda:" *The Divine Comedy of Dante Alighieri,* tr. John D. Sinclair, Italian and English (New York: Oxford University Press, 1948).

6. Cf. "Julian and Maddalo:" "Where . . . I met pale Pain / My shadow, which will leave me not again" (324–25); and "Invocation to Misery," which turns upon the idea of the poet's long and almost companionable intimacy with Misery.

7. The syntax carefully obscures the distinction between prayer and possibility: "Where for me, and those I love, / May a windless bower be built" (343–44).

8. For close verbal resemblances between "Lines written among the Euganean Hills" and *Prometheus Unbound,* see the Chorus of Furies, I, 495–577, esp. 550–60, 567–70, 574–77.

9. The experience described in the poem is clearly autobiographical. In June, 1822, Shelley wrote Trelawny asking if he could procure a small quantity of prussic acid: "I would give any price for this medicine. You remember we talked of it the other night . . . I need not tell you I have no intention of suicide at present,—but I confess it would be a comfort to me to hold in my possession that golden key to the chamber of perpetual rest—" (*Letters of P.B.S.,* II, 433). Many years later Trelawny told W. M. Rossetti that Shelley had attempted suicide in Naples (White, II, 570–71); he may have been remembering (or possibly exaggerating) the substance of their conversation that June. In a letter of December [17–18], 1818, to Peacock,

Shelley writes that he has "depression enough of spirits & not good
health" (*Letters of P.B.S.,* II, 64). His low spirits were probably
traceable to Clara's death in September, 1818, and Mary's unhappiness.

10. Cf. Wordsworth, "Composed upon Westminster Bridge, Sept. 3, 1802:"
"Ne'er saw I, never felt, a calm so deep! . . . / Dear God! the very
houses seem asleep; / And all that mighty heart is lying still!" Shelley
echoes another line from the Wordsworth sonnet: "This City now
doth, like a garment, wear / The beauty of the morning"—both in
"Stanzas written in Dejection," 3–4, and "Lines written among the
Euganean Hills," 169–70.

11. The word "untrampled" is thus glossed by F. S. Ellis, *A Lexical Concordance to the Poetical Works of Percy Bysshe Shelley* (London,
1892). The genesis of the image, as has often been noted, is probably
the boat trip described in Shelley's letter to Peacock: "We set off an
hour after sunrise one radiant morning in a little boat, there was not
a cloud in the sky nor a wave upon the sea which was so translucent
that you could see the hollow caverns clothed with the glaucous sea-
moss, & the leaves & branches of those delicate weeds that pave the un-
equal bottom of the water" (*Letters of P.B.S.,* II, 61).

12. Cf. Wordsworth, "Ode: Intimations of Immortality:" "No more shall
grief of mine the season wrong" (26).

13. Cf. especially "Ode to the West Wind," Stanzas IV and V; and the
self-portrait in *Adonais,* Stanzas XXXI–XXXIV.

14. White discusses the "Invocation to Misery" in relation to the painful
events of 1817–18, and their effects on Mary's spirits (II, chap. 20).
Several details from the "Invocation to Misery," especially Stanzas
VI–VIII, anticipate the allegory of Mary's "cold, chaste love" in
Epipsychidion.

15. "Je viens de trouver une admirable ode mélancolique de Shelley, com-
posée au bord du golfe de Naples, et qui se termine par ces mots: 'Je sais
que je suis de ceux que les hommes n'aiment pas; mais je suis de ceux
dont ils se souviennent!' À la bonne heure! voilà de la poësie."—letter
to Sainte-Beuve, March 30, 1865, in *Correspondance générale,* ed.
Jacques Crépet, V (Paris: Conard-Lambert, 1949), 77. See also
Baudelaire's definition of poetry in "Projets de Préfaces, II," *Les Fleurs
du Mal,* Edition critique établie par Jacques Crépet et Georges Blin
(Paris: Corti, 1968), p. 364.

CHAPTER FOUR

REVOLUTION & PROPHECY:
The Political Odes

---

*P**rometheus Unbound* appeared one year after the sheriff of Manchester had loosed the cavalry upon a peaceful assembly of workers, gathered in St. Peter's Field to hear the radical orator Henry Hunt appeal for parliamentary reform. Shelley wrote to Peacock of that "important news:" "These are, as it were, the distant thunders of the terrible storm which is approaching" (*Letters of P.B.S.*, II, 119). The image of that storm, in all its aspects, dominates *Prometheus Unbound* and the shorter poems accompanying it. "An Ode written October, 1819" is a call to the survivors of Peterloo to "arise" and "awaken:" "There is blood on the earth that denies ye bread!" (2). It is also a call to renounce revenge, to lift arms in self-defense only. "Ode to Liberty," which closes the volume, a celebration of the Spanish revolution of January, 1820, dramatizes Shelley's sense of his age as revolutionary, a "war of the oppressed against the oppressors" (canceled paragraph of preface to *Hellas*). The poet envisions the secular goddess Liberty rising triumphant in France, America, and Spain, after her long eclipse; he prays that the spark has been lit for other victims of empire, and calls to Italy to shake off her Austrian yoke, to "king-deluded Germany," to the England of Castlereagh, to awaken to the spirit of the times.

Shelley feared revolution in England and hoped it would prove unnecessary (her chains, unlike those of Spain, were "threads of gold," easier to loose than steel); still he felt bound in conscience to welcome the uprising of the poor. He wrote to Leigh Hunt in November, 1819: "*We* cannot hesitate which party to embrace; and whatever revolutions are to occur, though oppression should change names & names cease to be oppressions, our party will be that of liberty & of the oppre[ss]ed" (*Letters of P.B.S.,* II, 148). Five months later he was convinced that the English ministry was determined to resist the reforms that alone could prevent revolution. "The system of society as it exists at present must be overthrown from the foundations with all its superstructure of maxims & of forms," he wrote, in despair at the blindness of the government even to its self-interest; he intended to contribute to the revolution "*popular songs*" that might "awaken & direct the imagination of the reformers" (*Letters of P.B.S.,* II, 191).

Prometheus Unbound (1820) does not contain those popular songs; the volume constitutes Shelley's most serious and complicated poetry. Yet the historical urgency of the prayer to the West Wind, Destroyer and Preserver, agent of apocalypse, is unmistakable; it comes not from the autumn storm that Shelley observed from the woods near Florence but from his horror and exhilaration at the collision course set in England, and his desire to play a role in that conflagration.

> Drive my dead thoughts over the universe
> Like withered leaves to quicken a new birth!   (63–64)

The "dead thoughts" are his poems, most immediately the poems in the accompanying volume. *Prometheus Unbound* is a fable prophesying the spring that is to follow the unbinding of Prometheus from his long trial of suffering, and the liberation of man from false tyrannies without and within.

In this work and the shorter lyrics celebrating what Shelley believed to be the rising tide of liberty throughout Europe, it is clear that for Shelley, as for Blake or D. H. Lawrence, the true revolution is not in social structures but in the spirit of men, renewed through struggle and prayer; the true revolutionary is the new man. Political and social liberation are necessary but secondary; they follow from the liberation of man and cannot in themselves bring that liberation about. Shelley's practical political counsel tended to be moderate (he accepted gradual extension of the franchise rather than immediate universal suffrage, for example); his poetic vision was radical and apocalyptic. He believed that man is the victim not of his circumstances alone but of his nature; injuries cannot be removed merely by change of circumstance, the removal of tyrants, or the redistribution of wealth. For oppression is not only imposed from without but created from within; man, "on his own high will, a willing slave," makes of oppressed and oppressor "one world." The complexity of Shelley's revolutionary vision comes from his awareness of difficulties, the power of Life to "breed new wants." Prometheus, like Jesus, is an emblem of the power of good to bring forth evil:

> . . . those who do endure
> Deep wrongs for man, and scorn, and chains, but heap
> Thousandfold torment on themselves and him.
> (*Prometheus Unbound*, I, 594–96)

The condition of man matches the heroic emblem of the Titan or Divine Man whose action brings forth the reverse of his good intent:

> The good want power, but to weep barren tears.
> The powerful goodness want: worse need for them.
> (I, 625–26)

Yeats echoed Shelley's lines in his lament for the Irish revolution:

> The best lack all conviction, while the worst
> Are full of passionate intensity.
> ("The Second Coming," 7–8)

The lines apply equally to any time when the war between oppressor and oppressed has reached an intensity at which it appears to intelligent persons that any action, whatever its motive, can only hasten mutual destruction.

Shelley's poetry foretells an event that is destined but is obscure to the sleeping millions: the liberation of man. Shelley's letters make clear that he thought of liberation as a real and secular event, the overthrow of kings and priests and the self-determination of peoples. His faith in the inevitability of that triumph, however, was an act of will, a "solemn duty." In his poetry the line between hope and belief is deliberately eroded, and the poetry itself suggests that the difference is trivial, a matter of the false perspective of time.

Before we examine the shorter lyrics that accompanied the drama, we should look briefly at the drama itself as a political allegory. If *Prometheus Unbound* offers an enactment of the prophecy of man's liberation, it also offers a "justification" of his enslavement and a guide to conduct; it substitutes a radical political myth for orthodox religious explanations—those "codes of fraud and woe"—of the origin of evil, the suffering of man, and his ultimate salvation. Shelley deliberately places himself in the tradition of Milton, the great Republican and Protestant; his heroic theme, like Milton's in *Paradise Lost,* is the ultimate liberation of man, and his fable, like Milton's, reflects always upon the contemporary struggle for liberty. But Shelley reverses the terms of Milton's parable of just and unjust rebellion, just and unjust authority. Shelley's "great Father . . . the Supreme," is the tyrant Jupiter (I, 354, 374); his rebellious Angel, who "vainly [would] stand forth alone in strife / Against the Omnipotent" (I, 361–62), is not Satanic but Christlike, "The saviour and the strength of suffering man" (I, 817). Shelley's conception of "heaven-oppress'd mortality" is not unlike Milton's; enslaved to the false gods he has himself created, the tyrannies without and the lusts within, man's liberation, while he is subject to time and chance, depends upon that "true Liberty" which, in Milton's words, "always with right Reason dwells / Twinn'd, and from her hath no dividual being" (*Paradise Lost,* XII, 84–85). Although Shelley in "Ode to the West Wind" welcomes apocalypse, the destruction of the old world and creation of a new, the revolutionary virtue in *Prometheus Unbound* appears to be not rebellion but endurance— the great Miltonic virtue, man's triumph over his own "envy." Prometheus is the arch-rebel, who defies the gods to give their singular gifts to man (the same attempt Satan makes in the Garden); in Shelley's drama he appears not in his character of rebel but as the hero who endures all the pain his oppressor can inflict, and at last overcomes his own desire for revenge.

If we examine *Prometheus Unbound* as a political fable, we can distinguish in its action three classic stages of revolution: resistance (Prometheus bound to the rock); the overthrow of the tyrant (Jupiter's fall); and the liberation of man. As the drama opens, Prometheus is discovered chained powerless to a rock, destined to be tormented until he concedes defeat by revealing to the tyrant Jupiter the date of his overthrow, a secret known only to Prometheus. After an eon of torture, he suddenly finds that his hate has evaporated, leaving pure opposition alone, and he recalls his original curse on Jupiter with the charitable words: "I wish no living thing to suffer pain" (I, 305)—thus including the oppressor among the oppressed as potential victim. With the Titan's triumph over his own revenge, his beloved Asia, the other half of his soul, long exiled from him, is impelled by a vision to seek out the source of power beyond tyrant and victim alike, prior to and including Man, the Gods and the Titans. She is led by the voices of spirits to a region below the earth, where she confronts Demogorgon, a "mighty darkness," (II, iv, 2), whom she questions about the nature of ultimate power, ultimate evil.[1] That singular confrontation recalls "Mont Blanc" and the mind's effort to encompass the meaning of the Power that inhabits the inaccessible mountain top, hurling down life and death indifferently; for the "mysterious voice" of the wilderness, as interpreted by those few who understand its awful message, can repeal the "large codes of fraud and woe" that keep man enslaved. Similarly, Demogorgon is a "voice unspoken" (II, i, 191), which alone has the power to overthrow Jupiter but cannot do so until its "sleep" is broken by Asia. As in the earlier meditation, Asia's conclusion is that the heart must be its own oracle, the imagination must create its own symbol for faith: "the deep truth is imageless" (II, iv, 116). And with Asia thus turned back on her own powers (a return of self-knowledge comparable to Prometheus' "forgiveness" of Jupiter), the fatal hour is at hand, and the tyrant Jupiter is summoned to his fall by the greater power—Demogorgon—he has himself engendered. Prometheus is then unbound by Hercules—"strength" ministering to "wisdom, courage, and long-suffering love" (III, iii, 1–2)—and reunited with Asia; the sleeping Earth is awakened, its frozen winter yields to spring, and man is liberated not only from "Thrones, altars, judgement-seats, and prisons," the "foul shapes" that were "Jupiter, the tyrant of the world," but from the "guilt or pain, / Which were, for his [i.e. man's] will made or suffered them" (III, iv, 164, 180, 198–99).

If we look for a political moral, we find that resistance is twofold: it consists of a "patient and irreconcilable enmity with domestic and political tyranny and imposture" (Dedication to Hunt, *The*

Cenci); but it also includes conquering the tyrannical potential in one's own nature. One might cite Yeats again, also writing of revolution: "to be choked with hate / May well be of all evil chances chief" ("A Prayer for my Daughter," 52–53). Similarly, in *The Masque of Anarchy*, which Shelley wrote to commemorate Peterloo, slavery takes two forms:

> 'Tis to be a slave in soul
> And to hold no strong control
> Over your own wills, but be
> All that others make of ye . . .
>
> Then it is to feel revenge
> Fiercely thirsting to exchange
> Blood for blood—and wrong for wrong—
> Do not thus when ye are strong.
>
> (184–87, 193–96)

How then is the tyrant to be overthrown, if his victim forswears vengeance? The dethroning of Jupiter, which must be Prometheus' aim, is not in his power. It is destined in the original cycle of tyranny and rebellion; its hour is signaled by Prometheus' repentance and Asia's visionary journey. But it is the tyrant himself who has engendered his own overthrow: Demogorgon is his child, greater than he, given form by Asia's imaginings (as the dormant power of an enslaved people—the child of the tyranny that oppresses them—is created politically, given ideology and discipline, by poets and philosophers). Shelley is certainly not counseling accommodation; tyranny must be overthrown. But the revolutionary means is the nonviolent resistance whose greatest triumph is over its own anger and hatred, acting in alliance with the powers of love and imagination:

> To suffer woes which Hope thinks infinite;
> To forgive wrongs darker than death or night;
>   To defy Power, which seems omnipotent;
> To love, and bear; to hope till Hope creates
> From its own wreck the thing it contemplates;
>   Neither to change, nor falter, nor repent;

This, like thy glory, Titan, is to be
Good, great and joyous, beautiful and free;
This is alone Life, Joy, Empire and Victory.
(*Prometheus Unbound,* IV, 570–78)

Shelley's fear of revolutionary violence was founded on a practical as well as a poetic insight: the Aeschylean doctrine that "Men must reap the things they sow, / Force from force must ever flow" ("Lines written among the Euganean Hills," 231–32); that "Revenge and Wrong bring forth their kind" (*Hellas,* 729). The historical proofs always present to Shelley lay in the course of events in France following the Revolution—not the Terror alone, but the crowning of Napoleon as emperor by a people who had just purchased their freedom in blood. But Shelley was aware as well that tyranny is bound to issue in violence, that "the oppression which justifies, also produces resistance." He wrote in "A Philosophical View of Reform:" "The last resort of resistance is undoubtedly insurrection.—The right of insurrection is derived from the employment of armed force [i.e. by the government] to counteract the will of the nation." Against the use of this "last resort" he could urge only the obvious truth that every reformer or revolutionary must deal with as he can: "the true friend of mankind and of his country would hesitate before he recommended measures which tend to bring down so heavy a calamity as war" (*Works,* VII, 53–54).

The practical truth that lay behind Shelley's reluctant acceptance of violence was his awareness that the powerful do not relinquish power voluntarily. The oppressed cannot appeal to reason for redress, or accomplish revolution by the threat of violence alone: the stake of the oppressor, hence his resistance, increases with the possibility of insurrection. For historical proofs, once again, Shelley had not only the intransigence of the ancien régime on the eve of its overthrow, but also the "tyrannical obstinacy" of the English ministry in the face of increased popular agitation (*Letters of P.B.S.,* II, 153). And if the Aeschylean lesson was that one crime begets another, Shelley could find in Old and New Testaments a still darker vision: the world must be destroyed that it can be reborn; man must die that he can live.

The political poems published with *Prometheus Unbound,* especially "Ode to the West Wind" and "Ode to Liberty," and the "Ode to Naples," written too late for inclusion in the volume, represent the poet's attempt to serve in his own voice as hierophant of the newly awakened force of liberty rising in Europe. Each of these poems, like *Prometheus Unbound,* substitutes a radical political myth of liberation for the orthodox myths of revealed religion. As we examine each in turn, we shall analyze this myth-making in detail, always in relation to the poet's vow in "Hymn to Intellectual Beauty," that his poetic gift must oppose the "world's dark slavery" and help create the grounds for hope.

"Ode to the West Wind" is a central utterance not only of Shelley's poetry but of Romanticism, one of the great evocations of the sublime in nature and an impassioned expression of the poet's drive to be identified with and absorbed into elemental forces, whether they be creative or destructive. The youth's relation to nature is immediate and empathetic, as if he were an extension of nature or a natural creature himself; the adult's relation to nature must include understanding as well, and the adult experience of disillusionment and failure. As in the formal prayers of Coleridge and Wordsworth, the "sore need" of the poet arises from his sense of the separateness of human experience from the life of nature; mature thought—the distinctive human characteristic—implies the loss both of unreflective innocence and of direct apprehension of the divine. But the most distinctive quality of the poem is its revolutionary ardor; the whole poem drives toward its final prophecy, which expresses the essential impulse of revolutionary idealism.

The symmetrical, tightly-knit structure of "Ode to the West Wind" has impelled critics to look for earlier models in the Biblical psalms or in formal prayers addressed to the classical deities, and organized in similar fashion into an invocation to a deity, a lament of personal failure, and a prayer.[2] But sources and parallels fail to account for the powerful originality of the poem, the personal and vatic quality of its rhetoric. Shelley appears to be creating his own ritual, a modern realization of an ancient and familiar pattern.

The poet addresses his invocation and prayer to a deity whose powers are superbly evident in nature. But with the opening image of the Wind as the "breath of Autumn's being" the Wind's natural powers are assimilated to the supernatural, mythical and divine. The image of the night as a "vast sepulchre,"

> Vaulted with all thy congregated might

> Of vapours, from whose solid atmosphere
> Black rain, and fire, and hail will burst . . .
>
> (25–28)

evokes the wrath of Jehovah, visited on an erring Judah.[3] And the language that describes the response of nature to the fearful visitation of the Wind echoes the Psalms:

> The waters saw thee, O God, the waters saw thee; they were afraid: the depths also were troubled . . . The voice of thy thunder was in the heaven . . . thy path in the great waters . . .   (Psalm 77:16, 18–19)

The suggested analogy to the destructive powers of the righteous Hebrew god becomes more explicit in the third stanza:

> . . . Thou
> For whose path the Atlantic's level powers

> Cleave themselves into chasms, while far below
> The sea-blooms and the oozy woods which wear
> The sapless foliage of the ocean, know

> Thy voice, and suddenly grow grey with fear,
> And tremble and despoil themselves . . .   (36–42)

The Biblical allusions to the voice of the Destroyer cast their shadow back on the earlier imagery of destruction—the leaves as "pestilence-stricken multitudes" (5), the "congregated might / Of vapours" (26–27)—to lend to the natural power of wind on earth, air, and sea the weight of divine wrath. Thus it is natural for the lament and prayer that follow to take on the accents of Biblical devotion. The poet has "striven . . . with [the Wind] in prayer" (51–52), as Jacob strives with the angel; his lament, "I fall upon

the thorns of life! I bleed!" (54) echoes the tone and language of
the Psalmist; his prayer, like that of the sorely afflicted Psalmist, is
for strength to rise, to be restored to life.[4]

These powerful associations are imported into the service of a
deity sharply differentiated from the orthodox gods. The Wind is
not only strong and fierce, like Jehovah, but "wild," "impetuous,"
"Uncontroulable" (subject to no control), "tameless, and swift,
and proud." Not only does it embody power, the chief mark of
divinity, it is the emblem and embodiment of freedom. The final
extension of the poet's prayer, the supreme Romantic cry—"Be
thou, Spirit fierce, / My spirit! Be thou me, impetuous one!" (61–
62)—suggests the physical process of divine inspiration, God enter-
ing his prophet and speaking through his lips. But the spirit of
Shelley's prayer is directly contrary to the Biblical concept of obedience; his prayer is that of a prophet of revolution. Its meaning is not
only "inspire me," but "let me be free and impetuous as thou art;
let my spirit be fierce as thine; let my message be that which the
Wind symbolizes: freedom, the unconquerable will." Similarly, the
poet's prophecy, which has the ring of Biblical prophecies of the
new heaven and earth that follows upon the day of wrath, is
political and secular; an "awakened" earth is enlightened (rather
than obedient or purged), redeemed by the power of words and
thoughts, not by a miraculous sacrifice or divine gift of grace. "Ode
to the West Wind," in its total effect, attempts to supplant the Biblical vision of apocalypse with a vision that is politically radical, optimistic, and humane.

Shelley's great increase in poetic power becomes obvious if we
compare "Ode to the West Wind" with the earlier "Hymn to Intellectual Beauty." Both poems take the form of invocation and prayer
addressed to a fictive deity, combining traditional dress with a
modern and heretical substance. But in "Hymn to Intellectual
Beauty" the substitution of Shelleyan doctrine for orthodox Christian doctrine is largely a matter of direct statement. "Love, Hope,
and Self-esteem" replace "Love, Hope, and Faith" as the cardinal
virtues; "To fear oneself" replaces "to fear God" as the binding vow
of the believer. The machinery of the "Hymn to Intellectual Beauty"
is recognizably derivative; the "fair Spirit" is Collins' spirit of Evening superimposed on a Wordsworthian version of Platonic doctrine.

The "beating heart" and "streaming eyes" of the poet are appropriate to the neophyte of poetic tradition, but Shelley's references in letters of the time to weeping and trembling indicate that he experienced in the flesh the identical bardic ecstasy. And so, despite the grace of the poem and the consistency of its imagery, its vision can be considered a matter of dressing up reality rather than the creation of a poetic fiction that compels belief on its own terms.

The remarkable achievement of "Ode to the West Wind" is the adequacy of the secular image for divinity—power and freedom— in its effortless fusion of nature and myth. The very inclusiveness of the natural scene contributes to the religious character of the invocation. The first stanza evokes a sense of the curve of the horizon; the spring wind blows her clarion "o'er the dreaming earth" to fill "With living hues and odours plain and hill;" the Wind is "moving everywhere." In the second stanza the storm-clouds stream "from the dim verge / Of the horizon to the zenith's height;" in the third stanza the action moves from the surface of the sea (the wave's intenser day") to the very floor of the ocean. The panoramic description of the Wind's power is exact in every detail, even as it assimilates the Wind to greater conceptions of deity; the effect recalls the description of the sun in Psalm 19:6: "His going forth is from the end of the heaven, and his circuit unto the ends of it: and there is nothing hid from the heat thereof." The comprehensive description of the action of the Wind on nature lays the foundation for the poet's prayer:—"Drive my dead thoughts over the universe . . . Scatter . . . my words among mankind!"—which resembles in its scope the celebration of the heavens in the same Psalm: "There is no speech nor language, where their voice is not heard. Their line is gone out through all the earth, and their words to the end of the world" (19:3–4).

The heart of the poem lies in the last two stanzas—the poet's prayer—and in their relation to the first three stanzas of invocation. The lines of personal lament in Stanza IV form the emotional and rhetorical center of the "Ode." Its central, crucial position justifies the extremity of the cry:

> Oh! lift me as a wave, a leaf, a cloud!
> I fall upon the thorns of life! I bleed!

A heavy weight of hours has chained and bowed
One too like thee: tameless, and swift, and proud.

(53–56)

In these lines the natural forces invoked in the first three stanzas become metaphorical and symbolic. In line 53 the word "lift" echoes
the literal lifting described earlier—the clouds like hair "uplifted
from the head / Of some fierce Maenad," the winged seeds charioted
by the wind—but its meaning now is metaphorical: as the object of
the verb shifts from wave, leaf, and cloud to the poet, its meaning
shifts from the physical effect to the human and psychological one.
The verb of the next line follows naturally—"Oh! lift me . . . I
fall"—but deepens the metaphorical implications of both falling (or
failing) and being lifted. These implications are spiritual as well as
psychological; the words coincide with the Biblical terms for despair
and renewal. The reference is not to general despondency of the
kind analyzed in "Stanzas written in Dejection" but to a lack of
power. The wind is "Uncontroulable" but the poet, swift and proud
in his youth, has been tamed, "bowed," "chained" by life. This is
rather the inevitable human condition—that which differentiates
man's existence from the natural life of leaf, cloud, or wave—than
a failure peculiar to the poet, and it is the reason why he must look
to a strength beyond his own. (The emphasis is even clearer in the
draft reading of line 56: "One too like thee, yet mortal—.") And
it is the human condition that is stressed in the famous cry: "I fall
upon the thorns of life! I bleed!" The lines recall Genesis 3:17–18:
"cursed is the ground for thy sake . . . Thorns also and thistles
shall it bring forth to thee," and the parable of the sower, where the
thorns are explained as the "cares and riches and pleasures of this
life" (Luke 8:14).[5] Bleeding is a literal consequence of falling upon
thorns; it provides a dramatic metaphor for suffering, and more
specifically, for a weakening of powers, as the Psalmist laments, for
instance, that he is "poured out like water."

As the poet prays in Stanza IV that he may be "lifted" by the
Wind, so he prays in Stanza V that not only he but his poetry may
be infused with its power, that his poetry may share its "mighty
harmonies," and that it may be scattered and driven abroad by the
Wind. He prays that his poetry may be made effectual, that it be
given the power to hasten the good it prophesies. The poet's "sore

need" is a matter not only of a lack of strength in himself, but of an intrinsic lack of power in words and thoughts. Shelley's prayer, unlike the poems of Wordsworth and Coleridge that similarly call upon the wind for strength and inspiration or quickening, arises not from the failure of his imagination, not from his inability to write poetry, but rather from the failure of his poetry to effect change in the world.

The peculiarly mature character of the poet's lament and prayer can be seen by comparing it to the invocation to *Alastor,* in which the poet identifies himself with the "beloved brotherhood" of earth, ocean, air, as a child of nature, her lover and celebrant:

> . . . serenely now
> And moveless, as a long-forgotten lyre
> Suspended in the solitary dome
> Of some mysterious and deserted fane,
> I wait thy breath, Great Parent, that my strain
> May modulate with murmurs of the air,
> And motions of the forests and the sea,
> And voice of living beings, and woven hymns
> Of night and day, and the deep heart of man.   (41–49)

As in "Ode to the West Wind" the poet prays to be moved as a lyre by the breath of nature. But the confidence of the poet is pre-lapsarian, as it were; he has not "consciously injured" bird, insect, or beast, but has loved and cherished all living things. In "Ode to the West Wind" the poet has despaired of making his voice felt; in his youth nourished by nature, in manhood he has fallen on her thorns. As his vision of nature stresses not her harmonies but her terrible and indiscriminate destructive powers, so he conceives of the poet-suppliant not as one confident of adding his own note to the general harmonies of nature but as one who has been destroyed and must be made anew, who has fallen and must be lifted, who must be not merely breathed upon, or set in motion, but violently penetrated, made one with the source of power.

The very bareness of the last two stanzas, the absence of any statement comparable to that of the closing lines of "Hymn to Intellectual Beauty," the fact that the poet's prayer and prophecy as well as his lament are expressed entirely through metaphor, make the conclusion of the poem susceptible to a number of interpretations. Readings of the poem which stress the element of myth, psychology, or religion tend to obscure its political meaning, which probably would have been uppermost to a contemporary reader. The prophecy is clearly political; "Winter" refers to the destruction of the old (tyrants, palaces, priests, and kings), "Spring" to the birth of the new (justice, peace, love). The natural imagery of the invocation also has political overtones; the sleeping Mediterranean, "Lulled by the coil of his chrystalline streams," suggests the "sleeping" regimes along its shores, lulled by the beauty of the past, or by the illusion of permanence, and the "vast sepulchre" of the stormy night suggests the revolution that Shelley believed to be approaching.[6] The terms Shelley uses, however, are not local but general and all-embracing: not only "Baiæ's bay" but the Atlantic, not Italy and Greece but "the universe," not "Men of England" but "mankind." His prophecy, then, while it applies to the immediate political crisis, must be taken in the most inclusive sense as well.

The terms of the prophecy, "Wind," "Winter," "Spring," are given literal substance in the first three stanzas: when they become metaphors their content is deliberately unstated, left to suggestion and implication. The same terms are given a precise metaphorical meaning in a passage from *Laon and Cythna* which begins by describing the natural cycle:

> 'The blasts of autumn drive the winged seeds
> Over the earth. . . .
> Behold! Spring sweeps over the world again,
> Shedding soft dews from her ætherial wings . . .'
> (IX, 182–83, 186–87)[7]

The natural cycle is then turned into a metaphor for human regeneration, as in "Ode to the West Wind." But in *Laon and Cythna* every natural term is given its exact human and social counterpart. The analogy of Wind's seeding process to the fruitful dispersal of thought is made explicit:

> 'Has not *the whirlwind of our spirit* driven
> *Truth's deathless germs* to *thought's remotest caves?*'
> (IX, 202–03; my italics)

The symbolic meaning of Spring is similarly explicated:

'O Spring, of hope, and love, and youth, and gladness
Wind-winged emblem! . . .

(IX, 191–92)

(The corresponding associations are given Spring in "Ode to the West Wind" by the term "azure," and by the image of Spring as a shepherdess of "sweet buds"—that is, by metaphors of "hope, and love, and youth, and gladness.") Similarly, the human "Winter" that is analogous to the natural season is given a precise political content:

'Lo, Winter comes!—the grief of many graves,
The frost of death, the tempest of the sword,
The flood of tyranny . . .'

(IX, 204–06)

The passage from *Laon and Cythna* indicates the general meaning of the parallel terms in "Ode to the West Wind." But the fact that the tenor is so rigidly suppressed has the effect of making content secondary. The natural cycle becomes at last not a metaphor for a political doctrine (as it is quite clearly in *Laon and Cythna*) but a symbol of hope.

If we compare the sublime political odes of Shelley and Coleridge with their eighteenth-century predecessors, Thomson's "Liberty" and Collins' "Ode to Liberty," for instance, we discover the same kind of shift which marks the change in the nature poetry of the two periods. Thomson's long poem is cast as a dream vision, in which the Goddess of Liberty appears to the poet, describes her "chief establishments" through history, her triumphant rule in Greece, her defeat by the Roman tyrants, her disappearance from earth during the Dark Ages and reappearance in the Renaissance, and her subsequent establishment in Britain. The poem ends with a vision of the future and its "varied wonders," as Liberty reigns supreme over all. Collins' "Ode to Liberty" refers to the history of Liberty's rule in terms similar to those Thomson uses, but the historical material is absorbed into a rhapsodic Pindaric, allusive, highly rhetorical, metaphorical. The theme, as in Thomson's "Ode," is the victory of Liberty in Britain.

The most obvious difference between these poems and the political odes of Coleridge and Shelley is that the later poems are not patriotic but revolutionary. Coleridge's "Ode to the Departing Year" is a "loud Lament" for Britain which prophesies her destruction. "France: An Ode" (the "palinode" to the first "Ode") pleads that the poet be forgiven for celebrating the French Revolution and concludes that liberty and power are incompatible. Liberty exists only in clouds, woods and waves, in nature and the individual mind, not society. Shelley's "Ode to Liberty," written to celebrate the Spanish victory of January, 1820, against the Bourbons, is a call to action, explicitly political: "O Italy, / Gather thy blood into thy heart" (208–09). Because of the difference in motive, the Romantic sublime has an altogether different character from the eighteenth-century sublime, even when it resembles the patriotic odes in convention and vocabulary. The poet in the earlier poems who is borne on high to witness a vision is simply a specially gifted representative of society. In the Romantic sublime, although the function of the poem is social, the poet is outside society; he enters into an intense, direct relation with the divine that is analogous to the Biblical relationship between God and his chosen prophets. Thus the sublime machinery becomes a means of asserting the absolute importance of the truth which the poet has received and which a corrupt society fails to heed. And while the eighteenth-century sublime is a general poetic idiom—Collins' "Ode to Liberty" is in the same style as his "Ode to Fear" or "On the Poetical Character"—Coleridge and Shelley use the sublime for their political odes, and only incidentally elsewhere.

The style of "Ode to Liberty" is established in the opening stanza, which celebrates the return of Liberty in Spain, and its significance for the rest of Europe, still enslaved:

> A glorious people vibrated again
>   The lightning of the nations: Liberty
> From heart to heart, from tower to tower, o'er Spain,
>   Scattering contagious fire into the sky,
> Gleamed. My soul spurned the chains of its dismay,

And, in the rapid plumes of song,
Clothed itself, sublime and strong;
As a young eagle soars the morning clouds among,
Hovering in verse o'er its accustomed prey;
Till from its station in the heaven of fame
The Spirit's whirlwind rapt it, and the ray
Of the remotest sphere of living flame
Which paves the void was from behind it flung,
As foam from a ship's swiftness, when there came
A voice out of the deep: I will record the same.

(1–15)

In the opening lines, roused by an event and an apparition (the gleaming of Liberty o'er Spain—a reference to the successful rebellion), the soul of the poet clothes itself in song and soars aloft, leaving the mundane world behind. Then, as he is preparing to write ("Hovering in verse o'er [his] accustomed prey"), he is "rapt" or caught up, borne still further aloft, by "the Spirit's whirlwind."[8] Suddenly he hears a voice out of the deep, which he records as the substance of his vision. The final lines echo the prophecy of Revelation: "I was in the Spirit on the Lord's day, and heard behind me a great voice, as of a trumpet, Saying, I am Alpha and Omega, the first and the last: and, What thou seest, write in a book" (Rev. 1:10–11). (When the "voice" is recalled in the final stanza, it is called a "great voice.") The union of classical and Biblical inspiration, sophisticated literary myth and primitive religious doctrine, is sustained throughout the poem.

Not only the visionary machinery but the diction and the scale and scope of the action recall the sublime heroic odes of ancient and Biblical celebration. The perspective moves from peoples and nations to the sky above them, and thence to the Empyrean, the "heaven of fame," and the "remotest sphere of living flame / Which paves the void." All the verbs denote strong, swift, decisive action: Liberty *scatters* fire into the sky, the poet's soul *spurns* its chains, a young eagle *soars* into the sky, the ray of flame is *flung* behind. The Spaniards are "a glorious people," the poet's soul is "sublime and strong." The subjects of the two similes, soaring eagles and swift ships, are both conventional heroic images. The stanza contains a number of unusual words and common words used in an unusual sense, as well as words with Miltonic or Spenserian associations: "contagious fire," "station," "accustomed" for *customary*,[9] "dismay" —a recurrent Spenserian term for despair and paralysis of will. The term "vibrated" is especially striking in context: "A glorious people vibrated again / The lightning of the nations." "Vibrate" means to throw with vibratory motion, to launch or hurl (as a thunderbolt); the term supports the image of the lightning "From heart to heart, from tower to tower, o'er Spain, / Scattering contagious fire into the sky" (as the beacons announce the news of safe landing in the opening lines of *Agamemnon*). There is an implied analogy to the "vibrating" of the thunderbolt of Jove; the phrase "the lightning of the nations" is analogous to "the lightning of the gods." Here, as in the phrase "to fear himself" in "Hymn to Intellectual Beauty," a usage puzzling in itself is deliberately chosen to register a dissent from its customary context—for it is the people, not their God, who vibrate the lightning.

The style of the opening stanza embodies the excitement and urgency of the vision. Once we are well into the poem, the marks of the sublime compressed into the first stanza are diluted; the style becomes more direct, even though it remains highly metaphorical, and often Miltonic in vocabulary and usage. The body of the poem employs many tropes and conventions of the sublime: apostrophe, lament for the vanished Muse, personification, epithet, extended simile. Their total effect is to create of Liberty a divinity commensurate in her grandeur and conviction with the visionary preparations of the opening stanza.

The body of "Ode to Liberty," a history of Liberty's rule on earth and a prophecy of its return, challenges the received mythologies of literature, history, and theology by adapting their terms and images to a modern secular principle. "Ode to Liberty" can be read as a *Prometheus Unbound* in miniature, with a specifically political focus: its subject is not the human spirit but man in society. As in the drama, Shelley uses the tradition he loves and admires as a basis for a modern dissent. The oracle begins with a radically rewritten cosmogony, in which the rule of Chaos and the iron or postlapsarian age are telescoped into a single age of misrule and anarchy.

The Sun and the serenest Moon sprang forth:
The burning stars of the abyss were hurled

Into the depths of heaven. The dædal earth,
   That island in the ocean of the world,
Hung in its cloud of all-sustaining air:
      But this divinest universe
      Was yet a chaos and a curse,
For thou wert not: but power from worst producing worse,
   The spirit of the beasts was kindled there,
     And of the birds, and of the watery forms,
   And there was war among them, and despair
     Within them, raging without truce or terms:
The bosom of their violated nurse
   Groan'd, for beasts warr'd on beasts, and worms on worms,
   And men on men; each heart was as a hell of storms.

                                      (16–30)

Shelley's account is obviously analogous to traditional accounts of creation in Genesis, Hesiod, or Ovid. His version, however, deliberately omits any notion of a creator: the creative principle emerges from the will of man, after a period of anarchy. In the third stanza, which develops the image of society as a "chaos and a curse," brutal and dehumanized, the pivotal phrase once more echoes the creation myth of Genesis: "For thou [Liberty] wert not."[10] In effect, the opening stanzas establish Liberty rather than Light or the Spirit of God as the creative principle of a secular universe. The key phrase reappears in the stanza on Athens, the first "establishment" of Liberty:

   . . . Athens . . .
     Gleamed with its crest of columns, on the will
   Of man, as on a mount of diamond, set;
      For thou wert, and thine all-creative skill
  Peopled with forms that mock the eternal dead
     In marble immortality, that hill
    Which was thine earliest throne and latest oracle.

                                      (69–75)

Liberty, which alone can disperse chaos and create civilization, is associated first with art, later with song, the creative human impulses; Athens is set "on the will / Of man." The emphasis is entirely secular, yet the terminology remains religious: Athens' gleaming towers resemble a vision of the new Jerusalem, a "divine work";

Athens herself is "diviner yet," and the world is "this divinest universe."

The stanzas on Greece and Rome incorporate the Goddess of Liberty into the classical pantheon. The Acropolis is Liberty's "earliest throne and latest oracle."[11] Rome is suckled on the breast of Liberty (as on the breast of the she-wolf); in a "robe of vestal whiteness" Liberty rules from her Capitolian throne (site of the Temple of Jupiter, Juno, and Minerva), until driven from it by the defeat of the Roman Republic, as the maiden Astræa fled the earth with the onset of the Iron Age. The defeat of Liberty is sealed by the emergence of "the Galilean serpent," Christianity. The view of history presented in the poem coincides exactly with the sentiments Shelley expresses in a letter to Peacock: "O, but for that series of wretched wars which terminated in the Roman conquest of the world, but for the Christian religion which put a finishing stroke to the antient system; but for those changes which conducted Athens to its ruin, to what an eminence might not humanity have arrived!" (*Letters of P.B.S.,* II, 75).

The opening stanzas, then, use the imagery of classical theogonies to deify Liberty. The stanzas that recount her return in a reawakened England and Europe identify the return of Liberty with the promised millennium, the second coming of Christ. In synthesizing classical and Biblical myth Shelley is attempting to transcend the traditional machinery of the sublime ode, in which literary allusion is chiefly decorative and conventional, to create out of literary allusion and republican doctrine his own independent myth. The climactic stanza of this section describes Liberty arising in the French Revolution:

> The eager hours and unreluctant years
>   As on a dawn-illumined mountain stood,
> Trampling to silence their loud hopes and fears,
>   Darkening each other with their multitude,
> And cried aloud, Liberty! Indignation
>   Answered Pity from her cave;
>   Death grew pale within the grave,
> And Desolation howled to the destroyer, Save!
>   When like heaven's sun girt by the exhalation
>   Of its own glorious light, thou didst arise,
>   Chasing thy foes from nation unto nation

Like shadows: as if day had cloven the skies
  At dreaming midnight o'er the western wave,
  Men started, staggering with a glad surprise,
  Under the lightnings of thine unfamiliar eyes.

(151–65)

The opening lines recall the Biblical image of the multitudes assembled on a mountain top to await the coming of Messiah; the image of "heaven's sun" suggests Christ girded in his Father's might, driving the Satanic legions out of Heaven. The final metaphor also recalls the description in the opening stanzas of Tyranny as a "fierce cloud" hanging over a waste of waves; the "glad surprise" with which men are startled into hope is a reverse image to the "astonished [stupefied] herds of men" described earlier.

    The stanzas that follow trace the eclipse of Liberty in France, in the aftermath of revolution, and the conquests of Napoleon, the "Anarch" of Liberty's "bewildered powers" (175) (powers led astray). The poet appeals to the hope embodied in Spain and Greece and America, and urges action upon a sleeping England, a "King-deluded Germany" (201), a desolated Italy. The imagery of the apocalypse dominates this section, from the expectations of the "eager hours and unreluctant years" who stand, "Darkening each other with their multitude," to the cry of the Aeolian isles, " 'Be dim; ye lamps of Heaven suspended o'er us!' " (188), to the call to the Tomb of Arminius to "render up thy dead" (196), and the cry to the "free": "Disdain not thou, at thine appointed term, / To set thine armed heel on this reluctant worm [the name of King]" (224–25). The myth is given final shape in the Shelleyan reconstruction of the casting of Satan into hell, and the Day of Judgment:

O, that the wise from their bright minds would kindle
  Such lamps within the dome of this dim world,
That the pale name of PRIEST might shrink and dwindle
  Into the hell from which it first was hurled,
A scoff of impious pride from fiends impure;
    Till human thoughts might kneel alone,
    Each before the judgement-throne
Of its own aweless soul, or of the power unknown!
  O, that the words which make the thoughts obscure

> From which they spring, as clouds of glimmering dew
> From a white lake blot heaven's blue portraiture,
>   Were stript of their thin masks and various hue
> And frowns and smiles and splendours not their own,
>   Till in the nakedness of false and true
>   They stand before their Lord, each to receive its due.
>
>   (226–40)

The vehicle is Biblical myth, the tenor rational republicanism. The scene is the human mind and spirit, the actors thoughts and words, the moral standards truth and falsity. Liberty herself is the great judge; Wisdom, her coruler. And though Wisdom is deified in terms that recall the chariot Ezekiel witnesses in vision, the god emerges in actuality from "man's deep spirit:"

> Come Thou, but lead out of the inmost cave
>   Of man's deep spirit, as the morning-star
> Beckons the Sun from the Eoan wave,
>   Wisdom. I hear the pennons of her car
> Self-moving, like cloud charioted by flame;
>   Comes she not, and come ye not,
>   Rulers of eternal thought,
> To judge, with solemn truth, life's ill-apportioned lot?
>   Blind Love, and equal Justice, and the Fame
>   Of what has been, the Hope of what will be?
>
>   (256–65)

As Liberty is endowed finally with the attributes of the Biblical God, so Kings and Priests, enemies of Liberty, are the agents of Satan and Chaos. In the opening stanzas, the "chaos and . . . curse" are coextensive with the reign of "Tyranny" and "the sister-pest, congregator of slaves," Religion. When the Greek bards and sages thunder, inspired by Liberty, "Religion veils her eyes; Oppression shrinks aghast" (83). The Roman tyranny is followed by the emergence of "the Galilean serpent" Christianity (119); the Renaissance citadels of Italy rise "o'er the tempestuous sea / Of kings, and priests, and slaves" (127–28). France represents the alliance at its most powerful: "How like Bacchanals of blood / Round France, the ghastly vintage, stood / Destruction's sceptred slaves, and Folly's mitred brood!" (171–73). The double theme of Kings and Priests, the one representing physical, the other mental enslavement, reaches a climax in the parallel Stanzas 15 and 16:

> O, that the free would stamp the impious name
>   Of KING into the dust! . . .   (211–12)

> O, that the wise from their bright minds would kindle
>   Such lamps within the dome of this dim world,
> That the pale name of PRIEST might shrink and dwindle
>   Into the hell from which it first was hurled.   (226–29)

This is the double tyranny of the body and of the mind: the tyranny of the King must be destroyed by the free, the tyranny of the Priest by the bright light of reason. But the conclusion of the poem does more than prophesy the destruction of Kings and Priests; the two stanzas calling for their end are followed by a more sophisticated analysis:

> He who taught man to vanquish whatsoever
>   Can be between the cradle and the grave
> Crowned him the King of Life. O vain endeavour!
>   If on his own high will a willing slave,
> He has enthroned the oppression and the oppressor.
>   What if earth can clothe and feed
>   Amplest millions at their need,
> And power in thought be as the tree within the seed?
>   Or what if Art, an ardent intercessor,
>   Diving on fiery wings to Nature's throne,
>   Checks the great mother stooping to caress her,
>   And cries: Give me, thy child, dominion
> Over all height and depth? if Life can breed
>   New wants, and wealth from those who toil and groan
>   Rend of thy gifts and hers a thousandfold for one.
>   (241–55)

The opening lines of the stanza merge the Promethean myth and the myth of creation in Genesis. The great gifts of God are "vain" if man, on his own high (free) will, has enthroned oppression and the oppressor (defined as Kings and Priests), making of himself a willing (consenting) slave. Then follows a series of hypotheses, all connected with the Promethean gift, the ability to fulfill all natural and human potential. What if earth can clothe and feed all her millions; what if thoughts and ideas (that which distinguishes human life from all other life) can be translated into action, made effectual, as the seed develops naturally into the tree; what if Art, mediator between the human and the divine (or the divine in nature) can penetrate to the mysteries of life, attain dominion "over all height and depth?" What if such power is possible, and yet, life can make of power its own enemy? It is Life that is the great enemy to human aspiration; even though man be King over Life, Life takes its revenge. The last lines prophesy the breeding of "new wants" *despite* plenitude; wealth torn from those who toil and groan shall return a thousandfold for one of Life's gifts and Nature's. (The punctuation supports this reading: What if A, B, and C? if X.) If I am reading the lines correctly, they would seem to contradict Mary Shelley's statement that Shelley believed evil to be an external accident; he rather assumes that for every natural impulse toward good there is an equally natural impulse toward making good ineffectual, or turning it to evil. This dilemma provides the context for the final stanza:

> Come Thou, but lead out of the inmost cave
> 　　Of man's deep spirit, as the morning-star
> Beckons the Sun from the Eoan wave,
> 　　Wisdom. 　　　　　　　　　　　　　　(256–59)

The implication of these lines, and the final impression left by the poem, is that the struggle for liberty is internal as much as external.

　　The poem ends with the sudden silence of the voice. The stanza closing the vision is one of the most beautiful in Shelley's poetry.

> . . . 　The solemn harmony
>
> Paused, and the spirit of that mighty singing
> 　　To its abyss was suddenly withdrawn;
> Then, as a wild swan, when sublimely winging
> 　　Its path athwart the thunder-smoke of dawn,
> Sinks headlong through the aerial golden light
> 　　On the heavy-sounding plain,

When the bolt has pierced its brain;
As summer clouds dissolve, unburthened of their rain;
As a far taper fades with fading night,
As a brief insect dies with dying day,
My song, its pinions disarrayed of might,
Drooped; o'er it closed the echoes far away
Of the great voice which did its flight sustain,
As waves which lately paved his watery way
Hiss round a drowner's head in their tempestuous play.
(270–85)

The style complements and answers that of the opening stanza. Here are no abrupt changes, no violent jolting of language, no straining of metaphor, but a long, evenly sustained descent; to the earlier verbs of action, of violent upward motion, are opposed the quiet verbs of loss. The imagery of the opening stanza is heroic and cosmic; at the end the imagery is natural and mundane. In the opening stanza the poet preparing for song is compared to an eagle "Hovering . . . o'er its accustomed prey." As Shelley recapitulates the image it is modified; the "wild swan" also wings its way "athwart the thunder-smoke of dawn," but is itself the victim of greater forces.[12] The three parallel images that follow are a progressive narrowing; although each image is stated in terms of a natural, immediate dissolution, a sudden vanishing (hence like the "drooping" of the poet's song), the unspoken resemblance, which balances the pathos of death, is of fulfillment. "Disarrayed," a continuation of the negatives, the notion of something withdrawn, must be read in its literal sense as the reversal of "arrayed," recalling the earlier image of the poet's soul "clothed in song."

The closing simile has the terrible propriety of unconscious prophecy. But it also has the precision and finality of the expanded similes of classical poetry which Shelley took as his model. As the water sustains a swimmer along his path, so the great voice sustains the poet's song. Similarly, as the waters close over a drowning man's head, when the poet's song "droops," is no longer sustained aloft, the "waves" or echoes of the voice which carried him close far above him. The word "hiss" suggests the "closing" sound both of the waves and of the echoes (as of sound cut off). The simile implies that the abyss of the mighty Spirit, the realm it inhabits and to which it withdraws after its momentary descent, is to our terrestrial realm as the terrestrial world is to the world of the drowner. The comparison suggests the Platonic conception of life within the cave, which appears to be real and true until the aspiring spirit ascends into a daylight that blinds him with its clarity.

The imagery of the last stanza is in part simply Shelley's elaboration of oracular tradition. But its effect is to qualify the overt "doctrine" of the "Ode to Liberty," which asserts faith in the "high will" of man and hymns the great secular virtues. In the end we rest with a paradox that haunts Shelley's poetry. He has an overriding melancholy yearning to escape this "dim world" and a strong intimation of some light beyond it; at the same time he is, as he says of Julian in the preface to "Julian and Maddalo," "passionately attached to those philosophical notions which assert the power of man over his own mind, and the immense improvements of which, by the extinction of certain moral superstitions, human society may be yet susceptible." In the body of "Ode to Liberty" the vision is aggressively secular and is insisted upon by the revision of traditional religion. But it is characteristic of Shelley that he should be able to frame his secular myth in a metaphor that embodies the other half of his vision, familiar to us from "To Constantia," in which the poet, straining away from this dull world, is gifted with a momentary glimpse of the divine, seized, inspired, and at last returned to earth, his vision irrecoverable.

"Ode to Naples," like "Ode to Liberty," is a visionary celebration of an historical political event, the Neapolitan revolution of July, 1820. Like the earlier ode, it is dense with classical allusions, impassioned in rhetoric, daring in its metaphors, absolute and unsubtle in its sentiments. The form is the most complicated Shelley ever devised; like most of his metrical experiments, it appears to be a free and highly original development of conventional models.[13] The closest Romantic analogue is Coleridge's "Ode to the Departing Year," which was first printed with headings of "Strophe," "Antistrophe," and "Epode" in a variation of the Pindaric choral form revived by Gray and Collins. Shelley's metrical variation, too, may have been influenced by Coleridge's antiphonal patterning. Coleridge dropped the headings in *Sybilline Leaves* (1817); Shelley too evidently had second thoughts about their usefulness, and they are omitted from the holograph fair copy which probably represents his final revision. "Ode to Naples" in its contemporary printings consists of three parts: two introductory "Epodes" describing the onset of the poet's visionary seizure, in which he is inspired to prophesy; a middle section hailing the birth of freedom in Naples (three pairs of antiphonal "Strophes" and "Antistrophes," the complementary stanzas of which are derived from the epode stanza); and two concluding "Epodes" in which the poet warns of the dangers ahead and prays that Naples may remain free. In the central section the alternating patterns impart a rhythmical excitement to the fervor of celebration and the urgency of prayer. The reader is reminded of the lyrics of *Prometheus Unbound,* especially in Act IV, where Shelley experiments with an English version of the Greek lyric meters. Similarly, in "Ode to Naples" the rhythm seems designed to imitate, in a highly stylized manner, the function and the passion of the speaker.

The introduction of "Ode to Naples" describes Pompeii and the islands and bays surrounding Naples. Shelley draws upon the account of his expeditions to Pompeii and Baiæ in his letters to Peacock; the correspondences are close enough to suggest that Shelley had copies of the letters before him as he wrote. He writes of Pompeii, describing the view from the Temple of Jupiter:

> There was a magnificent spectacle. Above & between the multitudinous shafts of the . . . columns, was seen the blue sea reflecting the purple heaven of noon above it, & supporting as it were on its line the dark lofty mountains of Sorrento. . . . Between was one small green island. To the right was Capua, Inarime, Prochyta and Miseno. Behind was the single summit of Vesuvius. . . . The day was radiant & warm. Every now & then we heard the subterranean thunder of Vesuvius; its distant deep peals seemed to shake the very air & light of day which interpenetrated our frames with the sullen & tremendous sound . . .
>
> (*Letters of P.B.S.,* II, 73)

The first epode is based upon this description; the opening image, as editors point out, is derived from a passage later on in the same letter, in which Shelley compares the "shiver and rustle" of the late autumn leaves to the step of ghosts. While retaining the significant details of the prose account, he recasts the scene in the form of a dream vision. Thus the precise description of nature: "its distant deep peals seemed to shake the very air & light of day which interpenetrated our frames with the sullen & tremendous sound" (the attempt to render the exact quality of a thing perceived), becomes translated into the supernatural terms of vision, the casting off of the body and the entry of the divine into the soul, as in the ecstasy of "To Constantia:" "The oracular thunder penetrating shook / The listening soul in the suspended blood" (6–7). Similarly, the prose account of the tombs beyond Pompeii—"The radiance & magnificence of these dwellings of the dead, the white freshness of the scarcely finished marble, the impassioned or imaginative life of the figures which adorn them" (*Letters of P.B.S.,* II, 74)—is mythologized thus in the poem:

> Around me gleamed many a bright sepulchre,
> Of whose pure beauty, Time, as if his pleasure
> Were to spare Death, had never made erasure . . .
>
> (12–14)

The poem emphasizes the stillness of the scene, its clarity and purity, the absolute suspension of life; while the details are faithful to the original prose description, they suggest the pastoral landscape of dream vision. At the same time, the description evokes the sense of harmony which Shelley makes explicit in his comment on the view from the Temple:

> This scene was what the Greeks beheld. (Pompeii you know was a Greek city). They lived in harmony with nature, & the interstices of their incomparable columns, were portals as it were to admit the spirit of beauty which animates this glorious universe to visit those whom it inspired.
>
> (*Letters of P.B.S.,* II, 73)

The rest of the Ode is dominated by this perception, with Italy substituted for Greece as the land visited and animated by beauty.

The second epode introduces the vision proper, in which the poet is "rapt" or borne aloft. The ascent, which in "Ode to Liberty" is drawn in a single sharp image, is developed at length and is a means of evoking the scene around Naples, the bays, the clear skies, the sites of ancient myth and legend, Inarime (the island of Ischia), under which the giant Typhon was imprisoned, Lake Avernus, the abode of the Cimmerians and entrance to Hades. The divine and oracular seem to proceed from the natural, to be immanent in it or to issue out of it; every comparison suggests the indissoluble connection of nature and beauty and the divine in the classical world. Thus the comparison of one element to another—of sea and air to light, of poetic vision to angelic flight—suggests apparent and hidden analogies on every level of sense and being. As the motion of the Baian sea is "airlike," so the sunlight serves as "waves" for a boat made of "dewy air."[14] Similarly, emotion and poetry are "flowing" elements, their motion analogous to the eternal motion of air and sea. In fact the passage is a kind of mirror image to "Ode to the West Wind," in which the poet alone is set apart from the processes of nature; in "Ode to Naples" the winds are "gentle," the atmosphere "stormless;" and the poet is despite himself borne aloft on the combined impulse of natural and poetic inspiration. He recapitulates in his visionary air-borne pinnace the real boat trip described in the letter to Peacock.[15] But in the visionary scene nature is animated and will is attributed to the actors ("Aornos darkened . . . the . . . æther; Heaven stript bare / Its depth over Elysium"). The final words of the Introduction—"be they fate!"—mean "be they fulfilled;" the line is abrupt, like the corresponding line of "Ode to Liberty:" "I will record the same." The abruptness is deliberate, an imitation of the divine seizure of the poet, and also, in "Ode to Naples," a means of transition from the serene narrative of the Introduction to the highly wrought, impassioned invocation of the Ode proper.

The scene of the opening epodes is, of course, more than an occasion for the "picturesque and descriptive imagery" that Shelley's note mentions. If my reconstruction of the texts is correct, Shelley decided finally to omit these introductory epodes. But certainly in the first version of the poem, the description of Pompeii, the "City disinterred," frozen in the still beauty of the past, is a foil to the action and exuberant vitality of the strophes addressed to Naples, a "Heart of men" panting "Naked beneath the lidless eye of Heaven!"

From the opening image: "I stood within the City disinterred; / And heard the autumnal leaves like light footfalls / Of spirits passing through the streets"—Italy is presented as a land permeated with the spirit of the past, its art, literature, myth. The past informs the poet's vision of present Italy; the modern crisis is restated in terms of the history and myth of the ancient world. Homer and Virgil, invoked in the opening stanza, serve throughout as the context for the imagery of battle, historical and mythical; geographical names are consistently ancient rather than modern, as in "Ode to Liberty:" *Aornos, Inarime, Æaea, Ausonian, Cimmerian, Celtic*—all occur in Virgil. Images from the opening stanza are echoed in later stanzas; the "standard / Of some ætherial host" which announces the battle imagery is later recalled in the "banners blazoned to the day" of the barbaric legions (132). The theme of harmony, which permeates the stanza, is embodied in the metaphor of musical harmony (the "Kings of Melody;" the "mingled close" of sound and odor); this metaphor recurs in the "thrilling Paean" of Spain (102) which turns silence to music, the "Dissonant threats" of the enemy (134), the "harmonizing ardours" of Love and Beauty (165).

Shelley organizes the body of the poem, the "prophesyings" of which he is the inspired vehicle, as a sequence of alternating stanzas that answer one another in their refrain: "Hail, hail, all hail!" "All hail!" The first stanza of each pair prefaces the refrain with a somber qualification: "If Hope and Truth and Justice can avail." The ritual established by the repeated formula balances the elaborate, ecstatic metaphor of the invocation and prepares for the prayer with which the poem ends. One would expect a pattern so elaborate to have precedent; the closest analogue is perhaps Shelley's own "Ode to the West Wind," which similarly ends each invocation with the ritualistic "hear, O hear!" or a variant of it, and closes with a prayer.

The first stanza (lines 52–65) invokes Naples in a sequence of descriptive apostrophes. The opening metaphor suggests the present (Naples) as opposed to the past (Pompeii), the human (a Heart of men) as opposed to the natural and superhuman ("oracular woods and divine sea"). Succeeding metaphors place Naples geographically, politically, historically, as the harbor and metropolis of the Kingdom of Two Sicilies. At the same time they endow the proclamation of a constitutional government with mythic significance, as the hope of a restored Paradise, a Golden Age ruled by Love. The final tableau illustrates the closeness with which epic allusion is tied to historical event. Only bloodless sacrifices can be offered to Love;[16] the Victories Shelley describes in his letters (as in the Arch of Constantine) are traditionally associated with battles, conquering heroes, the gods of war. But the reform at Naples was won bloodlessly, by an ultimatum presented to Ferdinand by rebelling officers (hence "armed").

The rhetorical pattern of the opening stanza is sustained throughout the "hailing" strophes. Stanza II continues the invocation of Naples with a sequence of personifications drawn from classical and Christian myth. The opening image—"Thou youngest Giant birth / Which from the groaning Earth / Leap'st, clothed in armour of impenetrable scale!"—recalls Hesiod: "For all the bloody drops that gushed forth Earth received, and as the seasons moved round she bare . . . the great Giants with gleaming armour, holding long spears in their hands."[17] (Later in the poem the same myth is turned around: Naples is associated with the "ever-living Gods" threatened by the "Earthborn Forms," or "Anarchs of the North.") The "groaning Earth" is a conventional epithet in Hesiod, here applied to the misery of an enslaved Italy. The "proud Transgressors" of line 70 are kings and tyrants, Ferdinand in league with Austria. Naples defying Austria on behalf of Italy is associated with Christ pleading "before God's love" against Satan for man. The image of Naples "Arrayed in Wisdom's mail" refers to Pallas Athene emerging from the head of Jove dressed in golden armor, "Shaking a javelin keen" (Shelley's translation of the Homeric "Hymn to Minerva," 8). As Stanzas I and II link the parallel classical and Biblical images: "Elysian City" and "Paradise," "Love, the flower-enchained" (in the first version) and "God's love,"[18] the "youngest Giant birth" and "Last of the Intercessors," the effect is to make of the past, Greek, Roman, Biblical, a single heritage bearing directly upon the present, with an emphasis (appropriate to an ode for Naples) on the classical rather than the Biblical, the Roman rather than the Greek.

The second pair of strophes hail Naples as she is prepared for battle, arrayed in "Wisdom's mail," and in action, as the "Destroyer pale," conquering the enemy and establishing the rule of equality, freedom, and truth. Lines 77–90 urge Naples on to victory in a series

of images of weapons turned back against the wearer, battles won by
the mirror-like shield of Minerva rather than the sword, by a look
(as of a Basilisk or Gorgon) rather than a blood-letting. Lines 91–
101 complement these predominantly classical images with the
image of the Destroyer, the rending of false idols and "impious
gawds," the sending out of truth "even from the throne of God." The
final pair of strophes hail Naples as the hope of all Italy; each of the
captive Italian cities is personified in terms of its geography or its
long history of oppression. The sequence ends by recalling the defeat
of Republican Rome; modern Rome in the expectation of freedom
is:

> An athlete stript to run
> From a remoter station
> For the high prize lost on Philippi's shore.
>
> (122–24)

The prayer is that "Fraud and Wrong" may now avail as "Hope and
Truth and Justice" did then—that is, Fraud and Wrong may be defeated.

The body of the ode concentrates on the sense of crisis, the fact
that Naples is young in its promise and compassed round by dangers,
that there is no sure guarantee that "Hope and Truth and Justice"
will avail and "Fraud and Wrong" be conquered. The conditional
refrain is far from confident ("If Hope and Truth and Justice can
avail"); it is as much an incentive to courage as a celebration. The
mythical and historic past that is the source of analogy provides
more examples of defeat than of victory.

The final section turns to the contemporary danger, the Austrian
tyranny Shelley attacked so bitterly in "Lines written among the
Euganean Hills," imaged now in terms of the war of the Giants
against the Olympian Gods, the march of the Satanic legions against
Heaven, and the descent of the barbarian hordes into Roman Italy.
Lines 135–36 return to the opening image of Naples as an Eden,
wrapped by a "serene Heaven" (compare the "calm Serene" of line
36, the "Elysian City" of line 54). The image of the foe descending,
unhappily prophetic, recalls the "leagued Oppressors" of line 74,

moving "With hurried legions" from "their hundred gates" (as Satan's legions "hast on / With furious expedition," *Paradise Lost,* VI, 85–86). Austrian control over Italy is compared to "Chaos [moving] o'er creation, uncreating," a reversal of the primal act of creation, when the Spirit of God, or Freedom, or Love (Shelley uses several versions of the myth) moved over Chaos, giving it form. The "banners blazoned to the day" recall the banners of Milton's rebelling angelic legions who assemble in the "limits of the North:" "Ten thousand Banners rise into the Air / With Orient Colours waving" (*Paradise Lost,* I, 545–46). The Miltonic imagery complements the vision of volcanic vapour streaming "like the standard / Of some ætherial host" in the Introduction, lines 45–46. The concluding epodes, as these parallels indicate, are closely tied to the imagery of the Introduction, which opposes to the picture of "Famished wolves" glutting themselves on "Beauty's corse," a "pure beauty" that has remained untouched by time for two thousand years. As in all the political odes, past history is conceived as cyclical; the role of the poet is to reaffirm the eternal principle of freedom surviving the repeated secular (hence temporary) triumphs of tyranny, and to prophesy for present struggles the eventual breaking of the cycle, the final triumph of liberty.

"Ode to Naples" ends, like "Ode to the West Wind" and "Ode to Liberty," with a prayer addressed to a deity who is the creation of the poem itself, defined by the ceremonial invocation, given its distinctive character by a fusion of secular and religious metaphors. The prayer divides into an invocation (149–57); a twofold petition, a prayer for destruction (158–64) or for succour (165–73); a final prayer for freedom (174–76). The deity addressed is not sharply differentiated from more orthodox gods, as it is in the odes discussed above. The "Power" of "Ode to Naples," which "lull[s] all things" and "brood[s]" over the soul of the poet (22), which rules and moves "All things that live and are within the Italian shore" (150–51), can be assimilated to conventional ideas of a benign Providence, unlike Power in the earlier poems, where it is signalized by its detachment from human affairs, or by its flickering and intermittent appearances, and where the governing will is that of man, free and wise, "his own divine control." But it is difficult to say how much this represents a softening of Shelley's militant unorthodoxy, how much it is a matter of the appropriate dress for an ode to an Italian city. For the prayer, the climax of those "prophesyings" of which the poet is vehicle, is a development of his objective sense of Naples and her environs, as it is conveyed in the introductory epodes, where divinity is an emanation of art and nature. Love, the "great Spirit" (as he is called in the *Symposium* to distinguish him both from mortals and from the gods) is the tutelary deity of the stanzas that hail Naples' freedom. In the final epode, too, Love appears to be a composite deity: the Love of Greek cosmogony, first principle of order and harmony; Aphrodite, goddess of love and beauty, of dews and rain and sunlight; also "the love which heals all strife" ("Lines written among the Euganean Hills," 366).[18] The petition for grace: "with thine harmonizing ardours fill / And raise thy sons, as o'er the prone horizon / Thy lamp [Venus, the evening star] feeds every western wave with fire" (165–67) associates Love, "Spirit of Beauty," with the West Wind and its "azure sister of the Spring," who drives sweet buds to feed in air, and fills "With living hues and odours plain and hill." Above all, Love is the ruling god of Italy and of Naples, "This city of [Love's] worship" (176).

The sentiments of the first half of the petition ("Bid the Earth's plenty kill!") are pitched in the same violent key as the final stanzas on Kings and Priests in "Ode to Liberty" and the attack on the tyranny and corruption of the Italian cities in "Lines written among the Euganean Hills:" "If not, perish thou and they! . . . Earth can spare ye" (160, 163). Prometheus recalls his curse ("I wish no living thing to suffer pain"); *Hellas,* too, which contains passages of violent attack, pays tribute to forgiveness:

> In sacred Athens, near the fane
>   Of Wisdom, Pity's altar stood:
> Serve not the unknown God in vain,
> But pay that broken shrine again,
>   Love for hate and tears for blood.
>
> (733–37)

But the image of the Destroyer is central in Shelley's political poems. While forgiveness and compassion translate the human spirit into another realm, in the temporal world (where "light and darkness" bound the heavens) there is no doubt that tyrants must be forcibly overthrown, the foe eliminated.[19]

Even so, the violence that dominates the middle section of "Ode to Naples" (anticipating the violence of the final prayer) is mental rather than physical, like the pains of Prometheus, the rending of "the ministers of pain, and fear, / And disappointment, and mistrust, and hate" (*Prometheus Unbound*, I, 452–53). The suggestion is that the real battles are of the spirit rather than the flesh. Thus the "armour of impenetrable scale" which clothes Naples is "Wisdom's" (68, 71); the forces of evil are to be defeated by example rather than action, their own devices turned against them. It is Error that is to be rent so fiercely; the Destroyer is to sit sublime over "Falsehood's fallen state" and is to let sail not arrows or thunderbolts or cannonballs but "winged words . . . / Freighted with truth" (95, 98–99).

"Ode to Naples" is as closely constructed a poem as Shelley wrote; while its care is most clearly indicated by the ingenious multiple correspondences of the stanzaic form, the "Ode" shows the same kind of close thematic and imagistic development that gives structure to the poems discussed earlier. Beyond its technique, the special quality of "Ode to Naples" has to do with its sense of Italy, the land itself, its art, its history, its present crisis, and the source of the imagery in which all of these are clothed, its myth and literature. These are the same elements that lie behind the poet's apostrophe to Italy in "Ode to Liberty:"

> And thou, lost Paradise of this divine
>   And glorious world! thou flowery wilderness!
> Thou island of eternity! thou shrine
>   Where Desolation, clothed with loveliness,
> Worships the thing thou wert! . . .   (204–08)

Partly because of the actual geography and history of Italy, partly because of the coloring Shelley instinctively lent them, Italy was for him the living physical embodiment of beauty, and equally the living symbol of political oppression. This painful reality gives "Ode to Naples," despite its optimistic rhetoric, an elegiac undertone. In fact the Neapolitan revolution, like that of the Spaniards, was short-lived; the Austrian army invaded successfully the following winter,

NOTES

1. See Frederick A. Pottle, "The Role of Asia in the Dramatic Action of Shelley's *Prometheus Unbound,*" *Shelley: A Collection of Critical Essays,* ed. George M. Ridenour (Englewood Cliffs, N.J., 1965), pp. 133–43.
2. See M. H. Abrams, "The Correspondent Breeze: A Romantic Metaphor" (1957), in *English Romantic Poets: Modern Essays in Criticism,* ed. Abrams (New York, 1960), pp. 37–54. The closest contemporary analogue to the "Ode to the West Wind" is Coleridge's address to "Clouds, Ocean-waves, and Woods" in "France: An Ode;" see Harold Bloom, *The Visionary Company* (New York, 1961), p. 215.
3. Cf. the visions of destruction in the apocalyptic books: "And the Lord shall cause his glorious voice to be heard, and shall shew the lightning down of his arm, with the indignation of *his* anger, and *with* the flame of a devouring fire, *with* scattering, and tempest, and hailstones" (Isaiah 30:30); "When he uttereth his voice, there is a multitude of waters in the heavens, and he causeth the vapours to ascend from the ends of the earth; he maketh lightnings with rain, and bringeth forth the wind out of his treasures" (Jeremiah 10:13). Cf. also *Prometheus Unbound,* IV, 338–41: "Sceptred curse, / Who all our green and azure universe / Threatenedst to muffle round with black destruction, sending / A solid cloud to rain hot thunderstones." In "Ode to the West Wind," however, destruction is welcomed.
4. Frederick A. Pottle points out the resemblance of the poet's lament to that of the Psalmist, in the use of the words "strength" and "heaviness:" "The Case of Shelley," (1952) in *English Romantic Poets,* ed. Abrams, p. 292. For the metaphor "Oh! lift me . . . I fall" cf. Job 22:29: "When men are cast down, then thou shalt say, There is lifting up;" and Isaiah 40:30–31: "Even the youths shall faint and be weary, and the young men shall utterly fall; But they that wait upon the Lord shall renew their strength; they shall mount up with wings as eagles."
5. Cf. Byron, *Childe Harold's Pilgrimage:* "Meantime I seek no sympathies nor need; / The thorns which I have reap'd are of the tree / I planted,—They have torn me,—and I bleed; / I should have known what fruit would spring from such a seed" (IV, 10).
6. In the preface to *Prometheus Unbound* Shelley expresses faith in some social change to follow upon the great poetic activity of the age: "The great writers of our own age are, we have reason to suppose, the companions and forerunners of some unimagined change in our social condition or the opinions which cement it." He referred in a letter of October 28, 1819, to "this crisis of approaching Revolution" (*Letters of P. B. S.,* II, 132); on November 6 he wrote to the Gisbornes: "Every thing is preparing for a bloody struggle . . . we are on the eve of great actions" (*Letters of P. B. S.,* II, 149–50).
7. The parallel is suggested in George E. Woodberry, ed., *The Complete Poetical Works of Shelley* (Boston, 1901), p. 640.
8. Cf. Paul's account of himself "caught up to the third heaven . . . How that he was caught up into paradise, and heard unspeakable words"

(2 Cor. 12:2, 4); or Milton, *Paradise Lost,* VII, 1–39. The "heaven of fame" is the Empyrean, Milton's "Heav'n of Heav'ns:" the heaven of God's immediate presence.

9. "At th' accustom'd hour" (*Paradise Lost,* IV, 779); "o're th' accustom'd Oke" ("Il Penseroso," 60). For "contagious fire" (4) and "station" (10), cf. *Paradise Lost,* IX, 1036 ("*Eve,* whose Eye darted contagious Fire"); and VII, 563 ("The Planets in thir station list'ning stood"). Shelley uses the term "station" in this sense only in "Ode to Liberty;" "accustomed" appears elsewhere, also with epic associations.

10. Cf. Milton's address to Light: "before the Sun, / Before the Heavens thou wert . . ." (*Paradise Lost,* III, 8–9).

11. Although the "earliest throne" of Liberty suggests the Areopagus and the hill of Ares, the "marble forms" indicate that "that hill" is the Acropolis, "its bards and sages" the Athenian poets and philosophers. "latest oracle" refers to the Greek independence movement, which Shelley celebrates in *Hellas,* written the following year. The opening chorus of *Hellas* (46–92) summarizes the history of liberty as it is described in "Ode to Liberty."

12. For a possible source of the image of the bird falling to earth, its brain pierced, cf. the epic games in *Aeneid* V.513–18. But the "bolt" is there the hunter's arrow; in "Ode to Liberty" it is a lightning-bolt ("fulmine" in Shelley's Italian translation, Bodleian MS Shelley adds. c. 4, fol. 88).

13. The complicated stanzaic form and rhyme scheme are analyzed in Locock, *An Examination of the Shelley Manuscripts in the Bodleian Library,* pp. 14–18; and his errors are corrected by Hutchinson, pp. 903–04.

14. The "ever stormless atmosphere / Floats o'er the Elysian realm" as the Baian ocean "Welters" around its underground caverns; the comparison is based on the fact that the Bay of Baiæ is completely sheltered, thus unusually calm. "It," line 32, refers to the "Power divine" of the preceding stanza, "whose" to the Angel, thus: the Power divine bore me o'er the waves of sunlight, like an Angel whose swift pinnace of dewy air no storm can overwhelm. The poet is thus borne aloft in vision, as in "Ode to Liberty" he is "rapt" beyond the spheres.

15. "We passed Posilipo & came first to the eastern point of the bay of Puzzoli which is within the great bay of Naples & which again incloses that of Baiæ . . . We then went directly across to the promontory of Misenum . . . Here we were conducted to see the Mare Morto & the Elysian fields, the spot on which Virgil places the scenery of the 6th Æneid . . . After passing the Bay of Baiæ . . . we landed to visit Lake Avernus . . . & came to a calm & lovely basin of water surrounded by dark woody hills, & profoundly solitary" (*Letters of P.B.S.,* II, 61). "Aornos" is the Greek name for Avernus, retained by Virgil. The "Elysian realm" of line 31 is legendary; the "Elysium" of line 42 must be the "Elysian fields" of Misenum referred to in the letter.

16. Cf. the final chorus of *Hellas:* "Not gold, not blood, their altar dowers, / But votive tears and symbol flowers" (1094–95).

17. Hesiod, *Theogony,* 183 ff., in *Hesiod, The Homeric Hymns, and*

Homerica, tr. Hugh G. Evelyn-White, Loeb Classical Library (Cambridge, Mass., Harvard University Press, 1914).

18. Love is also human love, in the line "As sleep round Love, [is] driven;" the sleep of lovers occurs elsewhere in Shelley's poetry as an image of calm and perfection. Cf. *Epipsychidion,* 558–59.

19. The petition is clothed in the standard political rhetoric of the time, i.e., the Spirit of the Earth praying to the God of Nature in Coleridge's "Ode to the Departing Year:" "Avenger, rise! . . . And on the darkling foe / Open thine eye of fire from some uncertain cloud! / O dart the flash! O rise and deal the blow!" (93, 97–99). The idea of Nature defending her own against the enemy occurs again in *Hellas:* "Where'er the winds shall creep, or the clouds fly, / Or the dews fall, or the angry sun look down / With poisoned light—Famine, and Pestilence, / And Panic, shall wage war upon our side! / Nature from all her boundaries is moved / Against ye . . ." (437–42). See also Byron's *Prophecy of Dante:* "Oh! when the strangers pass the Alps and Po, / Crush them, ye rocks! floods whelm them, and for ever! / Why sleep the idle avalanches so, / To topple on the lonely pilgrim's head? / Why doth Eridanus but overflow / The peasant's harvest from his turbid bed? / Were not each barbarous horde a nobler prey?" (II, 101–07).

CHAPTER FIVE

NATURE HUMANIZED
& NATURAL MYTH

THE great range of the 1820 volume bears out the distinction Yeats made between Blake and Shelley as romantic visionary poets. Blake was a mystic, Yeats wrote, while Shelley's art shows that he was an unconverted man. "Shelley was not a mystic, his system of thought was constructed by his logical faculty to satisfy desire, not a symbolical revelation received after the suspension of all desire."[1]

There is a core of sanity to Shelley's thought, even when it is masked by his passion. The tentative nature of his myth-making reaches its logical extension in the unresolved dialectic of "Ode to Heaven" or "The Two Spirits: An Allegory." His poems should be read not as the working out of a system, or as different representations of a single ideal, but rather as fresh attempts to interpret an elusive, ever-changing reality, to discover its meaning for human life. As nature in Shelley's poetry is multiform, so are the several ideals discovered in nature, which represents, in turn, that "glass / Wherein man his nature sees" ("Ode to Heaven," 21–22). The laughter of the Cloud, the "gladness" of the Sky-Lark, the freedom of the West Wind, the "secret strength" that inhabits Mont Blanc— each has its special character, inseparable from the imagery that gives it life and from the questions raised by the "adverting mind" of the poet. If the political poems stress man's bondage, enforced by circumstance and self-willed, the nature poems represent a complementary aspect of Shelley's poetic vision, his extraordinary empathy for the natural world as it is free of that bondage, as it exists and rejoices in itself. The imagination of the poet invests nature with human impulse and form, creates of the natural world a human world, free from human limitation.

"Ode to Heaven" represents the dispassionate, philosophizing poet at his most engaging. Each section of the Ode offers a definition of Heaven in terms of a particular epistemology; the sequence of definitions thus turns into an argument on the nature of reality.[2] The terms of the argument are familiar from "Mont Blanc;" the universe (or the world of things) is set against the perceiving mind, and both are related to a Power behind things and thought. But the tone of "Ode to Heaven" is light, as might be appropriate to social discourse among minor spirits. The dialogue is marked by the kind of humor that Asia indulges in when she rebukes the Spirit of the Earth for aspiring prematurely to the pleasures of sexual love. The humor of the dialogue qualifies the philosophy and lends an academic, even pedantic, air to the argument. The poem illustrates particularly well the distinction Shelley made between philosophy and poetry; if philosophy seeks to arrive by rational means at the truth, poetry is equally at home in paradox, or can take a visionary leap to certainties that the heart alone can accept.

Each definition is a variation on the simple notion of heaven overhanging and hence surrounding or containing the earth. In the song of the opening "Chorus of Spirits," Heaven is infinite and unchanging, home to the temporal, the finite, the mortal. The first stanza makes of the arch of heaven (roof, canopy, dome) a series of regal and religious images: Heaven is "Presence chamber" and "Temple" of present and past, of time and place, "Dome" of the future—home of all we call reality. The second stanza turns from the container to the thing contained, "Earth and all Earth's company." Heaven is the primal Earth, or Paradise, with "deep chasms and wildernesses" —the landscape of "Kubla Khan" superimposed on the heavenly regions—in which "green worlds" and "swift stars" move and live. The last stanza makes explicit the contrast between the eternal dome and the "living globes" that people Heaven. Heaven remains the same; human generations and their "unremaining" gods pass away. Man worships blindly, invents his own gods—yet the Heaven that surrounds him is also the abode of the Power which alone reveals to man his divine nature, else obscured.

The "remoter voice" reduces the images of the Chorus of Spirits to their proper place in his perspective. The real is but the shadow of the absolute, to which the mind alone can attain; the shadow-world of life is a dim prelude to the glories beyond the grave. (A similar classification is made in the levels of reality in "Mont Blanc," as the poet moves from the physical scene to the world of images, and finally to the world of sleep and death.) The reduction in scale is achieved by a reinterpretation of the terms and images of the "Chorus of Spirits." Thus Heaven is not "Presence chamber" to the infinite but simply the "first chamber" of the mind (in the draft reading, "the mind which gazes on thee"—again echoing "Mont Blanc"); in a variation on the image of an enclosing roof, it is compared to a cave lighted dimly by stalactites, in which weak insects (like "young thoughts") clamber uncertainly; it is not an all-enclosing dome, but, in a variation of the arch image, a portal, or entrance to something beyond. The imagery challenges the joyous absolutes of the opening stanzas, the pure, intense color and motion of the spheres (green worlds, swift stars, icy moons); here all reality is dim, weak, shadowy, unsure.

The final and authoritative "voice" (louder and still remoter), rebukes the "Atom-born" for finding assurances of immortality either in life or death; life, it appears to say, is both much less and much more than they perceive or imagine. The final stanza is emotionally, rhetorically, philosophically definitive. The dialectic resembles that of the passage in Act IV of *Prometheus Unbound,* where, after the joyful epithalamium of Earth and Moon, Demogorgon rises out of the earth to address both. They acknowledge through an extraordinary reduction in scale of imagery the relation of that which exists to the Power greater than all:

> *The Earth.* I hear: I am as a drop of dew that dies . . .
> *The Moon.* I hear: I am a leaf shaken by thee!
> (*Prometheus Unbound,* IV, 523, 528)

In "Ode to Heaven" the final perspective does not deny the joy of creation but suddenly sets it in relation to the abyss, and to that spirit of which all creation is but a part. The "Ever-canopying Dome" of past and future becomes a "brief expanse," Heaven is a "globe of dew," its immensities of suns are furled in that "frail and fading sphere." The enthusiasm and optimism of the Chorus of Spirits yield to an austere, dispassionate objectivity. The correc-

tion of perspective is finely projected by the shift from the series of
appositives in the first two sections to the final precise image, which
includes and refutes all that has preceded it.

> What is Heaven? a globe of dew
> Filling in the morning new
> Some eyed flower whose young leaves waken
>   On an unimagined world.   (46–49)

The final twist is given to the notion that life, finite and temporal,
is contained in the infinite; it is the finite and perishable which
itself contains the measureless, the infinite. (This is another version
of the paradox explored in the question which closes "Mont Blanc:"
"And what were thou, and earth, and stars, and sea, / If to the
human mind's imaginings / Silence and solitude were vacancy?")
The globe of dew, the distillation of heaven in its most mutable
form, reflects "constellated suns unshaken," "orbits measureless"—
and in its own frailty reveals the nature of the cosmos it reflects. Yet
the image is one not only of mutability but of youth, freshness,
infinite possibility. The "eyed flower" (which suggests the perceiving mind), though perishable as the dew that briefly forms in its
center, contains all reality for its brief life and reflects (or perceives) the eternal as well as the mutable.

> Constellated suns unshaken,
>   Orbits measureless, are furled
>   In that frail and fading sphere,
>   With ten million gathered there
>   To tremble, gleam, and disappear!   (50–54)

The final line serves as a precise description of a globe of dew or
the reflection of stars in a globe of dew; it also stands as an image
of human life.

"Ode to Heaven" should be read not as doctrine but as the
dialectical exposition of the problem that moves Asia to cry:

> How glorious art thou, Earth! And if thou be
> The shadow of some spirit lovelier still,
> Though evil stain its work, and it should be

Like its creation, weak yet beautiful,
I could fall down and worship that and thee.
                              (*Prometheus Unbound*, II, iii, 12–16)

The same problem is explored in the fable of "The Sensitive Plant"
and the moral attached to it. Repeatedly Shelley expresses a delight
in life and the beauty of living things so intensely felt that it impels
him to believe in immortality. Yet he feels an equally certain and
intense apprehension of death, mutability, imperfection, as the
condition of life. There is not much distance in Shelley's poetry between his affirmation of hope and his pessimism, nor does he ever
try to resolve the problem of God and immortality. The moral to
"The Sensitive Plant" affirms as a "pleasant creed" that "love, and
beauty, and delight," are indeed immortal, but removed forever
from us, who can "endure no light." Yet the fable that precedes it
suggests that immortal beauty alone can nourish and sustain the
mutable. Similarly, if "Ode to Heaven" ends with an image of life
as a brief flash of light, the effect is not to deny but rather to qualify
sharply the expansive celebration of life in the opening stanzas.

"To a Sky-Lark," like "Ode to the West Wind," has long been
read as a classic statement of Romanticism. Shelley himself has
often been identified (mistakenly, I think) with the "blithe Spirit"
of the poem, the pure singer; certainly the lyric is his consummate
poetic rendering of the power of joy, that spontaneous lightness of
heart which he affirms to be the essential condition for poetry, as
perhaps for life itself.

What Shelley discovers in the song of the lark is in harmony
with the discoveries of Wordsworth and Coleridge, in their poems
on birds and bird songs:[3] the bird is conceived as spirit, unseen yet
heard; its song is the overflowing or disburdening of a full heart; its
song has profound implications for the poet or lover bound by the
flesh, whose singing is subject to paralysis or soured by self-love.
The lyrics of Wordsworth and Coleridge are primarily reflective:
the object is described so that the poet can consider his own relation to it, meditate on its implications. One is aware of the poet
standing firmly on the ground (hands clasped behind his back, eyes
toward heaven) even as he describes the bird soaring into the sky

or hidden in a grove; the permanent impressiveness of the poetry lies in the overt commentary, the honesty, integrity, and seriousness of the mind seeking to relate experience to universals. In Shelley's lyric, reflection is peripheral and after the fact; the heart of the poem is a straining after the precise quality of the experience, an extended attempt through description, image, and analogy, to embody the lark poetically, to fix its essence. When the poet turns at last to reflection, so intensely has he realized the lark in image, entered into its vision of life, so to speak, that the perspective on human life is altered: human ills become merely conditions excluded by the happy nature of the bird. "Mortals" are inconsequential; the sphere of analogy to human life, ideal and exemplary, becomes itself the subject of poetry.

The artistry of "To a Sky-Lark" has been often attacked.[4] The thesis of the poem, the glorification of inspiration above art, of ecstasy above knowledge, would seem to support the notion of what Keats called Shelley's "magnanimity"—that is, lack of discipline. Yet in the process of composition there is a shadowy area between "inspiration" and conscious artistry where the two impulses—the creator's and the compositor's—are barely distinguishable. Shelley's feeling for structure, for propriety of language, for sound, for development (all of which we would put under the heading of art— and all of which is absent from the bird's song) often seems as intuitive as the initial overflow of feeling which, according to his own account (or occasionally to Mary's reconstruction of events), impels him to put pen to paper. Yet analysis of his lyrics suggests that control is strong rather than weak, and discipline consistent.

Shelley's sense of artistic propriety is often expressed as a form of imitation, in which the subject radically affects the style of the poem. While this seems a function of conscious art in a "sublime" poem like "Ode to Liberty," it is equally evident in the simplicity and naturalness of "To a Sky-Lark." As the bird is "Spirit" rather than bird, a "Scorner of the ground," so the language that describes it is pure, simple, monosyllabic, stripped of complication. The image of the bird as purity, singleness of impulse, affects the conception of human ills, which are described simply and dispassionately:

> We look before and after
> And pine for what is not—   (86–87)

One might compare the tone of these lines to the passionate lament of "Ode to the West Wind," which appears an extension of the passion of the elements. The imagery of the poem, too, which has often been attacked as Shelley's "favorite imagery" of stars and clouds, radiates out from the image of the bird itself. While most of the images are drawn from nature, like the bird, they are (again like the bird) the least earthbound of natural things, the most bodiless and pure—moonlight, raindrops, flower, poet, and maiden. Even the apparent spontaneity of the poem, in its stanza form, its profusion of images, its structure, is calculated—a conscious imitation of the pure spontaneity that the bird's song represents.

The opening stanzas describe the soaring flight of the bird and the quality of its song, as it is glimpsed in the heavens at sunset (lines 11–15). Each statement of fact ("Higher still and higher / From the earth thou springest . . . Thou dost float and run . . . Thou art unseen,—but yet I hear thy shrill delight . . . All the earth and air / With thy voice is loud") is reinforced by a comparison, as if description alone is inadequate to convey the intense quality of the experience. Comparisons, drawn from other phenomena of the heavens at other times of day and night, appear to be suggested quite simply by the scene, usually by contraries. The bird vanishing into the sunset suggests the star that is unseen in "broad day-light;" the "pale purple even" suggests the "white dawn clear;" the "golden lightning" of the sun suggests the moon raining out her beams. Yet the apparently associative imagery works on another level as well; in effect it surrounds the notion of the bird (or spirit) as something invisible, yet heard, or felt, with other instances of natural phenomena inaccessible to the eye and yet real—in fact more real, or "keen" (intense), than ordinary sense perceptions.[5] The morning star, for instance, vanishes to sight through a narrowing or intensification of its rays—"Until we hardly see—we feel that it is there." The suggestion is that the highest certainty is not of the eye, but of the "feeling"—not visible but invisible. Just so the Spirit of Intellectual Beauty "floats tho' unseen amongst us;" the "dim sense of unapprehended things" is the primary source of the poet's sense of beauty and value, rather than sense perception or a priori religious formulations. The image of the morning star serves as physical evidence for the objective reality of that which can be known only through intuition; the lark itself serves as a symbol of just such divination. In the absence of faith in a benevolent Providence, the poet's perception of the bird's spontaneous happiness, uncalled-for, uncaused, is an assurance of a divinity in nature, perhaps the only kind of assurance available to him.

As the poet moves from the description of the bird in the heavens (its song heard, itself unseen, its presence intuited or felt) to the attempt to discover its essence, the character of the similes changes. A series of extended comparisons is framed by a question and answer which imply the inadequacy of all attempts to define the lark:

> What thou art we know not;
>   What is most like thee? . . .
>   All that ever was
> Joyous and clear and fresh, thy music doth surpass.
>   (31–32; 59–60)

To recapitulate the rationale behind the intervening figures (lines 33–58): each simile presents a figure which is like the skylark in that it is hidden, and yet its song (or hue or scent) through a spontaneous excess overflows its secret place into the world; each is like the bird in that it sings (or gives of itself) unbidden and unbeholden, as if song is simply an extension of its nature.[6] Beyond the common element of meaning, the sequence itself suggests that the poet is engaged in the process described in "Mont Blanc," as the poet's thoughts seek images for the scene, or in *Epipsychidion:* "I measure / The world of fancies, seeking one like thee" (69–70). The poet is driven to seek for images or analogies because of the difficulty of apprehending reality—the bird vanishing to sight, the "Dizzy Ravine," the inexpressible Emilia—and because of his need to surmount that difficulty. The image-making itself is self-conscious, remains tentative, hypothetical. So in "To a Sky-Lark," the chain of similes, while they are instances drawn from the world of things, human and natural, are also preformulated images, poetic fancies drawn from the "still cave of the witch Poesy." Their primary associations are with the poetry of Wordsworth and Coleridge.[7] The frequency with which glowworms, maidens, flowers, rainbows, vernal showers, occur in the earlier poets provides Shelley with a poetic context for his own precise vignettes.

In the last part of the poem, the human poet pays tribute to the natural poet. Accounts of the poem which take the bird to be a symbol of joy, or a Platonic ideal, obscure the fact that the bird is from the first a singer. The opening reference to "unpremeditated art" suggests the connection with poetry; the first extended simile ("Like a Poet hidden / In the light of thought") makes the resemblance explicit, and the last section of the poem develops the comparison in detail. The poet matches the different kinds of human song against that of the lark, and finds them wanting (as the natural sound of the rain or freshness of the flowers is surpassed by the lark), and he speculates on the possible objects of the lark's song—objects of praise, love or knowledge appropriate to bird or spirit. As in the earlier part of the lyric, the effect is of intense empathy, that "going out of our own nature" which Shelley affirmed in the "Defence of Poetry" to be the secret of morals and virtue of the imaginative faculty, and which he consciously sought to achieve in his own poetry. The standard of all is the "clear keen joyance" of the bird, and human vanity, sorrow, and fear seem the most transient and ephemeral of things. The emphasis throughout is on the bird (representing innocence, joy, purity) as unsurpassable, beyond reach, as it is from the first beyond sight. Yet the poem ends with a modest prayer that suggests hope—a matter not of the logic of the imagery or argument, nor of doctrinaire belief, but rather of Shelley's conscious adherence to that "solemn duty which we owe alike to ourselves & to the world" (*Letters of P.B.S.*, II, 125).

> Teach me half the gladness
>   That thy brain must know,
> Such harmonious madness
>   From my lips should flow,
> The world should listen then—as I am listening now.
>
>   (101–05)

The "harmonious madness" suggests the intoxicated poet of Coleridge's "Kubla Khan:"

> And all should cry, Beware! Beware!
> His flashing eyes, his floating hair!
> Weave a circle round him thrice,

And close your eyes with holy dread,
For he on honey-dew hath fed,
And drunk the milk of Paradise.   (49–54)

But the lines should be read too as complementing "Ode to the West Wind" in affirming the role of the poet as mediator between nature and society, as one who, himself awakened and inspired, has the power to awaken a sleeping earth. If he is weak, if he has fallen on thorns, if his strength is gone from him and delight fled, his "sore need" is not only for divine strength but for the joy of the natural creature.

Despite its fame and familiarity, critical interest in "The Cloud" has been rather one-sided. Modern critics tend to emphasize the meteorological fact in the poem, presumably because earlier critics, admiring Shelley's flights of imagination, failed to note his precise observation of nature.[8] But to interpret Shelley's nature poetry primarily as a record of his observation remains a mistake. The weakness of the common-sense view is that it is unhistorical. Shelley had a far more serious view of the nature of poetry; its function is to present "beautiful idealisms of moral excellence" (preface to *Prometheus Unbound*); to "[redeem] from decay the visitations of the divinity in man" ("A Defence of Poetry," Para. 40). And by and large his poetry conforms to his conception of high seriousness. In "To a Sky-Lark," "The Cloud," and "Ode to the West Wind," as in "Mont Blanc," a natural object becomes the embodiment and symbol of a human ideal, a human characteristic carried to its absolute pitch.

"The Cloud" should be read not as a nature poem but as a mythological poem—nature humanized. It is closely related to "The Witch of Atlas," and, even more strikingly, to "Song of Apollo." "Song of Apollo" is a self-portrait of a sublimely egoistic divinity; in his song the natural world is given reality wholly through its relation to the god. Both "Song of Apollo" and "The Cloud" move from an account of the subject's manifold activities and powers to a definition of its essence. In "Song of Apollo" the account of the speaker's activities and the definition of his essence are based both on natural fact and on the traditional mythology of the sun. In "The Cloud" there is, of course, an abundance of natural fact; the mythology, however, is invented.

The Cloud is in its substance always the same and indestructible, in its form ever changing. As if to embody its paradoxical nature in the very form of his myth, Shelley makes of the Cloud not a single figure (like Apollo, or the Witch of Atlas), but rather an elusive, chameleon-like shape or spirit, identified only by its activities, its visible effects. It has no formal identity but is given conceptual unity by its delight in its own ever-changing existence. Sky, earth, and sea are peopled with kindred natural spirits, the creation of the Cloud's own imaginative and joyous rendering of natural fact: the dancing earth, the genii that move in the sea, the pilot Lightning, the sanguine Sunrise and ardent Sunset, the maiden Moon, the Powers of the air.

The quality of the Cloud's delight is illuminated by certain qualities of the Witch of Atlas. Like the Cloud, the Witch is free from gravitational pull, the normal lot of mortal things. Her immunity provides an index to her special nature. For instance, her whims or impulses enjoy an absolute freedom from impediment; the deed is simultaneous with the thought. The human norm is very different, of course; one recalls Julian's passionate outcry against the limitations which he refuses to recognize as the human condition: "if we were not weak / Should we be less in deed than in desire?" ("Julian and Maddalo," 175–76). Both the Cloud and the Witch are singularly detached from the effects of their power, and are in general amused by the spectacle of life. The resemblance in spirit between the two can be seen in the following passage:

> These were tame pleasures; she would often climb
>   The steepest ladder of the crudded rack
> Up to some beakèd cape of cloud sublime,
>   And like Arion on the dolphin's back
> Ride singing through the shoreless air;—oft-time
>   Following the serpent lightning's winding track,
> She ran upon the platforms of the wind,
> And laughed to hear the fire-balls roar behind.
>   ("The Witch of Atlas," 481–88)

This image of joy is quite different from the joy of the sky-lark, which is a matter of a "full heart." Here joy is freedom—freedom of movement, of spirit, freedom which comes both from power and from immunity to cause and effect.[9] The complementary image to the Witch in free motion is the Witch still in a "windless haven" in the eye of the storm:

> There she would build herself a windless haven
>   Out of the clouds whose moving turrets make
> The bastions of the storm, when through the sky
> The spirits of the tempest thundered by.   (429–32)

The parallel image in "The Cloud" is of the Cloud asleep "in the arms of the blast" (16)—the natural child of the elements.

The poem begins with the simplest of things: the Cloud as bringer of rain and shade and dews:

> I bring fresh showers for the thirsting flowers,
>   From the seas and the streams;
> I bear light shade for the leaves when laid
>   In their noon-day dreams.
> From my wings are shaken the dews that waken
>   The sweet buds every one,
> When rocked to rest on their mother's breast,
>   As she dances about the sun.   (1–8)

The opening lines, simple as they are, indicate the quality of the Cloud's imaginative perception of its world: every natural phenomenon is given a metaphorical counterpart. The perspective of the Cloud, which we may assume to be truer than our own, is that of myth and metaphor—these are prior to natural fact. The metaphors of the opening stanza are fairly close to traditional metaphors for natural phenomena—the Earth as mother of life, the Sun as male fertilizing principle and object of worship—but the first extended metaphor, in lines 17–28, is highly original. Critics have suggested that Shelley's image of the Lightning piloting the Cloud over earth and ocean, "Lured by the love of the genii that move / In the depths of the purple sea," is the metaphorical counterpart to the current theory of cloud formation, as explained, for instance, in

Giovanni Battista Beccaria's *A Treatise upon Artificial Electricity* (English translation 1776) or Adam Walker's *A System of Familiar Philosophy* (1799).[10] What remains with the reader, in any case, is not the meteorological "fact," which is mistaken, but the image of the eternal desire of the Lightning for the Spirit he loves in seas and streams. As the poem progresses, stanza by stanza, through a complete survey of the natural world—earth, water and sky, sun, moon and stars, at all times of day and night, at all seasons, in all kinds of weather—the metaphor in which fact is enclosed repeatedly provides human or divine motivation for that which human beings think of as being uncaused or naturally caused. The rhythms of natural life, sleep and awakening, generation and dissolution, are imagined not as inevitable cycles but as a spontaneous, joyous interchange of elements, moved by love. This is the vision of nature dramatized in "The Sensitive Plant" and "The Witch of Atlas," and always given poignancy by its barely explicit relation to human life. In "The Cloud" there is simply a glancing reference to "mortals" who, through ignorance or because of their earthbound vision, call "That orbed maiden with white fire laden" the moon. But all nature is animated by human instincts that are freed from the stain of human self-interest (anxiety or fear of consequences) and hence made beautiful: the maternal love of the earth as she rocks the sweet buds to sleep, the Sunset's "ardours of rest and love," the delight in pageantry, the laughter of the elements at their own "quips and cranks" and immortality.

Almost any stanza will serve to illustrate the freedom and spontaneity of the imagery and its inventiveness in relation to natural fact. Take the tableau of the third stanza, for instance.

> The sanguine Sunrise, with his meteor eyes,
>   And his burning plumes outspread,
> Leaps on the back of my sailing rack,
>   When the morning star shines dead;
> As on the jag of a mountain crag
>   Which an earthquake rocks and swings,
> An eagle alit one moment may sit
>   In the light of its golden wings;
> And when Sunset may breathe, from the lit Sea beneath,
>   Its ardours of rest and love,

> And the crimson pall of eve may fall
>   From the depths of Heaven above,
> With wings folded I rest, on mine aëry nest,
>   As still as a brooding dove.   (31–44)

The stanza is perfectly balanced between two personifications, the "sanguine Sunrise" and the ardent "Sunset," morning and evening. The imagery moves as if by the power of its own suggestion: the "burning plumes" of the Sunrise, a metaphorical intensification of the rays of dawn, suggest the golden eagle to which the Sunrise is compared; this in turn suggests the final image, the "brooding dove" with folded wings. Yet the primary effect of the images (which appear to be spawned almost accidentally) is to evoke the natural rhythms of morning and evening, awakening and rest: the momentarily poised eagle suggests power, pride, energy, something about to happen, the unpredictable; the dove is an image of rest and renewal, a drawing in of powers. One suggests the aggressive male passion for adventure; the other is warm and domestic, comforting and comfortable—the home instinct. Incidental metaphors, too, are constantly surprising and precise: there is almost nothing of the cliché here, the automatically appropriate adjective or phrase. "The morning star shines dead" is a concise way of capturing the same phenomenon described in "To a Sky-Lark," 18–25; "the lit sea" (as if it has caught fire) is visually evocative and precise; "mine aëry nest" is a pun—the nest is high in the air, also made of air.

  The final stanza defines the Cloud as child of the elements and intermediary between them, in its Hermes-like role as immortal agent provocateur, disguised and infinitely adaptable, immune to the effects of its own irrepressible whimsy. After the account of its manifold activities, the Cloud stands named in myth, identified as to genealogy, the key to its unity revealed.

> I am the daughter of Earth and Water,
>   And the nursling of the sky;
> I pass through the pores of the oceans and shores;
>   I change, but I cannot die—
> For after the rain, when with never a stain
>   The pavilion of Heaven is bare,

And the winds and sunbeams, with their convex gleams,
    Build up the blue Dome of Air—
I silently laugh at my own cenotaph,
    And out of the caverns of rain,
Like a child from the womb, like a ghost from the tomb,
    I arise, and unbuild it again.   (73–84)

The paradoxical conclusion of the stanza offers an image of rebirth
that is also an image of destruction, a cheerful equation of life and
death ("Like a child from the womb, like a ghost from the tomb").
The Cloud ends as it begins, in laughter. Human beings are the
prisoners of their own materialism, their inability to deny either
sense-perception or logic; even minor natural divinities are superior
to both. Though the Cloud is temporarily dissolved, it is not dead;
similarly, the stainless blue dome of Heaven can be unbuilt, though
we might fondly wish to believe it permanent. As in "Ode to
Heaven," Shelley counters delusions of permanence and immortality
with an image of eternal flux. At the same time he qualifies his delight in life and beauty with an austere and unsentimental vision of
eternity.

    The mythological lyrics that Shelley composed for Mary Shelley's
"Proserpine" and "Midas" illustrate the same kind of mythmaking
that characterizes "The Cloud" and "The Witch of Atlas," the intensely sympathetic realization of a natural and mythological world
existing entirely apart from human life. Although Shelley appears
to be merely interpreting a well-established tradition, his rendering
of the myth in each case is distinctive. In "Arethusa," for instance,
the metamorphosis of nymph and river god is spiritual as well as
physical; lust turns to love, fear to friendship, when the perils of
the flesh are removed. The lust of Pan, similarly, and its reward,
become an instance of the search for the ideal and its insupport-
ability, the universal worship of a "delusive flame."
    The two lyrics that Mary Shelley entitled "Hymn of Apollo" and
"Hymn of Pan" are sung for the contest between the two gods
precipitated by the luckless Midas. In the Ovidian myth that Mary
adapts, Pan has the temerity to challenge Apollo's superiority in
song; Apollo is awarded the victory by the judge, old Tmolus, and

Midas, who is charmed by Pan's rustic notes, is punished for his dull hearing with asses' ears. As we might expect, Shelley's interpretation of the contest represents a radical revision of the classic fable. In his version Apollo sings first rather than last, and is answered more than adequately by the clever Pan. The two songs emerge as antiphonal definitions of poetry: the harmony of the lyre set against the sweetness of the pipe, the powers of light set against the powers of darkness; *ethos,* the moral element, set against *pathos,* the element of feeling. Apollo, god of the Sun, stands for power and truth; his realm is eternity. Pan, god of the natural world, is the enchanter, the teller of tales; his realm is life in process. Apollo is the source of energy and light, the masculine principle to a female Nature; he symbolizes poetry as self-consciousness, issuing in a revelation of divinity:

> I am the eye with which the Universe
> Beholds itself, and knows it is divine.   (31–32)

But Pan merely sits and plays as the darkness gathers, and all the creatures of Earth, nymphs and satyrs and fauns, even the gods themselves, are drawn irresistibly to "attend and follow." He is hierophant of the Universe; he sings its motions, its life processes, Love, Death, and Birth. And his role is not to proclaim the divinity of the natural world, but rather to lament its mortality:

> Gods and men, we are all deluded thus!—
> It breaks on our bosom and then we bleed.   (32–33)

His unsuccessful pursuit of Syrinx is emblematic of the universal error and condition of human life. Man's nature lies in his incompleteness; he "desires what [he] has not, the Beautiful!" ("The Sensitive Plant," 77). And out of this desire arises all love, all poetry. The error, as Shelley wrote in a letter to his friend Gisborne, a month before his death, "consists in seeking in a mortal image the likeness of what is perhaps eternal" (*Letters of P.B.S.,* II, 434).

The antiphonal character of the two songs is reflected in every quality of the verse. The six-line stanza of Apollo's song, with its rhymed iambic pentameter, is steady, secure, weighty, a sonorous procession of statements. The twelve-line stanza of Pan's song, divided irregularly into groups of five and seven lines, imitates the spontaneity of the pipes, ever-shifting in rhyme and emphasis, circling back on its changing refrain. Apollo is defined in terms of his power, his effect upon nature; he is the subject of each sentence. Pan is defined allusively, in terms of the response nature spontaneously makes to his seductive song. The setting of Apollo's dominion is the cosmos, the blue dome of Heaven, with sea and earth spread below in panorama. In Pan's song the setting is local and particular, Arcadia described with its rivers and mountains and vales (Peneus, Olympus, Tempe, Mænalus), its river-girt islands, moist river-lawns, dewy caves. Classical flora and fauna are named: the bees on the bells of thyme; cicadae and lizards; myrtle and lime.[11] The scale of the action is smaller, the real rather than the sublime.

In both songs, as in "The Cloud," nature and myth are humanized, animated, and driven by love and desire. Natural events are not determined; they are given psychological motivation. The clouds "grieve" for the ending of day, Apollo "soothes" them with his smile:

> I stand at noon upon the peak of Heaven;
>   Then with unwilling steps, I linger down
> Into the clouds of the Atlantic even;
>   For grief that I depart they weep and frown—
> What look is more delightful, than the smile
> With which I soothe them from the Western isle?
>
>   ("Song of Apollo," 25–30)

The human elements of the action, the reluctance of Apollo and the grief of the clouds, are Shelley's addition to traditional myth, as rendered, for instance, in the Homeric "Hymn to the Sun," which Shelley translated:

> His rapid steeds soon bear him to the West;
> Where their steep flight his hands divine arrest.
>
>   (21–22)

But the humanizing of Apollo is more than an appealing touch of fancy; it serves as a metaphor for the scene, the slow waning of a long afternoon, the darkening of the clouds, the last brief glow of sunset.

In "Song of Pan," the humanizing is more extensive, and represents a radical revision of the classical conception of the goat god and his Arcadian retinue. An element of cunning remains; the great reign of Apollo is cleverly reduced to "the light of the dying day," speeded by the sweet pipings of Pan in preparation for the evening rites to come. But the tone of the whole is softened and idealized:

> And all that did then attend and follow
> Were as silent for love, as you now, Apollo,
>   For envy of my sweet pipings.   (22–24)

The most startling modification of traditional myth occurs in the final stanza. In the Ovidian story, the transformation of Syrinx serves as the origin of Pan's pipes; he sighs in disappointment, and the reeds give forth a low sound, which suggests the musical instrument.[12] Shelley halts the tale halfway and draws its moral explicitly, in a way that links the poem with all Shelley's laments for the rash pursuit of love and beauty in mortal form. The curious dislocation of grammar in lines 32–33 contributes to the effect of spontaneity, as well as to the poignancy of the lines: "it" appears to have no reference. The reader must supply a phrase to make sense of the lines grammatically: "we are all deluded thus!—[we pursue a maiden and clasp a reed]; It breaks on our bosom and then we bleed." The central metaphor of these lines is similar to one of the most extreme and passionate of Shelley's metaphors: "I fall upon the thorns of life! I bleed!" The image of the dying or crucified God lies behind both. Yet in the "Song of Pan" the pathos is controlled by the dramatic framework, the fact that the lines are a clever appeal for sympathy and a sly dig at Apollo, as well as a poignant reflection on life. The difference in tone is symptomatic of the movement in Shelley's poetry from passionate commitment and a proportionately intense despair to the reflective melancholy of the late lyrics.

NOTES

1. W. B. Yeats, "Prometheus Unbound" (1932), *Essays and Introductions* (New York: Macmillan, 1961), pp. 421–33.
2. Mary Shelley refers to "Ode to Heaven" as evidence that Shelley was at one time a convert to the "Immaterial Philosophy" of Berkeley: preface to *Essays, Letters from Abroad* (1840) in *Works,* V, ix–x. C. D. Locock, ed., *The Poems of Percy Bysshe Shelley,* 2 vols. (London, 1911), provides a brief explication, stanza by stanza: II, 505.
3. See, for instance, Wordsworth's "To the Cuckoo," 1–4, 13–16, and "The Green Linnet," 21–22. See also Coleridge's "The Nightingale," 46–68.
4. Cf. F. R. Leavis: "['To a Sky-Lark'] is a mere tumbled out spate ('spontaneous overflow') of poeticalities, the place of each one of which Shelley could have filled with another without the least difficulty and without making any essential difference." *Revaluation: Tradition and Development in English Poetry* (London: Chatto & Windus, 1947), p. 215.
5. The objects to which Shelley compares the song of the lark are materially real, a point emphasized by Frederick A. Pottle in "The Romantic Imagination Revisited," *Yale Review,* 39 (1950), 346–49. The star fading out in the dawn, as long as you keep your eye on it, is an intense point of light, just as the song of the lark, so long as you can hear it, is shrill.
6. Leone Vivante offers a philosophical reading of the similes, in *English Poetry and Its Contribution to the Knowledge of a Creative Principle* (London: Faber & Faber, 1950): "Shelley seems to search here—yet as one who only looks after beauty!—for a high and still higher degree of indeterminacy. . . . Invisibility, secretness and intimacy, which we here find expressed, are in fact essential aspects of indeterminacy" (p. 172).
7. Coleridge's "The Nightingale" includes in its imagery "vernal showers," "many a glow-worm [lighting] up her love-torch," "a most gentle Maid," the moon suddenly emerging from a cloud. The *Concordance to the Poems of William Wordsworth,* ed. Lane Cooper (London, 1911), lists a good many glowworms; many maidens, including at least two who are love-sick; many roses, including an "embowering" rose; vernal showers and airs in plenty. Shelley carries the image of the love-sick maiden to a fine extreme in the love-duet of Earth and Moon in Act IV of *Prometheus Unbound,* where the Moon describes herself as "a most enamoured maiden / Whose weak brain is overladen / With the pleasure of her love" (467–69). I would generalize broadly that Wordsworth uses the terms named above as if they were the vocabulary of common life and day-to-day experience, Coleridge as if they were the materials of poetry alone (romantic and unreal), Shelley as if they were the property of a poetic storehouse that includes both common images (glowworm, rose) and fanciful (poet, highborn maiden) for the sophisticated poet to use as he will—the whimsical "dell of dew," the witty image of the winds deflowering the rose—a term which, incidentally, appears neither in Wordsworth nor in Coleridge.
8. Cf. Carl Grabo, *A Newton among Poets* (Chapel Hill, 1930), pp. 119–

21; and Desmond King-Hele, *Shelley: His Thought and Work* (London, 1960), pp. 220–27.

9. Cf. "To Constantia:" "Secure o'er woods and waves I sweep, / Rejoicing, like a cloud of morn" (17–18).

10. Grabo, pp. 119–20, quotes at length from Beccaria's *Treatise;* King-Hele, pp. 222–25, cites Walker's *System of Familiar Philosophy.*

11. Many of these details occur in Virgil's 10th Eclogue, part of which Shelley translated, probably at about this time.

12. Ovid, *Metamorphoses* I.689–712. The contest between Pan and Apollo is described in XI.146–71; in Ovid's version Pan sings first. Mary Shelley reversed the order in her play, and Shelley clearly designs Pan's song to follow and answer Apollo's.

CHAPTER SIX

WORLD, LIFE, & TIME

ALTHOUGH SHELLEY published three major works after *Prometheus Unbound,* only one short lyric was printed with them, "Lines written on hearing the News of the Death of Napoleon," which accompanies *Hellas.* Most of the short lyrics of 1820–22, as well as a number of earlier ones, were published by Mary Shelley in *Posthumous Poems* (1824), several from manuscript drafts. Some of these lyrics may have been conceived as songs in the major works, or in uncompleted works like the "Fragments of an Unfinished Drama" or "Tasso" or "Charles the First;" they were either discarded by Shelley or allowed to take their own independent form. In the late lyrics the poet as prophet has all but vanished; the voice is quiet, direct, and intimate. The subjects of the lyrics are the classic themes of love, death, time, mutability, rendered not in a social or cosmic context but rather as they affect the solitary self. Although they were not intended to produce a consistent or cumulative effect, taken together they seem to express the essence of Romantic sensibility.

"The Two Spirits: An Allegory" is a metaphorical analysis of human aspiration, presented as a dialogue between two Spirits. The debate juxtaposes the themes of "Ode to the West Wind" and "To a Sky-Lark" and "The Cloud," sets against the terrors of apocalypse the joys of freedom, and against metaphors of destruction (the swift clouds of the hurricane) metaphors of transcendence.

FIRST SPIRIT
O Thou who plumed with strong desire
Would float above the Earth—beware!

A shadow tracks thy flight of fire—
Night is coming!

(1–4)

SECOND SPIRIT
The deathless stars are bright above;
If I should cross the shade of night
Within my heart is the lamp of love
And that is day—

(9–12)

As the debate unfolds, it becomes clear that the First Spirit is the
voice of caution, the reality principle, warning the aspiring Second
Spirit of the destruction that attends on pursuit of the impossible.
And yet, like a good friend, reluctantly abandoning a position once
held by both, the First Spirit is not too far behind the Second Spirit
in its appreciation of the delights of freedom, the bright regions of
the air. The Second Spirit, faith answering reason, asserts that it
has that within which transcends time and death, namely "the lamp
of love," which turns night into day. Reason will not be appeased,
even though her objections have been answered adequately in terms
of her own metaphors, and she offers further doubts.

FIRST SPIRIT
But if the whirlwinds of darkness waken
Hail and Lightning and stormy rain—
See, the bounds of the air are shaken,
    Night is coming!   (17–20)

SECOND SPIRIT
I see the glare and I hear the sound—
I'll sail on the flood of the tempest dark
With the calm within and light around
    Which make night day . . .   (25–28)

The First Spirit warns the Second Spirit not merely of known
dangers but of those unknown as well, the "Hail and Lightning
and stormy rain" of "Ode to the West Wind." The Second Spirit
does not deny the dangers, but welcomes apocalypse, reaffirming its

faith in the transcendent power of love and desire, the "calm within and light around / Which make night day." And the Second Spirit scornfully dismisses the "trembling throng / Whose sails were never to the tempest given" (*Adonais,* 489–90), those bound by their dull apprehensiveness to the earth and its mortal cycles of day and night, birth and death.

Although the metaphors can be translated rather freely (the title, which appears in the holograph draft, invites the reader to explicate as he will), the dialogue is restricted so closely to the terms of the metaphors that their full meaning must wait on the stanzas with which the poem ends. These, one feels, should provide the "key" to the allegory, and a resolution of the debate. The first stanza of the final pair offers as one possibility—"some say"—the terrible enactment of the First Spirit's prophecy, embodied in an image that draws to their logical extreme the metaphors of storm and darkness. The Second Spirit, it is suggested, has achieved immortality of a kind, as a perpetual image of enforced flight, ever-renewed destruction. The second stanza offers the alternative possibility, that the Second Spirit (to keep to the terms of the metaphor) has succeeded in turning night into day; the transcendent power of love is affirmed, not perhaps to achieve what it desires (to reach the "bright regions of the air"), but, in the form of an image, shape, or vision, to awaken love, or to keep alive the memory of love in others. The final image is a reversal of Keats's "La Belle Dame sans Merci;" the traveller awakes from his dream not to the "cold hillside" but to a renewed life.

These final stanzas preserve the character of the debate, which, of course, can never really be settled. Temperamentally and even intellectually Shelley's sympathies lie with the instincts of the heart, its aspirations toward freedom, happiness, the ideal and eternal. In his earlier poetry Shelley tends to argue that the ideal can be realized on earth; later on, the question appears to lose urgency. The longing itself is primary, not its satisfaction: the desire to "cross the shade of night," the movement of the heart toward freedom and delight, the belief in the transcendent power of love. In his political poetry love turns out into the world; it is the chief agent of social and political regeneration. The final image in "The Two Spirits" is of the solitary human being, the "traveller." There is no suggestion of a social or political context; hope moves fortuitously, and yet miraculously, from human heart to human heart.

"To Night" is possibly the most perfect example of the theme of aspiration; it is an intense evocation of desire which entirely suppresses the rational equivalent of desire, the knowledge of what is longed for, and why. The poem expresses the quintessence of Romantic longing, a passive languor in which the will and the intellect (reason, reflection, the moral sense) are extinguished, and the whole being is driven by desire. The object of desire remains deliberately obscure, like the figure of Night itself, which is associated but not identified with annihilation, love, joy, and fear.

The context of the poem is unmistakably erotic. The traditional association of the night with love, the images of seduction in the second stanza, the contrast between the "lone daylight," the "unloved guest," and the Night, who is addressed throughout as a beloved, suggest intense sexual longing. Erotic love is the suppressed tenor of a metaphor sustained throughout the poem. The "Epithalamium" that Shelley wrote the same year for a play by Edward Williams resembles "To Night" in several details.

> Night! with all thine eyes look down!
>   Darkness! weep thy holiest dew! . . .
> Haste, coy hour! and quench all light,
> Lest eyes see their own delight!
> Haste, swift hour! and thy loved flight
>   Oft renew! . . .
>
> O joy! O fear! there is not one
> Of us can guess what may be done
> In the absence of the sun . . .
>
> Oh! linger long, thou envious eastern lamp
>   In the damp
>   Caves of the deep!
>   (Rossetti version, 1–2, 5–8, 13–15, 17–19)

The terms of "To Night" are used in the "Epithalamium" with explicit reference to a bridal night. The urgency of the lover's desire for night, his impatient endurance of the day, are conventional in an epithalamium; the "joy and fear" which make Night "terrible and dear" refer to the anticipation of love, joyful because of its pleasure, fearful because it is unknown. Yet the obvious similarities hardly explain the peculiar power of "To Night." While the "Epithalamium" is a formal celebration of love, "To Night" can be read without reference to love or sexual desire, as a poem about the creative imagination, or death. The intensity of the poet's passion is partly the result of removing its human and conventional rationale, of keeping the erotic terms just beneath the surface. For although the poet's passion is appropriate to love, his longing is displaced entirely onto Night, the agent of love. It is Night, darkness, which is imagined with the prophetic eye of the lover, which is "terrible and dear," "long-sought," "beloved." The reader is prevented from taking the poet's longing for Night to be a conventional displacement (as in the epithalamium) by the turn of the plot, the sympathetic volunteering of Death and Sleep, who might very well mistake the poet's longing for Night as a desire for their own light-and day-denying powers. This the poet explicitly, even triumphantly denies, without identifying the object of his desire. Sleep will come when Night is fled (as, in a conventional epithalamium, the lover expects confidently to remain awake until dawn); Death will come when Night is dead (the particular night, hence love and life). Both Death and Sleep will come in their own time; the poet's longing is for something which must be granted (a "boon"), and which requires prayer and devotion. The reader can only surmise that while the poet finds the slow passage of day unendurable, it is not because he yearns for oblivion, temporary or permanent, but because he anticipates the coming of "dreams of joy and fear."

The reader may be tempted, because of the power of the lyric, to take it as a direct expression of need and longing on the poet's part, analogous to "Ode to the West Wind," where Shelley assumes in his own voice a role as poet and prophet, or to a poem like "To Edward Williams" or "Song: 'Rarely, rarely, comest thou'," where Shelley is obviously lamenting his personal distress. But the speaker in "To Night" is given no special identification; he is simply the vehicle of an emotion. The lyric could conceivably be a pure "song," or it could serve in a drama (for instance, Shelley's "Unfinished

Drama" about an Indian enchantress); its tone of rapture is assumed, its urgency not an "overflow of feeling" on the poet's part but conventional.[1]

The form of the lyric is an almost magical embodiment of its passion, a musical representation of desire. The lingering refrain, singled out by the pauses that precede and follow it (in all but the third stanza), carries the weight of the emotion, the lyric cry: "Swift be thy flight!" "Come, long-sought!" "Come soon, soon!" Yet the refrain is incorporated into the general rhyme pattern, so that despite the pauses, the movement of the stanza is sustained in a single line to the end. The dramatic modulation of tone from the first two stanzas of direct address and entreaty to the third stanza, which suddenly shifts to the poet and his longing (in a movement somewhat similar to that of "Ode to the West Wind") is beautifully caught in the shift from the falling rhythm of the first two stanzas, especially marked in the refrain, to a rising rhythm, again established by the refrain: "I sighed for thee." The effect is of a change of pace, a sudden arousal of expectation.

Romanticism is associated for the common reader not with conventions or technical mastery but with the direct expression of intense personal emotion, joy or sorrow, hope or despair; not with reflection and analysis but with the overflowing heart. The most famous of Shelley's lyrics in this vein is probably "O World, O Life, O Time," appropriately entitled by Mary Shelley "A Lament."

> O World, O Life, O Time,
>   On whose last steps I climb,
> Trembling at that where I had stood before—
>   When will return the glory of your prime?
>   No more, O never more!
>
>   Out of the day and night
>   A joy has taken flight—
> Fresh spring and summer [   ] and winter hoar
>   Move my faint heart with grief, but with delight
>   No more, O never more!

As in "Hymn to Intellectual Beauty," the mark of Wordsworth's "Ode: Intimations of Immortality" lies on the poem, in its vocabulary of loss, its familiar terms for the primary emotions: "joy," "grief," "delight." But the moral drawn by the "philosophic mind" is wanting; the lyric is Wordsworthian nostalgia carried to its furthest expressive extreme. The lines place the speaker (poet or lover) at that point of no return, that outermost verge, which could perhaps be considered Shelley's peculiar realm of being. The same quality of despair is found in *Adonais:*

> Why linger, why turn back, why shrink, my Heart?
> Thy hopes are gone before: from all things here
> They have departed; thou shouldst now depart!
> A light is passed from the revolving year,
> And man, and woman; and what still is dear
> Attracts to crush, repels to make thee wither.   (469–74)

But the lament that in *Adonais* has the support not only of the occasion but of a long elegiac tradition as well is in the brief lyric sustained by rhetoric alone: invocation ("O World, O Life, O Time"); question ("When will return the glory of your prime?"); answering refrain ("No more, O never more!"). The power of the lyric comes from the projection of a personal, known despair onto that which is most abstract and inclusive: World, Life, Time. We have no way of knowing, of course, to what degree the lines are personal in the narrow sense of the term. Shelley wrote to John Gisborne, in a letter of June 18, 1822: "I stand, as it were, upon a precipice, which I have ascended with great, and cannot descend without *greater, peril* . . ." (*Letters of P.B.S.,* II, 436); the thought of those Dantesque "last steps" was never far from his mind. Indeed, the words "I am despair" are scrawled across the notebook page on which the first draft of the lyric appears. On the other hand, the draft occurs opposite a page of "Ginevra," and resembles lines 208–10 of the "Dirge" which concludes that fragment: "One step to the white death bed, / And one to the bier, / And one to the charnel—and one, oh where?" The peculiar compression of the lines in question— "O World, O Life, O Time, / On whose last steps I climb, / Trembling at that where I had stood before"—exemplifies the bonding of the literal and metaphorical which Shelley analyzed in Sophocles' line: "Coming to many ways in the wanderings of careful thought" (Mrs. Shelley's note on *Prometheus Unbound*). The small human figure stands in a landscape that has been abstracted and refined, as in a surrealist painting, to suggest simultaneously a human and a cosmic or divine perspective. Time is at once linear and cyclic; the movement of the seasons is superimposed on the motions of the heart, the trembling of the flesh. Both the personal and cosmic dimensions of sorrow are "explained" by a statement at once absolute and oblique: "A joy has taken flight." The lyric can be set against the urbane rendering of the same set of terms in "Song: 'Rarely, rarely comest thou.' " [2] In the longer poem the poet, an abandoned lover, courts Delight, aware that like a flesh and blood mistress, she is likely to return, if at all, not for pity but for pleasure; he must therefore assume a gaiety he cannot feel. The brief lyric is absolute and despairing, the direct expression of unassuageable grief; the longer lyric leaves an opening for hope: "Oh, come, / Make my heart once more thy home." But hope is a note heard less and less often in the late lyrics, which lament instead the irreversibility of life's processes.

The most familiar of Shelley's love lyrics fall into the last two or three years of his life. A few poems are translations or free imitations, exercises in a recognizable literary style or idiom: "The Indian Girl's Song," "From the Arabic: An Imitation," "Love's Philosophy" or "An Anacreontic," "Buona Notte." Some of these were circulated in manuscript, and printed in Leigh Hunt's periodicals.[3] All the love lyrics, whether conventional or personal, are constructed with a high degree of artifice.[4] Each lyric has not only its distinctive prosodic pattern but usually its own kind of verbal ingenuity as well. This is a matter partly of the closeness with which the central argument or analogy is carried out, partly of verbal tricks, the pun on "good" in "Buona Notte," the repeated comparatives in "Thou art fair and few are fairer" (*fair-fairest, faint-faintest, weak-weakest*), the doublets of "When passion's trance is overpast." These lyrics, which appear to be so simple in thought, so spontaneous in form, show a remarkable development of the kind of artistic skill that Shelley undervalues in theory, in the fashion of his time, but demonstrates in practice above all the Romantics.

The common reader has usually cherished the love poems for their humanity as well as their charm. They are not simply love complaints; they express rather a sophisticated awareness of social complexities, and the recognition that human passions operate in a framework of limited possibilities. Although some lyrics, like "The Indian Girl's Song" or "From the Arabic," are intensely erotic, with a metaphorical equivalent to the sexual "swoon" at their center, other love poems, like "When passion's trance is overpast" or "One word is too often profaned,"[5] are reflective, elegiac; they "look before and after," qualify and propitiate.

The life remains beyond our reconstruction, to a degree. But it is tempting to correlate the sad love poems of 1820–22 with the biographical evidence of the letters. The lyrics anatomize the loss of love, the decay of passion into indifference, the persistence of relationship despite disillusionment, the heavy sense of obligation the lover feels toward one he can no longer make happy. Behind them would seem to lie the central event of Shelley's life, his elopement with Mary and their attempt to live together as lovers and comrades in complete freedom. The passionate intensity of their first love is unmistakable in the letters of 1814–15, and in Shelley's idealization of his 18-year-old beloved in *Laon and Cythna*. But signs of distress appear in some unfinished lines penciled faintly in one of Shelley's notebooks, which Mary transcribed at last for the public in *Poetical Works* (1839), dating them "Livorno, August 1819." Shelley had written in a letter of August 5, two months after William's death: "Mary's spirits still continue wretchedly depressed—more so than a stranger . . . could imagine" (*Letters of P.B.S.,* II, 107). It seems clear that her depression had cut her off not only from Shelley's love but from her own feeling for him. I present the lines as they appear in Shelley's notebook.

My dearest M. wherefore hast thou gone
And left me in this dreary world alone
Thy form is here indeed a lovely . . .

But thou art fled,—gone down the dreary road
Which leads to Sorrow's most obscure abode
Thou sittest on the hearth of pale despair
It   where
For thine own sake I cannot follow thee
Do thou return for mine—

As Shelley knew well, such a return cannot be willed; neither love nor delight answers to the need of the lover or the one bereft. And the last love poems accept the claims of life, even as they lament life's inexorable erosion of love and happiness.

It seems likely that Mary never regained her spirits fully after William's death, and in her prolonged depression a certain natural rigidity of character emerged, often found in persons of an idealistic and passionate nature. She describes her state in a poem written after Shelley's death, an accurate account of pathological depression and its alienating effects:

> My heart was all thine own,—but yet a shell
> Closed in its core, which seemed impenetrable.[6]

To Shelley she became "poor Mary;" he remained devoted to her, and pained by her pain, but he sought and found what he refers to as "consolation" elsewhere, with his friends the Gisbornes, and in a series of brief romantic episodes, the most serious of which undoubtedly was with Jane Williams.[7]

"The Indian Serenade," as the poem is entitled in Mary Shelley's transcripts, has long been read as a confessional lyric, a typically Romantic cri de coeur. The early new-critical attack on Shelley's "sentimentality" depended on discovering in the exclamation "I die, I faint, I fail!" emotion in excess of its occasion.[8] The wide currency given the autobiographical reading has to do primarily with the two contradictory accounts of the poem's genesis: Medwin's assertion that it was written for Jane Williams (presumably in 1821) for an Indian air; and a statement by Sophia Stacey's son, C. S. Catty, that it was written for Sophia in November, 1819, when she was visiting Shelley and Mary in Florence.[9] If Shelley wrote the poem either for Sophia or for Jane, then conceivably he might be projecting his own romantic feelings in the cry of the Indian lover. But the only holograph fair copy of the poem known to survive is headed "The Indian girls song," a fairly sure indication that the lines were to be sung by a woman. And Medwin notes as a source "the Persian air sung by the Knautch girls." I would accept the 1821 date that Mary assigns to the lyric; the draft of the poem occurs in a notebook largely devoted to *Hellas,* which was written in October, 1821. Indeed, it is possible that "The Indian girls song" is not a title but rather a stage direction, and that Shelley considered inserting the poem in the drama. In the opening scene of *Hellas,* the chorus of Greek captive women and the Indian slave address the sleeping Mahmud antiphonally, in lines similar in tone to the famous "Serenade:"

Chorus.

Sleep, sleep! our song is laden
With the soul of slumber;
It was sung by a Samian maiden,
Whose lover was of the number
Who now keep
That calm sleep
Whence none may wake, where none shall weep.

Indian.

I touch thy temples pale!
I breathe my soul on thee!
And could my prayers avail,
All my joy should be
Dead, and I would live to weep,
So thou mightst win one hour of quiet sleep.

(*Hellas,* 14–26)

But whatever its genesis, there seems no reason to doubt that the lines were sung "to an Indian air" by Jane and circulated among the Shelley circle.

Whether we entitle it "The Indian Girl's Song," or "Lines to an Indian Air" (the title of the first posthumous printings) or "The Indian Serenade," the song bears consideration as one of Shelley's most perfect lyrics. We can assume now that the complaint is uttered by a lovesick maiden rather than a lovesick youth; the lyric is a mirror image of Coleridge's "Lewti, or the Circassian Love-Chant," which confesses that "maids, as well as youths, have perished / From fruitless love too fondly cherished."[10] The Serenade is sung under the window of the beloved, and is given the appropriate—and obviously derivative—nocturnal setting: starlight, soft

winds, "champak odours," nightingale song. The opening stanza
suggests that the lover and a sympathetic nature are at one in mood
and impulse:

> I arise from dreams of thee
> In the first sleep of night—
> The winds are breathing low
> And the stars are burning bright.
> I arise from dreams of thee—
> And a spirit in my feet
> Has borne me—Who knows how?
> To thy chamber window, sweet!—   (1–8)

Nature not only is sympathetic but offers metaphors of sexual passion, in the low breathing of the winds, the stars "burning bright";
the singer surrenders to the seductive elements of nature and to the
dreaming spirit within, which conspire together, in the fashion of
dream vision, to transport her to the side of the beloved. In the
second stanza, nature takes on the colors of the lover's agitation and
provides her with analogies to her lovesickness:

> The wandering airs they faint
> On the dark silent stream—
> The champak odours fail
> Like sweet thoughts in a dream;
> The nightingale's complaint—
> It dies upon her heart—
> As I must die on thine
> O beloved as thou art!   (9–16)

The erotic terms of the first stanza are recalled: the "wandering
airs" echo the "winds" of line 3; the "sweet thoughts in a dream"
echo the "first sleep of night" (indeed, the word "sweet" slipped
into line 2 in Mary Shelley's transcripts). And the hidden sexual
metaphor, a poetic (perhaps characteristically feminine) imitation
of unfulfilled desire, unfolds in the movement from sleep, awakening, and visionary transport, to the dying winds, odors, song—
images of impulse that falls short of its object, hence dies. The
champak may have been suggested by Moore's *Lalla Rookh;* the

nightingale's complaint is a stock image in Eastern love poetry, as
in Moore's lyrics. But the pattern of three parallel analogies and
their application to the speaker is typically Shelleyan, as is the
development of the pattern in the third and final stanza.[11]

> O lift me from the grass!
> I die, I faint, I fail!
> Let thy love in kisses rain
> On my lips and eyelids pale.
> My cheek is cold and white, alas!
> My heart beats loud and fast.
> Oh press it close to thine again
> Where it will break at last.   (17–24)

In lines 17–18 the lover's cry identifies her with the failing impulses
of nature; such restorative powers as there may be, however, lie
not in nature but in the beloved. And the sexual theme is made explicit in the images of intense excitement ("My heart beats loud
and fast"), life-renewing energy (a "rain" of kisses) and deathly
swoon ("My cheek is cold and white, alas!"), and the image of
union and dissolution in the last two lines.

Certainly this last stanza is highly emotional; its rhetorical pattern and the metaphor itself ("O lift me from the grass!") inevitably recall the confessional cry of "Ode to the West Wind:"
"Oh! lift me as a wave, a leaf, a cloud! / I fall upon the thorns of
life! I bleed!" But like "Ode to the West Wind," "The Indian Girl's
Song" has the satisfying undertone of a reasoned argument based
on analogies between the human and natural cycles of sleep and
awakening, life and death; its passion is controlled by its structure.
The broken phrases imitate spontaneity, as if the lover's cry is a
pure outbreak of feeling; but the exclamation ("I die, I faint, I
fail!") arises naturally from the parallel images of Stanza 2:
"The wandering airs they faint . . . The champak odours fail . . .
The nightingale's complaint— / It dies upon her heart—."

It might be added that the song is more sophisticated than Shelley's Victorian readers assumed; evidently it is sung after an ex-
change of love—hence the "dreams" from which, in a draft reading,
the singer arises "wild & joyous." The lovers have presumably returned to their own chambers; the final plea of the girl is that she

be pressed to her lover's heart "again." That is, the song is a cry not so much for love as for a permanent union: "Where it will break at last." For the Shelleyan lover, love and death are a single ecstatic consummation; the "Indian girl" is one in this respect with the Arab maiden of Alastor and the Samian maiden of *Hellas*—as with the lyric speaker of *Epipsychidion*.

It is not difficult to imagine "When passion's trance is overpast" in a dramatic context, as part of "Julian and Maddalo," for instance, or the fragmentary "Tasso;" indeed it bears a strong resemblance to the incomplete "Song for Tasso." Yet it seems personal, unlike "The Indian Girl's Song;" it agrees with the treatment of love in the self-portraits, and can be read as an early treatment of the recurrent theme of the late lyrics, the irreversible character of the death of love. The poem, like many of the love lyrics, explores the analogy between the natural cycle and the cycle of human love. Tenderness and truth, the "flower" of love, grow out of "passion's trance" and the "wild feelings" that, like all mortal things, subside when their date is past. The poet entertains the hope that the analogy is a true one: that tenderness and truth can live on, while passion slumbers (as the seed lives on in the sleeping earth), that they can revive after their apparent destruction, as the woodland violets reappear in the spring. If the poet could thus recover the innocence of the past, he would be content to "dream the rest," to accept tenderness in lieu of love, truth in lieu of passion. But mortality in human love, as in human life, is absolute. Tenderness and truth cannot live once the passion that creates them is dead; the last stanza confirms the finality of their loss. The "moral" is supported by the chief formal device of the lyric, the repeated doublets. These suggest the primacy of interrelationship, which the lover would deny (hoping to separate passion from tenderness, wild feelings from rational feelings), but which life confirms. Just as love is of the whole being, the flesh as well as the spirit, so its loss is total. The lyric recognizes the intransigence of passion, the arbitrariness of its course; the frailty lamented is, quite simply, the frailty of the flesh.

The late lyric that Mary Shelley entitled "Mutability" provides another example of the distinctive character of Shelley's lyric art,

the extraordinary compression of the cosmic and the personal, the
effortless adaptation of traditional poetic elements to an intensely
personal idiom. The poem is Shelley's version of carpe diem. The
most immediate traditional elements, perhaps, lay in the Calderon
lyrics he was translating at the time; indeed, the lyric could well
have begun as a translation.[12] Carpe diem poems usually have two
parts; a statement of the brevity of life's pleasures, and an admonition to enjoy them while they last; and Shelley's lyric follows the
pattern. He begins with the traditional emblem, the flower that
blooms today and dies tomorrow, and in its brief course illustrates
the transitory nature of all life and beauty:

> The flower that smiles today
>   Tomorrow dies;
> All that we wish to stay
>   Tempts and then flies;
> What is this world's delight?
> Lightning, that mocks the night,
>   Brief even as bright.—

It is a classic statement of the theme but unmistakably reminiscent
of the fair spirit of Intellectual Beauty and the inconstant visitations
of her light. It is Shelleyan in its touches of psychology: the temptation and mockery that human desire reads into the appearance of
nature. It is Shelleyan, too, in the simple irony: "All that we wish
to stay / Tempts and then flies." This is the same irony that shapes
"To a Sky-Lark:" "We look before and after / And pine for what
is not." The second stanza moves from the flower, emblem of "this
world's delight," to the frailty of its human equivalents:

> Virtue, how frail it is!—
>   Friendship, how rare!—
> Love, how it sells poor bliss
>   For proud despair!
> But these though soon they fall,
> Survive their joy, and all
>   Which ours we call.—

Virtue, friendship, love—the "flower" of human relationship—are
also uncertain, doomed. But they "fall" with a difference: unlike
the flower, which is "Brief even as bright," these outlive the joy

which they briefly occasion, and the illusion of possession. Love flowers as bliss, but lingers as despair.[13]

The final stanza turns to the conventional admonition, again given an additional irony. The brevity of the flower's life is recalled, and associated with the brevity of love and the fickleness of the beloved; the moral is, as usual, to seize the day.

> Whilst skies are blue and bright,
>   Whilst flowers are gay,
> Whilst eyes that change ere night
>   Make glad the day;
> Whilst yet the calm hours creep
> Dream thou—and from thy sleep
>   Then wake to weep.

"Dream thou" we read at first to mean *Enjoy these before they flee, as they must;* second to mean *Dream that they will last.* But "from thy sleep / Then wake" implies that delight itself is a dream, and lasts as long as the dream lasts. We wake to find light gone (a return to the night mocked briefly by lightning), the flower dead, Love betrayed, and possession an illusion; we weep because we endure and remember. Loss is total: "All that we wish to stay / Tempts and then flies;" or stays only to torment us. The emphasis in the lament is not for the frailty of gaiety and love but for our own endurance past their date, the fact that we "wake to weep." It is a favored theme for Shelley, as his repeated essays at dream vision attest. The paradoxes latent in the form correspond perfectly to his melancholy and his need to escape the bonds of self, and to his conviction that escape and transcendence are bound to be temporary. The dominant impression in the last poems seems to be twofold: that without the vision, waking reality is insupportable, but that it is also our inescapable condition.

One of the last lyrics Shelley completed, "When the lamp is shattered," is similarly a lament for "The frailty of all things here," the inability of light, music, love, to survive their source and occasion. Though the lyric consists mainly of a sequence of simple statements expressing logical relationship (when A then B; when C then D; as A and B, C and D, so X and Y), generalization breaks into passion, and the final effect is of the most intense expressiveness and lyricism. The lyric is a lament not merely for the death of love but for the death of the spirit that illuminates life, gives it beauty and meaning, and, after its departure, leaves the "noblest things vacant and chidden" ("The Zucca," 30).

The first two stanzas quietly demonstrate the inability of music, splendor, light, the natural effluence of the joyous spirit, to survive their source. The world survives—the motes of dust, the water vapor that causes the rainbow—but it is no longer illuminated, no longer made beautiful. Similarly, when the spirit is mute, the natural overflowing music of the heart ceases; it becomes an empty vessel and can only echo mournfully to the winds that buffet it. The analogies in a famous fragment probably written at about the same time, "Music, when soft voices die," urge that music and odor, although mortal in origin, endure in their effects; so poetry survives its source and serves as a nest for the immortal god of Love. In "When the lamp is shattered" the contrary assertions, that sweet notes are not remembered and loved accents soon forgotten, in the absence of the lover, are made analogous to objective fact: reflected light is in fact extinguished with its source, the rainbow's glory dissipated with the cloud. What is perhaps only a subjective mood is supported by incontestable evidence. Indeed, in the reasonableness and logic of the lyric's argument lies its strength:

> As music and splendour
> Survive not the lamp and the lute,
> The heart's echoes render
> No song when the spirit is mute—   (9–12)

How reasonable—and yet there is an ambiguity arising from the distancing of the "I," the specific context for this death; the syntax insists on the general meaning. One is forced to keep strictly to the terms of the given metaphors, which insist simply on the transience of music, splendor, love. The concluding lines of Stanza 2 are equally allusive:

> No song—but sad dirges
> Like the wind through a ruined cell
> Or the mournful surges
> That ring the dead seaman's knell.

Since its own spirit is mute, the only echo given by the heart, now an empty chamber, is a response to random outside forces, the wind echoing through a ruined cell (perhaps an echo of the "Bare ruin'd choirs" of Shakespeare's Sonnet 73), the waves tolling the buoy bell for death. When the heart is no longer possessed by love, when the spirit is broken or shattered, then it continues to register experience without any power to alter or transfigure it.

The opening line of Stanza 3, "When hearts have once mingled," is grammatically parallel to the opening line of the poem, "When the lamp is shattered," which suggests that the thought is parallel. Indeed the first draft moves directly from one to the other, from the broken lute, to forgotten accents, to the nest abandoned by Love. The subject of the last two stanzas, the "weak one," the "frailest" heart, who serves as the cradle, home, and bier of Love, is identical with the subject of the first two stanzas, the heart which, after its spirit is muted, can render no song but sad dirges. Love departs freely from the stronger heart, leaving it untouched; it remains perversely in the weaker heart, no longer as an illuminating or joyous principle but as a "living grave" ("Remembrance") that must be endured (as the "light in the dust" has not disappeared, but rather "lies dead"). The strong one forgets, the weaker remembers and laments. In Shelley's other love poetry, too, the source of love, joy, and happiness, is the stronger, the one who is free, while the weak one is susceptible, fated from the start to "endure" rather than "possess." The last stanza plots the course of this doomed love. The death of love is already an irreversible fact; the nest in which Love has chosen to die simply lies open to its own despair, the hostile elements, the passage of time.[14]

The conclusion of the poem (beginning "O Love! who bewailest") is an extended address to Love. In the voice of reason, the poet questions a perverse and self-destructive deity: Why do you, who know best the frailty of all mortal life (the law of nature demonstrated so conclusively in the first two stanzas), choose the frailest heart of all for your nest? Its unruly passions (its woe, desire, its throbs) will rock Love as the ravens on high are rocked by the storm; the rafters which support it will rot, leaving Love naked to the elements when winter comes.[15] The difficulty of the lines is in part a matter of Shelley's usual practice of referring at will to either the tenor or the vehicle of his metaphor. Thus given the metaphor of a heart as a nest, he speaks either of "its passions" or of the rafters that support it. Indeed, the concluding line ("When leaves fall and cold winds come") seems to mark a sudden shift to the sphere of analogy—the storms of winter—as the real subject. The final transition back to the tenor, the human subject—the weak heart—is left to the reader. The equation between the seasonal winter and the winter of the heart or spirit should be familiar from other poems; Shelley uses a similar image in the fragmentary "Lines": "Far, far away, O ye / Halcyons of Memory, / Seek some far calmer nest / Than this abandoned breast! / No news of your false spring / To my heart's winter bring" (1–6).

Despite the ambiguity of the last stanza, the power of the lyric lies in the displacement of passion, as the long, despairing question and prophecy is addressed to Love, rather than to the human being at the center of the poet's thought. Love is traditionally free to choose his habitation, and thus the poet can address him as if his present state is the result of a free choice, an instance of folly or perversity. But the human situation behind the metaphor is not a matter of choice at all, as the earlier stanzas imply; rather it is in the nature of life itself. The indirection of the lyric is what makes it so moving; the question asked is, after all, unanswerable. Sorrow and pity are diverted from the lover to Love; it is Love who suffers the storms that buffet the heart, who lies exposed to laughter. It is not merely the foolish, weak heart but the God himself who defies bright reason, logic, the lessons of nature and time. Once more we hear the cry of Pan: "Gods and men, we are all deluded thus!" We are left with the paradox that action is determined not by free choice, as we like to assume, but by desire, which takes its own course regardless of common sense and reality.

NOTES

1. Bloom, *Shelley's Mythmaking*, pp. 5–8, reads the lyric as an example of "primitive mythopoeic poetry" about the writing of poetry. The Huntington draft suggests a more personal element than the finished poem: "Once I called on Death, or Sleep . . . I thought they had what thou dost keep" (draft, lines 22–24) could be read as a reference to the autobiographical passages of "Hymn to Intellectual Beauty," possibly "Stanzas written in Dejection" as well.

2. The holograph of "Song: 'Rarely, rarely, comest thou' " is reproduced in *The Shelley Notebook in the Harvard College Library*, ed. G. E. Woodberry (Cambridge, Mass., 1929); *Works* prints a corrected text.

3. "Love's Philosophy," an adaptation of the Anacreontic drinking song also translated by Cowley and Moore, was published in the *Indicator* (December 22, 1819); "The Indian Girl's Song" was published posthumously as "Song, written for an Indian Air," in the *Liberal*, I (1822); "Buona Notte," in its English version, was published in the *Literary Pocket-Book* (1822). "The Question," another literary exercise, was also published in the *Literary Pocket-Book* (1822).

4. R. D. Havens, "Structure and Prosodic Pattern in Shelley's Lyrics," *PMLA*, 65 (1950), 1076–87, analyzes the structure of these short lyrics in detail. "An Exhortation" is particularly interesting; it is constructed around a group of five or six monosyllabic nouns, which are repeated and redistributed in new patterns in each stanza. "Lines written on hearing the News of the Death of Napoleon" is comparably ingenious, repeating and interweaving five or six rhyme words and three phonemes, in a Shelleyan adaptation of a sestina.

5. "One word is too often profaned" is one of the few late lyrics for which Shelley's holograph seems to have disappeared. The poem was first printed in *Posthumous Poems* (1824), from the fair copy in Mary Shelley's notebook, Bodleian MS Shelley adds. d. 7.

6. "The Choice," 35–36, quoted in White, II, 55. Shelley's analysis of his deteriorated relations with Mary is compassionate but clear-sighted: "I only feel the want of those who can feel, and understand me. Whether from proximity and the continuity of domestic intercourse, Mary does not. The necessity of concealing from her thoughts that would pain her, necessitates this, perhaps. It is the curse of Tantalus, that a person possessing such excellent powers and so pure a mind as hers, should not excite the sympathy indispensable to their application to domestic life" (letter of June 18, 1822, to John Gisborne, *Letters of P.B.S.*, II, 435).

7. White provides a judicious account of Shelley's relationship with Jane Williams, II, 343–47. Shelley's earlier romantic history is allegorized in *Epipsychidion*, 267–345.

8. Cf. the attack by Cleanth Brooks and Robert Penn Warren in *Understanding Poetry* (New York, 1938), pp. 319–23. This classic attack has been countered by readings that stress the conventional nature of Eastern love poetry and its fashionable imitations; see B. A. Park, "The Indian Elements of the 'Indian Serenade,' " *Keats-Shelley Journal*, 10 (Winter, 1961), 8–12; and G. M. Matthews, "Shelley's Lyrics," in *The Morality of Art: Essays Presented to G. Wilson Knight*, ed. D. W. Jefferson (London, 1969), pp. 195–209. Matthews is the first critic, as far as I know, to identify the speaker as female.

9. C. S. Catty, "Shelley's 'I arise from dreams of thee' and Miss Sophia Stacey," *Athenaeum*, No. 4199 (April 18, 1908), p. 478. W. M. Rossetti, ed., *Poetical Works of Percy Bysshe Shelley* (London, 1878), III, 402–03, states that Catty sent him a copy but it contained no variants which suggests to me that it was not a Shelley holograph. Catty's note appears to be the sole source of the account of the poem in Helen

Rossetti Angeli, *Shelley and His Friends in Italy* (London, 1911), though Mrs. Angeli saw Sophia Stacey's diary; and Angeli's account in turn is the source of White's discussion: "There can be no question about his first and most famous poetic gift to [Sophia Stacey], the passionate lyric 'I arise from dreams of thee' " (White, II, 174). Medwin is not always reliable, but I see no reason to doubt his attribution of the poem, which is supported by references in letters both by Shelley and Mary to the "Indian air." See Thomas Medwin, *The Life of Percy Bysshe Shelley*, ed. H. Buxton Forman (London: Oxford University Press, 1913), pp. 317–18; see also Shelley's letter to Claire Clairmont, [March 31, 1822], *Letters of P.B.S.*, II, 403 ("Mary will . . . send you the Indian air"), and Mary's letter to Hunt, August 18, 1823 ("all at once I heard chords on the harp—the co[mmence]ment of the Indian air you have so often heard me mention that [Shelley and] Jane used to sing together"), *Letters of M.W.S.*, I, 256. Additional evidence (admittedly slight) is provided by the holograph, which bears two addresses, both in Pisa, to which Shelley and Mary moved in January, 1820 (Sophia had parted from them in December, 1819, in Florence).

10. "Lewti, or the Circassian Love-Chant," 49–50. Cf. Byron, "Stanzas to a Hindoo Air," which is sung by a female, and Moore's "The Young Indian Maid."

11. Shelley's use of Calderon's pattern of parallel analogies (as in Shelley's translation of *El Magico prodigioso*, III, 45–78) is discussed in Neville Rogers, *Shelley at Work*, 2nd ed. (Oxford: Clarendon Press, 1967), p. 329.

12. Matthews, "Shelley's Lyrics," p. 205, suggests that "The flower that smiles today" was written for the opening scene of *Hellas*, and several verbal resemblances, as well as the lyric's place in the notebook containing drafts of *Hellas*, would seem to support his argument. But the lyric appears to be self-sufficient, and I am not convinced that it was ever intended as part of the drama.

13. Line 12 reads in *Posthumous Poems* (1824) and all subsequent editions, "But we, though soon they fall," which changes the sense; Mary Shelley evidently felt that some editorial change was necessary, though she transcribed the line correctly in her original copy.

14. The image of Love dwelling in the heart, as a bird in the nest, is common in Italian love poetry; cf. Guido Cavalcanti, Ballata XII; Tasso, Sonnet 2; or Guido Guinicelli, Canzone ('Al cor gentil, ripara sempre Amore'); in *Lyric Poetry of the Italian Renaissance*, ed. L. R. Lind (New Haven, Conn., 1954). But the draft suggests that the thought was originally less obscure: when hearts have mingled, the "wild bird" flees the love nest first, leaving the "weak one" behind.

15. See Pottle, "The Case of Shelley," pp. 303–05, in *English Romantic Poets*, ed. Abrams.

CHAPTER SEVEN

THE MAGIC CIRCLE:
Poems to Jane Williams

THE POEMS to Jane Williams were written in the winter and spring
of 1822,[1] when the intimacy between Shelley and Jane and Williams was too close, perhaps, to sustain the easy friendship in which
it had begun. Since October the two families had lived on separate
floors of the same house on the Lung'Arno, in Pisa; in early May,
Shelley and Mary moved to Casa Magni for the summer, and Jane
and Williams moved in as their temporary guests[2]—a living arrangement fraught with danger when one couple is reasonably
happy and the other miserable. For Mary was pregnant and ill; she
loathed the isolation and discomfort of the house and hated the sea,
and Shelley was unable to break through her misery. He was driven
despite his sympathy for her to suspect that her coldness signified
not only that she was unhappy but that she no longer loved him.
The poems to Jane were to be kept from Mary's eyes (they are
headed: "For Jane and Williams alone to see;" "Not to be opened
unless you are alone"—and to Williams: "If any of the stanzas
should please you, you may read them to Jane, but to no one
else");[3] and their implied or explicit subject is not only the delight
the poet takes in Jane's singing, or her hand on his forehead, but
his embittered "life and love," his "cold home." Jane appears to
have had none of Mary's intellectual or Emilia Viviani's spiritual
refinement; Shelley must have been drawn to her at least in part because she and Williams were devoted to each other. This meant
that she could be kind to Shelley in a disinterested way (a "friend"),
and that she could never be his—ideal circumstances, in a way, for
Shelley, and thus celebrated and lamented in the poems. By July

162

he was in love with Jane—guilty enough in imagination, at least, to write in the last letter Mary was to receive from him, four days before he sailed for Leghorn; "You have no idea how I am hurried & occupied—I have not a moments leisure—but will write by next post—" (*Letters of P.B.S.*, II, 444), and immediately afterward, to Jane: "[I] shall urge [Williams] to sail with the first fair wind without expecting me. I have thus the pleasure of contributing to your happiness when deprived of every other—and of leaving you no other subject of regret, but the absence of one scarcely worth regretting . . . Adieu, my dearest friend—I only write these lines for the pleasure of tracing what will meet your eyes . . ." (*Letters of P.B.S.*, II, 445).

The poems to Jane include "The Magnetic Lady to her Patient" and "The keen stars were twinkling;" "With a Guitar" (written to accompany a gift from Shelley), an epistle in tetrameter couplets, marked by the whimsy that characterized Shelley's social relations; the lovely pastoral, "The Invitation," and its companion poem, "The Recollection;" and "Lines written in the Bay of Lerici," possibly the last lyric Shelley wrote. We could include too the stanzas "To Edward Williams," addressed really to Edward and Jane ("Dear friends, dear *friend*").[4] These are the most intimate as well as the most charming of Shelley's love poems. In them he breaks away from the brief lyric form, with its simplifications, into sustained analysis of the themes that dominate all the late lyrics: the perversity of human desire, its illogic and self-destructiveness, the illusory and fragile nature of happiness and love, the conflict between reason and desire, between desire and obligation. It is unlikely that Shelley would ever have turned away completely from political and prophetic poetry; but these poems, representing as they do his last work, suggest the deepening pessimism of his vision of life. For poetry in these lyrics has nothing to do with changing the world, nor does it impinge on the larger world in any way; it is rather a means of cherishing the moment of happiness, of celebrating and perhaps immortalizing "one moment's good" after long pain.

The social context of the poems is drawn in a letter Shelley wrote to John Gisborne:

> I like Jane more and more, and I find Williams the most
> amiable of companions. She has a taste for music, and an
> elegance of form and motions that compensate in some degree
> for the lack of literary refinement. Mrs. Gisborne knows my
> gross ideas of music, and will forgive me when I say that
> I listen the whole evening on our terrace to the simple melodies
> with excessive delight. I have a boat here . . . Williams is
> captain, and we drive along this delightful bay in the evening
> wind, under the summer moon, until earth appears another
> world. Jane brings her guitar, and if the past and future could
> be obliterated, the present would content me so well that I
> could say with Faust to the passing moment "Remain, thou,
> thou art so beautiful."
> (Letter of June 18, 1822, *Letters of P.B.S.,* II, 435–36)

The poet's momentary happiness, his general unhappiness, the fact,
more or less apparent to him, that he was falling in love with Jane
—these are the materials of the poems, their ostensible occasion
and subject. They analyze complicated adult relationships; above
all they demonstrate the poet's insight into his own nature, his
acute sense of the personal necessities that made it imperative for
him to tame his ardor, not to "break his chain." Yet the privacy of
actual lives is protected, the personal details disguised (especially
those having to do with Mary), even as the emotions they cause
in the poet are analyzed. In their subtlety, the poems reveal a quality of Shelley's mind he hints at with reference to his strained relations with Byron: "What is passing in the heart of another rarely
escapes the observation of one who is a strict anatomist of his own"
(*Letters of P.B.S.,* II, 324).

"The Magnetic Lady to her Patient" is frank in its portrait of
the relationship between Jane and Shelley. Jane is made to say at
least three or four times that she pities Shelley but cannot love him,
that her role is that of friend and physician, not of mistress. The
explicitness of the poem (she reminds him at the outset of her own
happy relationship with Williams) is part of its charm, the tone of
affectionate raillery and wholly disinterested tenderness. The patient's ills are the same as those which plague the poet of "Stanzas
written in Dejection"—"lost health," "the world's dull scorn"—but
they are validated by the fact that it is not the poet but the Lady

who names them. The cure, again, is forgetfulness, but the self-pity
of the earlier poem ("I could lie down like a tired child") is modified by the poet's awareness of the several players in the drama, not
only Jane and himself but Edward and Mary.

The occasion of the poem—Jane practicing hypnotism on the
ailing poet—becomes a metaphor for their relationship, both for
what Jane insists that it be, and for what he would like it to become. The metaphor of love as a sickness, the mistress as physician,
is one of the oldest staples of love poetry, and it is a function of the
poem's wit to raise possibilities even as their implications are denied. In hypnotism the subject is laid to sleep and forgetfulness
induced; when he is entirely receptive, a new spirit is infused into
him. In this last stage, the physician-patient relationship is easily
confused with that of mistress and lover: "By mine thy being is to
its deep / Possest" (35–36).

The entry of the hypnotist's spirit into the subject suggests unmistakably the spiritual or physical union of love, a thought which
no doubt the poet briefly, wistfully, entertains, before he descends
to earth:

> "The spell is done—how feel you now?"
>   "Better, quite well" replied
>   The sleeper—"What would do
> You good when suffering and awake,
>   What cure your head and side?"
> "What would cure that would kill me, Jane,
> And as I must on earth abide
> Awhile yet, tempt me not to break
>   My chain."   (37–45)

The effect of the stanza lies in the shift from Jane's concern to the
poet's oblique play on her words: "What would cure that would
kill me, Jane." As her frankness comes from a free heart, his allu-
siveness, in the form of pun and metaphor, comes from the knowledge of burdens he cannot shake off. The "chain" he must not
break is the chain of life; also, undoubtedly, it is the chain of his
marriage.

"The keen stars were twinkling" is a poetic rendering of the experience Shelley describes in the letter to Gisborne: "we drive along

this delightful bay in the evening wind, under the summer moon, until earth appears another world." The poem concentrates upon the presentness of the scene, even though the poet's delight has its source in something more, the yearning for "some world far from ours." The lyric is reminiscent of "To Constantia," both in its occasion and in the relationship suggested between song and feeling, between the singer and the instrument. In both lyrics the erotic component is submerged; the emphasis is on the power of song to move the spirit to delight and to transport the hearer to another world. But the later lyric is more personal and circumstantial, not an extended analysis of the experience, like "To Constantia," but a musical imitation of it.

The structure of the poem depends on the analogy between the moon, which gives splendor to the stars, and Jane's voice, which gives life to the guitar's soulless notes. Each stanza interweaves the same terms—keen stars, fair moon, sweet tones—until they are given final shape in the last lines:

> Though the sound overpowers
> Sing again, with your dear voice revealing
> A tone
> Of some world far from ours,
> Where music and moonlight and feeling
> Are one.   (19–24)

The present scene, the rising moon, the stars, the guitar, Jane's life-giving presence—all are turned into an emblem of the poet's desire for love and harmony and his sense that although the elements are present, a particular human magnetism is needed to bring them into relationship. The stanza, with its ingenious verbal and metrical patterning, its rhythmical pauses, is an imitation of the song Jane might have played (as Shelley's description of it, "words for an ariette," suggests); the syncopated rhythm approximates the pattern of a voice singing against strummed chords. The stress pattern compels one to read with "rests" included, so that the short lines are isolated: *Tonight; Delight; A tone; Are one.* In the final lines, the three stresses, which summarize the three elements of the scene, "music and moonlight and feeling," literally become "one."

The remaining three poems inscribed to Jane are essays in light tetrameter couplets, conversational in tone, intimate, analytic. Each poem idealizes Jane, partly as a compliment to her peculiar grace and serenity, partly in response to the poet's needs, to which Jane is merely an accessory. For in these poems Jane, the "spirit of peace in our circle of tempests," is identified with the harmonizing and life-giving spirit described in "The Zucca," that which the poet, or in the allegorical framework of the poem, the human soul, desires beyond all else. It is this spirit which the poet or lover adores—

> In winds, and trees, and streams, and all things common,
> In music and the sweet unconscious tone
> Of animals, and voices which are human . . .
> In the soft motions and rare smile of woman,
> In flowers and leaves, and in the grass fresh-shown
> ("The Zucca," 33–35, 37–38)

—and whose sudden and unpreventable flight he laments, since he cannot follow after.

"With a Guitar" represents the happiest side of this spring interlude. It has the overtones of social intercourse, the affectionate nicknaming and play-acting in which the Shelley circle always indulged (and which Shelley alludes to in the last section of *Epipsychidion*). Its theme, like that of "The keen stars were twinkling," is the happy union of love, music, poetry, nature.

The opening section imagines the group of friends as immortal spirits temporarily imprisoned in their present bodies. Jane and Edward are Miranda and Ferdinand (ideal love), Shelley is Ariel (their guardian spirit, devoted servant, agent of poetry), and Mary, one is tempted to say, is "the silent Moon / In her interlunar swoon," sadness personified. True to the fiction, Miranda and Ferdinand are quite unaware of Ariel's long service, of which he must gently remind them; this is his excuse for the long introduction, with its ingenuous declaration of "more than ever can be spoken."

The second part of the poem turns to the guitar itself, which, in a kind of mirror image to the opening fiction (Ariel, we remember, was imprisoned for twelve years in a pine), is seen as the second and happier life of a tree. To those who know how to question it, the guitar will reveal the secrets of nature and the oracles it conceals:

> For it had learnt all harmonies
> Of the plains and of the skies,
> Of the forests and the mountains,
> And the many-voiced fountains,
> The clearest echoes of the hills,
> The softest notes of falling rills,
> The melodies of birds and bees,
> The murmuring of summer seas,
> And pattering rain and breathing dew
> And airs of evening;—and it knew
> That seldom heard mysterious sound,
> Which, driven on its diurnal round
> As it floats through boundless day
> Our world enkindles on its way—   (65–78)

The natural world is conceived in terms of its sounds—many-voiced fountains, echoes, pattering rain; these merge naturally into the sounds of the guitar, which both echoes and interprets natural sound. The pastoral survey, like that in "Lines written among the Euganean Hills," climaxes in the intuition of a transcendent principle of unity or harmony, a "mysterious sound" (like the "soul of all" or the inconstant Spirit of Intellectual Beauty), which, though seldom heard, can be divined or sensed through its analogy with that which can be heard. The poem ends with what amounts to a definition of poetry or art, lighter in tone than those in "A Defence of Poetry" but in agreement with Shelley's general insistence on "the wise heart" and the "mind's imaginings" as the ultimate source of love, beauty, and truth:

> All this it knows, but will not tell
> To those who cannot question well
> The spirit that inhabits it:
> It talks according to the wit
> Of its companions; and no more
> Is heard than has been felt before
> By those who tempt it to betray
> These secrets of an elder day.—   (79–86)[5]

Nature and natural mythology on the one hand, the grace and intuitive feeling of the pure spirit on the other—these remain Shelley's absolutes. The tribute Shelley pays them in this poem balances the sadness of other poems of this time, the despair of "When the lamp is shattered," the recurrent lament for the loss of love and happiness.

The companion poems "The Invitation" and "The Recollection" are perceptibly the work of the author of "Lines written among the Euganean Hills." Again the poet's mood is described in relation to a scene lovingly and accurately set down, to which he is intensely responsive and yet which serves to establish beyond all question his isolation from nature. In the poems to Jane, unlike "Lines written among the Euganean Hills," other persons figure in the poet's thoughts: the woman he is falling in love with, whom he identifies with all that is happy, free, and life-giving, and his wife, who has come to be associated only with "low-thoughted care," past tragedy, the poet's inescapable responsibilities. While the poet concentrates on the image of his own happiness or grief—the day, the scene—the human relationships in the background, barely hinted at, color all that he says. In addition to the human quality of these lyrics, their tenderness and nostalgia of tone, we notice as in all the late lyrics the quiet disappearance of apocalyptic hope, the ambition to change the world. The pine forest in the Cascine and the day spent there provide just such a "green isle" in the sea of agony as the day the poet spends in the Euganean Hills, but his modest joy in it—"To-day is for itself enough"—does not radically alter his initial pessimism; he has no hopes of permanent relief, change, or transcendence. For in these poems the poet's personal distress takes the form of a stoicism most closely akin to that of Keats's great Odes. From a world of care and sorrow the poet imaginatively enters a closed and secret and delightful world, of nature, art, or love, from which he must at last return, tolled back to his "sole self." The psychological and artistic movement of the poems is similar to Keats's characteristic procedure. The poet first holds the image of perfection in his mind—for Keats the song of the bird, the Greek urn, for Shelley the hour spent in the forest with Jane—then, through the process of imagining it, he appears to be physically absorbed into its reality, which becomes exclusive and absolute:

"Already with thee! tender is the night . . ." But as the intensity of the imagined moment fades, as the song of the nightingale recedes over the hills, the vision dissolves, and the world's reality breaks in upon the poet with the return of his self-consciousness.

"The Invitation" is organized, like "Lines written among the Euganean Hills," on an extended analogy between the physical rhythms of nature and the emotional rhythms of human life. The fair day, unexpectedly breaking into the winter, come to smile at the "rough Year," is sister to the fair Jane, come miraculously to ease the poet's sorrow:

> Best and brightest, come away—
> Fairer far than this fair day
> Which like thee to those in sorrow
> Comes to bid a sweet good-morrow
> To the rough year just awake
> In its cradle on the brake.—   (1–6)

The poet offers a pseudo-mythological genealogy for the sweet morning, which draws closer and closer to the thought of the ministering Magnetic Lady, until the analogy is made explicit:

> The brightest hour of unborn spring
> Through the winter wandering
> Found, it seems, the halcyon morn
> To hoar February born;
> Bending from Heaven in azure mirth
> It kissed the forehead of the earth
> And smiled upon the silent sea,
> And bade the frozen streams be free
> And waked to music all their fountains
> And breathed upon the frozen mountains
> And like a prophetess of May
> Strewed flowers upon the barren way,
> Making the wintry world appear
> Like one on whom thou smilest, dear.   (7–20)

The analogy between the frozen earth, wintry and barren, and the desolate state of the poet leads to the second analogy, between the nature of the day—a rare halcyon day in February, with winter

soon closing in again—and the nature of the poet's experience, a
brief moment of peace and happy forgetfulness interrupting cares
to which he must return. Given this simple framework, it is easy to
see why the poem should be so modest in scope compared to "Lines
written among the Euganean Hills," where the terms are on the one
hand the physical vista of all Italy, its cities islanded in the fair
plains, on the other a metaphor for the human condition, green
isles of happiness in a sea of agony. The tone reflects the difference
in scope; Shelley turns next to a confession Cowperesque in its
modesty and humor, its defiance of the "accustomed" demons. Yet
the poetic sensibility is the same as that of "Stanzas written in Dejection," "Invocation to Misery," and "Song: ('Rarely, rarely
comest thou')":

> Hope, in pity mock not woe
> With smiles, nor follow where I go;
> Long having lived on thy sweet food,
> At length I find one moment's good
> After long pain—   (41–45)

"The Invitation" ends with a brief description of the "wild woods
and the plains" reminiscent of the noon moment described in "Lines
written among the Euganean Hills." But in "The Invitation" the
description is limited to the physical scene, and the felt unity is an
appearance, momentary and fragile:

> Where the earth and ocean meet,
> And all things seem only one
> In the universal Sun.—   (67–69)

The account of wintry woods and sea is the kind of natural description at which Shelley is unsurpassed, in which physical life, and the
meaning it embodies and evokes, effortlessly pass one into the other.
The whole of nature—land, sea, and sky—seems to have a life of
its own, whose secrets are bare to the eye of the poet. It is as if
nature, in its multiplicity and continual process, revealed to him the
secret of unity and timelessness—in the "wild woods" where nature
is not bound or limited, where day and night, winter and summer,
earth and ocean, meet and appear to be merged into one. The na-

tural scene represents innocent relationship, the more innocent, perhaps, because the elements that meet or reflect one another in love do not merge, barely touch, and bear no fruit, scent, or color. Nature under such an aspect offers still another inducement to Jane to join the poet, and demonstrates the innocence of his request.

"The Recollection" is, as Shelley says, "The epitaph of glory fled" and is therefore more serious, more complicated. It is an attempt to fix the exact quality of the scene and of the poet's happiness; more precisely, it seeks to find an image that can permanently stand for the day in the pine forest. Its formal introduction sustains the tone of epistolary verse; with an inversion of rhyme the passage ends on a sad, suspended cadence: "A frown is on the Heaven's brow." The "frown" recalls the "smile" with which "The Invitation" begins; the reader will guess that it is not only the earth that has returned to its wintry state. And the experience, as it is now recalled, takes on more and more the character of an interlude, a pause, marked by a silence and stillness, a profound calm, which is gradually elaborated and deepened until it takes on magical properties, like the trance of dream vision or revelation. Land, sea, and sky are drawn, each soothed to peace and harmony by the "smile of Heaven," the waves "half asleep," the clouds "gone to play," the twisted pines stilled by the "azure breath" of the wind, the "treetops . . . asleep / Like green waves on the sea, / As still as in the silent deep / The Ocean woods may be." The universal calm is finally made to include the human beings who perceive it; its source, imaged as the lovely day, the "smile of Heaven," is identified more precisely as the "Radiant Sister of the day" of "The Invitation."

> There seemed from the remotest seat
>   Of the white mountain-waste,
> To the soft flower beneath our feet
>   A magic circle traced,
> A spirit interfused around
>   A thrilling silent life,
> To momentary peace it bound
>   Our mortal nature's strife;—
> And still I felt the centre of
>   The magic circle there

> Was one fair form that filled with love
> The lifeless atmosphere.   (41–52)

The "magic circle" recalls the windless bower envisaged by the poet at the end of "Lines written among the Euganean Hills," its peace made permanent by "the love which heals all strife / Circling, like the breath of life, / All things in that sweet abode" (366–68). But where the island paradise is an image of an Elysium, a universal source of hope, the "magic circle" is drawn around an hour of present life, the peace is momentary, the source of love is embodied in human form, hence transient and frail. And as if the statement alone is not sufficient, Shelley draws the "magic circle" in terms of a new circle image of sky and forest reflected in the forest pools (like the reflection of "old palaces and towers" in "the wave's intenser day," in "Ode to the West Wind"). The still reflection, while real, has the perfection and truth as well as the illusory character of dream or vision; it strangely approximates a Platonic absolute— "purer," "more boundless," "more perfect"—to which the "upper world," "our world above," is but a dim shadow.

> We paused beside the pools that lie
> Under the forest bough—
> Each seemed as 'twere, a little sky
> Gulfed in a world below;
> A firmament of purple light
> Which in the dark earth lay
> More boundless than the depth of night
> And purer than the day,
> In which the lovely forests grew
> As in the upper air,
> More perfect, both in shape and hue,
> Than any spreading there.   (53–64)

Just as in lines 33–52 the notion of absolute peace yields imperceptibly to the idea of the love which is its source and which emanates from Jane, so in lines 53–76, as the description of the reflected Elysium continues, its perfection and truth become identified with physical love: the water's desire to receive the surrounding woods.

> Sweet views, which in our world above
>   Can never well be seen,
> Were imaged in the water's love
>   Of that fair forest green;
> And all was interfused beneath
>   With an Elysian glow,
> An atmosphere without a breath,
>   A softer day below—   (69–76)

The poem ends with a return to reality, the "frown . . . on the Heaven's brow," the poet's melancholy; the shift is accomplished aphoristically by pun and metaphor:

> Like one beloved, the scene had lent
>   To the dark water's breast,
> Its every leaf and lineament
>   With more than truth exprest;
> Until an envious wind crept by,
>   Like an unwelcome thought
> Which from the mind's too faithful eye
>   Blots one dear image out.—
> Though thou art ever fair and kind
>   And forests ever green,
> Less oft is peace in ——'s mind,
>   Than calm in water seen.   (77–88)

To paraphrase: as a passing wind blots out from the pool the reflection of the scene (by ruffling the surface, distorting the reflection), so an "unwelcome thought" erases Jane's image from the poet's "too faithful" mind—"too faithful," I think, simply as the water reflects the scene with "more than truth," though the line is ambiguous. One might guess that the lines allude to the poet's marriage, to which he is "too faithful;" in his relations with Mary he must have felt that patience and endurance were indicated, but there was no reason for him not to indulge his happiness in Jane's companionship. The final quatrain seems to be a frank statement of the poet's dilemma, but the meaning is still restricted to the terms of the metaphor, and one knows no more than at the beginning. As the green forest is to the water that images it in love, so is the fair Jane to Shelley; but (to return to the opening analogy of the poem) the peace of the day is but a moment's respite from the poet's "long pain;" the waters of his spirit are troubled indeed, and whatever beneficent effect Jane may have is bound to be merely temporary.

As "The Invitation" and "The Recollection" suggest comparison with "Lines written among the Euganean Hills," "Lines written in the Bay of Lerici" suggests "Stanzas written in Dejection" in its simplicity of statement, its directness. As in the earlier poem, the poet's agitation of spirit is measured against a scene so lovely and so intensely felt that it becomes an image of the serenity from which he is excluded. The displacement of emotion in the opening lines of the poem is characteristic of Shelley's last poems. Brooding about Jane, he addresses the Moon: "Bright wanderer, fair coquette of Heaven;" suffering the effects of her recent presence and her departure, he analyzes the nature of time and the relationship of the present to past and future. Thus before turning directly to the beloved, his thoughts linger over the moment of departure, which turns into an image of suspended time. And the image of this "silent time," when the moon hovers between its rise and its setting, "like an albatross asleep," anticipates the thought of the moment of happiness, the "time which is our own," suspended between past and future, which, the poet implies, possess or enchain us. It is a moment caught and imprisoned, like the noon moment of "Lines written in the Euganean Hills," or the hour spent in the pine forest in the Cascine, when flux, process, physical reality are for a moment transcended by feeling and memory. The images that render this moment are similar to those which dominate "Music, when soft voices die:" they have to do with the analogy between the vibrations of feeling and those of sound and odor, the relation of physical cause to nonphysical effect. The effects of love are imperceptible, immeasurable, but felt by the "enchanted heart," which is not dependent upon physical presence. But the demon reassumes his throne, despite a momentary enchantment; the poet's "antient pilot, Pain" takes control of his "frail bark" once more, in the image which represents Shelley's persistent vision of the solitary human life. No sooner does he mention his "faint heart," though, than he turns again to the scene, displacing his need onto the landscape:

> . . . I dare not speak
> My thoughts; but thus disturbed and weak
> I sate and watched the vessels glide
> Along the ocean bright and wide,
> Like spirit-winged chariots sent
> O'er some serenest element
> For ministrations strange and far . . .   (35–41)

As in "Stanzas written in Dejection," the very solitude of the poet
sharpens his sensibility to the harmonies of the natural scene, as
well as to its analogy with human life. The enumeration of the
elements of the scene—the gliding vessels, the wind, the scent of
the flowers, the coolness of dew, the sweet warmth left by day—
seems to parallel the enumeration earlier in the poem of the beloved's ministrations, her tones, the "soft vibrations of her touch,"
her healing presence. Both passages imply the gulf between the
suffering poet and the harmony of spirit toward which he yearns,
whether represented by his "guardian angel" (who, like the moon,
is bound after her brief stay for her own "nest"), or by the natural
scene in its clarity and freshness.

The poet has instinctively turned to the scene for some easing
of his pain, perhaps for a continuation of the peace ministered by
his beloved, who serves in all these poems as an extension of a
beneficent nature. And the scene finally supplies its more than
adequate image. With a sudden twist or tautening the quiet description ends with the vision of the fisherman with lamp and spear—
the human figure in the landscape, the natural predator, as the fish
are natural victims. And to this image the poet appends a moral,
somewhat in the fashion of the wry aphorism that ends "The
Recollection:" "Less oft is peace in [Shelley]'s mind / Than calm
in water seen:"

> Too happy, they whose pleasure sought
> Extinguishes all sense and thought
> Of the regret that pleasure [   ]
> Seeking life not peace.   (55–58)

The final contrast is between not happiness and despair but the
simplicity of nature, even in the urge of natural creatures toward

death, and the complexity of human life, which, subject always to "sense and thought," must endure the departure of pleasure, and which survives all it loves. What the poet envies in the luring of the fish, which otherwise seems to mirror his own foolish pursuit of pleasure, is the singleness of animal instinct, the sureness of its consequences.

The image of the "delusive flame" is the last variation on a theme that runs through Shelley's poetry, the desire of every living creature:

> . . . ever from below
> Aspiring like one who loves too fair, too far,
> To be consumed within the purest glow
>
> Of one serene and unapproachèd star,
> As if it were a lamp of earthly light,
> Unconscious, as some human lovers are,
>
> Itself how low, how high beyond all height
> The heaven where it would perish!
> ("The Woodman and the Nightingale," 25–32)

Yet the image of temptation, desire, and destruction in Shelley's last poem has a special quality entirely different from the soaring affirmations of *Adonais* and *Epipsychidion,* an objective, ironic detachment. The appended moral suggests that the choice for the aspiring soul is simply between the seeking of life—i.e., of its necessity, of light, love, delight—and the sensible pursuit of peace. Life and peace are incompatible; by implication, peace is possible only in the grave. The earlier images of present peace and happiness are set in a most somber perspective. And for the first time, the image of the flame is qualified by the suggestion that it is indeed a false lure, and that the heart which follows the flame does so because it is a "weak heart of little wit" ("Love, Hope, Desire, and Fear," 49).

These last lyrics confirm the darkening of spirit that is suggested so strongly by "The Triumph of Life." One senses an increasing pessimism on Shelley's part, the gradual withdrawal of the poet's bright Elysium until it appears to be no more than an image of what the soul in vain desires, counter to all reason, all evidence. Yet as Shelley's hope of permanent change in society and in private life recedes and its place is taken by the notion of endurance, the ideal for which his spirit longs seems suddenly to take shape in the present moment, the beloved Italian scene, the brief presence of a woman. Hence the poignancy of these poems, which celebrate present happiness in the certainty of loss, which do not seek beyond the "present and tangible object" but rather draw a magic circle around that which is mortal and doomed.

Even as Shelley's perspective seems to shift, his art is strengthened. In these last poems there is always a hard core of thought at the center, whether the poem appears to be a simple description of a natural scene, an expression of nameless joy or sorrow, or an ecstatic approximation of an ideal beyond sense experience or rational inference. Though Shelley's unique qualities as a poet come from his intense sensibility to just these things, though he is preeminently a poet of passionate feeling and commitment, his intelligence, which is essentially abstract and logical, is always in control. The precision of his thought should never be underestimated; as it is the source of difficulty, sometimes of ambiguity, so it is what finally gives his poetry its strength.

NOTES

1. Only one of the poems is dated, but the others can be placed roughly. "The Recollection" is dated "Feb. 2, 1822" (the day commemorated, according to Williams' *Journal*); "The keen stars were twinkling" can be dated by its close verbal resemblances to Shelley's letter of June 18; "Lines written in the Bay of Lerici" must have been written in late June as well. "With a Guitar" was written sometime after January 25 (when Shelley asked Horace Smith to purchase a pedal harp for Jane) and before "The keen stars were twinkling." "To Edward Williams" was sent to Williams on January 26, according to Williams' *Journal*. The poems and their dates are discussed in White, II, 343–47. Medwin includes among the poems to Jane "When the lamp is shattered" and "I arise from dreams of thee" (Medwin's *Life of Shelley*, ed. Forman, pp. 317–18). The relationship between Jane and Shelley is analyzed in G. M. Matthews, "Shelley and Jane Williams," *Review of English Studies*, n.s. 12 (1961), 40–48; and Donald H. Reiman, "Shelley's 'The Triumph of Life:' The Biographical Problem," *PMLA*, 78 (1963), 536–50. I would agree with Reiman that it is unlikely that anything more passed between Shelley and Jane than conversation and vibrations from Jane's cool hand—at least as

of the writing of "Lines written in the Bay of Lerici" ("Memory gave me all of her / That even fancy dares to claim," 26–27). But the tone of Shelley's last letter to Jane unquestionably suggests infatuation.

2. Shelley wrote to Byron: "The Williamses, with all their furniture embarked, and no place to sleep in, have taken refuge with me for the present; and they are, in my actual situation, [a reference to Claire's presence, and the recent death of her daughter Allegra] a great relief and consolation" (letter of May 3, 1822, *Letters of P.B.S.*, II, 416). According to Mary, no other house was to be found nearby, and therefore the temporary arrangement was continued (*Letters of M.W.S.*, II, 169–70).

3. That the secret was well kept is indicated by the fact that Mary did not publish complete texts of these poems until the second edition of *Poetical Works* (1840).

4. I do not present the new text of "To Edward Williams;" the holograph is transcribed literally, along with Shelley's letter to Williams, in *Letters of P.B.S.*, II, 384–86; and the text in *Works* is an edited version of the MS.

5. As Locock points out in his note (Locock, *Poems*, II, 529), Shelley imitates his own translation of Homer's "Hymn to Mercury," lxxi–lxxxiii. But in "With a Guitar" Shelley puts "perfect skill" beneath Jane's natural feeling.

Texts

Key to Critical Apparatus

1817   *History of a Six Weeks' Tour* (London, 1817)

1819   *Rosalind and Helen* (London, 1819)

*1820*ᵃ   *Prometheus Unbound* (London, 1820)

*1820*ᵇ   Leigh Hunt's copy of *Prometheus Unbound,* in the Huntington Library, San Marino, California, cat. no. 22460

1824   *Posthumous Poems* (London, 1824)

1829   *Poetical Works of Coleridge, Shelley, and Keats* (Paris, 1829)

1839   *Poetical Works,* ed. Mrs. Shelley, 4 vols. (London, 1839)

1840   *Poetical Works,* ed. Mrs. Shelley, 2nd edition (London, 1839 [1840])

1903   *An Examination of the Shelley Manuscripts in the Bodleian Library,* by C. D. Locock (Oxford, 1903)

1904   *Poetical Works,* ed. T. Hutchinson (Oxford, 1904)

*1911*ᵃ   *Note Books of Percy Bysshe Shelley,* ed. H. B. Forman (Boston, 1911)

*1911*ᵇ   *Poems,* ed. C. D. Locock (London, 1911)

1926   *Complete Works,* ed. Roger Ingpen and W. E. Peck (London, 1926–30)

1929   *Shelley Notebook in the Harvard College Library,* ed. G. E. Woodberry (Cambridge, Mass., 1929)

1934   *Verse and Prose,* ed. Sir John C. E. Shelley-Rolls and Roger Ingpen (London, 1934)

Ex.   *Examiner*

Lib.   *Liberal*

M.R.   *Military Register and Weekly Gazette*
O.H.   *Oxford University and City Herald*

CITATION OF MANUSCRIPTS

The following abbreviations are used for manuscripts frequently cited:

B = Bodleian Library
H = Harvard College Library
Hn = Huntington Library, San Marino, California

The notebooks in the Bodleian Library are either paginated or folioed; the two notebooks in the Harvard College Library are folioed; the three Huntington notebooks are folioed from front to back and back to front, with asterisks used to differentiate the two systems. In each case, reference is given to the form followed by the library. For unnumbered manuscripts, library shelf-mark alone is given. A page or folio reference followed by "rev." indicates that the page must be inverted to read the lines in question.

In the variants and expanded textual notes, holograph deletions are printed in italic type; italics in the texts proper indicate Shelley's italics. Substantive editorial additions are in square brackets; conjectural readings are preceded by a query. *Tr* refers to a transcript in a hand other than Shelley's. "M.W.S." is Mary W. Shelley.

Hymn to Intellectual Beauty

First published in the *Examiner,* January 19, 1817 (*Ex.*); reprinted with
alterations in *Rosalind and Helen* (1819).

HOLOGRAPHS:
> Bodleian MS Shelley adds e. 16, pp. 57–61; draft, lines 37–48
> omitted
> Corrections made on a clipping of the *Examiner* text, in Harvard
> MS Eng. 258.3, fols. 2–3 (*H*)

The text is based on the corrected *Examiner* text. According to M.W.S.,
"Note on Poems of 1816," "Hymn to Intellectual Beauty" was conceived
during Shelley's trip around Lake Geneva with Byron, in June, 1816;
Shelley sent it to Leigh Hunt the following October, with the pseudonym
"Elfin Knight," but allowed Hunt to print it with his name. Shelley apparently bore no responsibility for the *1819* text. He wrote in the "Advertisement" to *Rosalind and Helen:* "I do not know which of the few
scattered poems I left in England will be selected by my bookseller to
add to this collection." "Hymn to Intellectual Beauty" was one of these,
and Peacock, who revised proof for the volume, was most likely responsible for changes in punctuation (chiefly the removal of dashes)
and in form ("amongst" changed to "among," line 2; "doth" changed
to "dost," line 13; "art" changed to "are," line 44). (See Forman,
The Shelley Library, pp. 88–89.) *1904* and most modern editions are
based on the unrevised *Examiner* text; *1926* prints *1819*. The corrections in the Harvard notebook are discussed by Stuart Curran, "Shelley's
Emendations to the *Hymn to Intellectual Beauty,*" *English Language
Notes,* 7 (1970), 269–72. *B* contains several draft readings of interest,
and confirms the corrections in *H;* it is printed in full in Appendix B, I.

HYMN TO INTELLECTUAL BEAUTY

1

The awful shadow of some unseen Power
  Floats tho' unseen amongst us,—visiting
  This various world with as inconstant wing

As summer winds that creep from flower to flower.—
Like moonbeams that behind some piny mountain shower,   5
    It visits with inconstant glance
    Each human heart and countenance;
Like hues and harmonies of evening,—
    Like clouds in starlight widely spread,—
    Like memory of music fled,—   10
    Like aught that for its grace may be
Dear, and yet dearer for its mystery.

2

Spirit of BEAUTY, that doth consecrate
  With thine own hues all thou dost shine upon
  Of human thought or form,—where art thou gone?   15
Why dost thou pass away and leave our state,
This dim vast vale of tears, vacant and desolate?
    Ask why the sunlight not forever
    Weaves rainbows o'er yon mountain river,
Why aught should fail and fade that once is shewn,   20
    Why fear and dream and death and birth
    Cast on the daylight of this earth
    Such gloom,—why man has such a scope
For love and hate, despondency and hope?

3

No voice from some sublimer world hath ever   25
  To sage or poet these responses given—
  Therefore the name of God and ghosts and Heaven,

27 name of God and ghosts] names of Demon, Ghost, *Ex.*

---

27. In *H* the "s" on "names" is canceled, "Demon, Ghost" is canceled, and
"God & ghosts" inserted in the margin. The corrected line approximates the draft
reading: "names of Ghost & God & Heaven" (*B*). It may be that Shelley sent the
poem to Hunt with the line written as it appears in *B,* and that Hunt requested
him to soften the attack on religion. Shelley could have obliged with "names of
Demon, Ghost, and Heaven," but then restored the sense of the earlier reading in
his private copy. Presumably Shelley could have made changes in the poem
sometime in December, when he paid several visits to Hunt in London (*Letters
of P.B.S.,* I, 373 n.). The change is similar to those Shelley was obliged to make
in the atheistic passages of *Laon and Cythna* to conform to Ollier's suggestions

Remain the records of their vain endeavour,
Frail spells—whose uttered charm might not avail to sever,
    From all we hear and all we see,   30
    Doubt, chance, and mutability.
Thy light alone—like mist o'er mountains driven,
    Or music by the night wind sent
    Thro' strings of some still instrument,
    Or moonlight on a midnight stream,   35
Gives grace and truth to life's unquiet dream.

4

Love, Hope, and Self-esteem, like clouds depart
    And come, for some uncertain moments lent.
    Man were immortal, and omnipotent,
Didst thou, unknown and awful as thou art,   40
Keep with thy glorious train firm state within his heart.
    Thou messenger of sympathies,
    That wax and wane in lovers' eyes—
Thou—that to human thought art nourishment,
    Like darkness to a dying flame!   45
    Depart not as thy shadow came,
    Depart not—lest the grave should be,
Like life and fear, a dark reality.

5

While yet a boy I sought for ghosts, and sped
    Thro' many a listening chamber, cave and ruin,   50
    And starlight wood, with fearful steps pursuing
Hopes of high talk with the departed dead.
I called on poisonous names with which our youth is fed,
    I was not heard—I saw them not—
    When musing deeply on the lot   55
Of life, at that sweet time when winds are wooing

---

33 sent, *Ex.*   43 lovers'] lover's *Ex.*

(see *Letters of P.B.S.*, I, 433–36 and nn.). See also note to lines 41–42 of the holograph draft (lines 53–54 of *Ex.*) in Appendix B, I.
    33. There is no comma after "sent" in *B;* I follow modern editors in omitting it.

All vital things that wake to bring
News of buds and blossoming,—
Sudden, thy shadow fell on me;
I shrieked, and clasped my hands in extacy!   60

6

I vowed that I would dedicate my powers
To thee and thine—have I not kept the vow?
With beating heart and streaming eyes, even now
I call the phantoms of a thousand hours
Each from his voiceless grave: they have in visioned bowers   65
Of studious zeal or love's delight
Outwatched with me the envious night—
They know that never joy illumed my brow
Unlinked with hope that thou wouldst free
This world from its dark slavery,   70
That thou—O awful LOVELINESS,
Wouldst give whate'er these words cannot express.

7

The day becomes more solemn and serene
When noon is past—there is a harmony
In autumn, and a lustre in its sky,   75
Which thro' the summer is not heard or seen,
As if it could not be, as if it had not been!
Thus let thy power, which like the truth
Of nature on my passive youth
Descended, to my onward life supply   80
Its calm—to one who worships thee,
And every form containing thee,
Whom, SPIRIT fair, thy spells did bind
To fear himself, and love all human kind.

58 buds] birds *Ex.*   66 loves *Ex.*

---

58. *buds:* in *H* "ir" in "birds" is canceled, and "u" written in the margin. "birds" is probably a compositor's error; Shelley's "u" and "ir" are very similar. The word is unmistakably "buds" in *B*. The same error occurs in the *1820*ᵃ text of "The Cloud," line 6.

Mont Blanc

LINES WRITTEN IN THE VALE OF CHAMOUNI

First published in *History of a Six Weeks' Tour* (1817); reprinted in *Posthumous Poems* (1824), with some changes in punctuation.

HOLOGRAPHS:
> Bodleian MS Shelley adds. e.16, pp. 3–13

The text is taken from *1817*. *B* is a nearly complete draft, much-canceled; it is very likely the draft composed at the time of the journey to Mont Blanc, in July, 1816. It is possible that Shelley did not revise the poem until the following summer; no attempt was made to publish it, evidently, until the fall of 1817. *History of a Six Weeks' Tour* was begun during the summer of 1817; M.W.S. records writing out the 1814 Journal in August (*Mary Shelley's Journal,* p. 83); on September 28 she wrote to Shelley, who had left Marlow for London: "I think you took up my journal of our first travels with you if you did tell me if you have done any thing with it or if you have any prospect—if you have I will go on instantly with the letters" (*Letters of M.W.S.,* I, 35). Shelley returned to Marlow on October 10, and M.W.S. records: "write out letters from Geneva. Shelley transcribes his Poem" (*Mary Shelley's Journal,* p. 85). Although the "Poem" usually referred to prior to this entry is *Laon and Cythna,* it seems reasonable to assume, given the context and the fact that Shelley finished *Laon and Cythna* on September 23, that the "Poem" here mentioned is "Mont Blanc," and that Shelley was responsible not only for transcribing it but for seeing it through the press during the next month. For this reason I follow *1817* closely. But since the draft has never been deciphered in full and possesses distinct literary interest, I present it in Appendix B, II.

MONT BLANC
LINES WRITTEN IN THE VALE OF CHAMOUNI

I.

The everlasting universe of things
Flows through the mind, and rolls its rapid waves,
Now dark—now glittering—now reflecting gloom—
Now lending splendour, where from secret springs
The source of human thought its tribute brings   5
Of waters,—with a sound but half its own,
Such as a feeble brook will oft assume
In the wild woods, among the mountains lone,
Where waterfalls around it leap forever,
Where woods and winds contend, and a vast river   10
Over its rocks ceaselessly bursts and raves.

II.

Thus thou, Ravine of Arve—dark, deep Ravine—
Thou many-coloured, many-voiced vale,
Over whose pines, and crags, and caverns sail
Fast cloud shadows and sunbeams: awful scene,   15
Where Power in likeness of the Arve comes down
From the ice gulphs that gird his secret throne,
Bursting through these dark mountains like the flame
Of lightning thro' the tempest;—thou dost lie,
Thy giant brood of pines around thee clinging,   20
Children of elder time, in whose devotion
The chainless winds still come and ever came
To drink their odours, and their mighty swinging
To hear—an old and solemn harmony;
Thine earthly rainbows stretched across the sweep   25
Of the ethereal waterfall, whose veil
Robes some unsculptured image; the strange sleep
Which when the voices of the desart fail
Wraps all in its own deep eternity;—
Thy caverns echoing to the Arve's commotion,   30
A loud, lone sound no other sound can tame;
Thou art pervaded with that ceaseless motion,

Thou art the path of that unresting sound—
Dizzy Ravine! and when I gaze on thee
I seem as in a trance sublime and strange   35
To muse on my own separate phantasy,
My own, my human mind, which passively
Now renders and receives fast influencings,
Holding an unremitting interchange
With the clear universe of things around;   40
One legion of wild thoughts, whose wandering wings
Now float above thy darkness, and now rest
Where that or thou art no unbidden guest,
In the still cave of the witch Poesy,
Seeking among the shadows that pass by,   45
Ghosts of all things that are, some shade of thee,
Some phantom, some faint image; till the breast
From which they fled recalls them, thou art there!

III.

Some say that gleams of a remoter world
Visit the soul in sleep,—that death is slumber,   50
And that its shapes the busy thoughts outnumber
Of those who wake and live.—I look on high;
Has some unknown omnipotence unfurled
The veil of life and death? or do I lie
In dream, and does the mightier world of sleep   55
Spread far around and inaccessibly
Its circles? For the very spirit fails,
Driven like a homeless cloud from steep to steep
That vanishes among the viewless gales!
Far, far above, piercing the infinite sky,   60
Mont Blanc appears,—still, snowy, and serene—
Its subject mountains their unearthly forms
Pile around it, ice and rock; broad vales between
Of frozen floods, unfathomable deeps,
Blue as the overhanging heaven, that spread   65
And wind among the accumulated steeps;
A desart peopled by the storms alone,

45 pass by *1817;* pass by, *1829*

Save when the eagle brings some hunter's bone,
And the wolf tracts her there—how hideously
Its shapes are heaped around! rude, bare, and high,   70
Ghastly, and scarred, and riven.—Is this the scene
Where the old Earthquake-dæmon taught her young
Ruin? Were these their toys? or did a sea
Of fire envelope once this silent snow?
None can reply—all seems eternal now.   75
The wilderness has a mysterious tongue
Which teaches awful doubt, or faith so mild,
So solemn, so serene, that man may be
But for such faith with nature reconciled;
Thou hast a voice, great Mountain, to repeal   80
Large codes of fraud and woe; not understood
By all, but which the wise, and great, and good
Interpret, or make felt, or deeply feel.

IV.

The fields, the lakes, the forests, and the streams,
Ocean, and all the living things that dwell   85
Within the dædal earth; lightning, and rain,
Earthquake, and fiery flood, and hurricane,
The torpor of the year when feeble dreams
Visit the hidden buds, or dreamless sleep
Holds every future leaf and flower;—the bound   90
With which from that detested trance they leap;

69 tracts] tracks *1829, 1839*   74 fire, *1817;* fire *1824*

---

69. *B* reads "And the wolf watches her;" the last two words could be read as
"tracts her there." It may be that Shelley did, in fact, misread his first draft, and
changed the preceding line to conform, changing "where" (*B*) to "when" (*1817*).
M.W.S. retains "tracts" in *1824*, but substitutes the more familiar "tracks" in
1839 ("tracks," in *1829*, along with some punctuation changes, may have been
her suggestion as well). "Tracts," though obsolete now and probably in Shelley's
time as well, is used by Spenser in the sense of "traces" or "tracks" in a similar
context (*The Faerie Queene*, II, i, 12); I therefore retain it. Shelley probably
means "trace" rather than "track," insofar as "tracks" suggests "following the
physical tracks of."
74. *sea of fire:* I follow *1824* in omitting commas after "fire" (line 74), "birds"
(line 115), "man" (line 118); these are conceivably editorial emendations, and
uncharacteristic of Shelley's usual punctuation (as of modern punctuation). The
draft agrees with *1824* punctuation.

The works and ways of man, their death and birth,
And that of him and all that his may be;
All things that move and breathe with toil and sound
Are born and die; revolve, subside and swell.   95
Power dwells apart in its tranquillity
Remote, serene, and inaccessible:
And *this,* the naked countenance of earth,
On which I gaze, even these primæval mountains
Teach the adverting mind. The glaciers creep   100
Like snakes that watch their prey, from their far fountains,
Slow rolling on; there, many a precipice,
Frost and the Sun in scorn of mortal power
Have piled: dome, pyramid, and pinnacle,
A city of death, distinct with many a tower   105
And wall impregnable of beaming ice.
Yet not a city, but a flood of ruin
Is there, that from the boundaries of the sky
Rolls its perpetual stream; vast pines are strewing
Its destined path, or in the mangled soil   110
Branchless and shattered stand; the rocks, drawn down
From yon remotest waste, have overthrown
The limits of the dead and living world,
Never to be reclaimed. The dwelling-place
Of insects, beasts, and birds becomes its spoil;   115
Their food and their retreat forever gone,
So much of life and joy is lost. The race
Of man flies far in dread; his work and dwelling
Vanish, like smoke before the tempest's stream,
And their place is not known. Below, vast caves   120
Shine in the rushing torrents' restless gleam,
Which from those secret chasms in tumult welling
Meet in the vale, and one majestic River,

115 birds, *1817;* birds *1824*   118 man, *1817;* man *1824*
121 torrent's *1817, 1824, 1839;* torrents' *1829*

---

121. "torrents'," as the subject of "Meet," line 123, must be plural; modern
editions make this correction.

The breath and blood of distant lands, forever
Rolls its loud waters to the ocean waves,   125
Breathes its swift vapours to the circling air.

V.

Mont Blanc yet gleams on high:—the power is there,
The still and solemn power of many sights,
And many sounds, and much of life and death.
In the calm darkness of the moonless nights,   130
In the lone glare of day, the snows descend
Upon that Mountain; none beholds them there,
Nor when the flakes burn in the sinking sun,
Or the star-beams dart through them:—Winds contend
Silently there, and heap the snow with breath   135
Rapid and strong, but silently! Its home
The voiceless lightning in these solitudes
Keeps innocently, and like vapour broods
Over the snow. The secret strength of things
Which governs thought, and to the infinite dome   140
Of heaven is as a law, inhabits thee!
And what were thou, and earth, and stars, and sea,
If to the human mind's imaginings
Silence and solitude were vacancy?

To Constantia

First published in the *Oxford University and City Herald,* January 31, 1818 (*O.H.*), signed "Pleyel." A draft version was published in *Posthumous Poems* (1824), entitled "To Constantia, Singing."

HOLOGRAPHS:

  Bodleian MS Shelley e. 4, fols. 36v rev.–34 rev.; draft
  Harvard MS Eng. 258.3, fols. 43 rev.–42v rev.; fair copy

The text is based on *O.H.,* with some capitalization and orthography taken from *H. H* appears to be drawn directly from *B,* and probably served in turn as the text for the copy sent to the *Herald.* Claire Clairmont mentions copying part of the poem, in her journal for January 19 (*Journals of Claire Clairmont,* p. 79), and either Claire or the editor may have been responsible for some changes in accidentals. *O.H.,* which was unknown to Shelley's editors, is reproduced in my "Shelley's 'To Constantia,' A Contemporary Printing Examined," *TLS* (February 6, 1969), 140. *1824* is based on a transcript of *B* by M.W.S. in Bodleian MS Shelley adds. d. 7, pp. 38–40; *B* was transcribed again, and some errors corrected, in *1903,* pp. 60–63. The *1903* text is adopted in *1904* and other modern editions; *H* is the basis of *1926.* Both *1824* and *1903* misinterpret the order of stanzas in *B,* which is in fact the same as the order in *H;* Shelley ran out of clean pages and was thus obliged to write the third stanza on the verso of the folio preceding the first stanza, and the fourth stanza on the recto of the same folio.

---

title: "To Constantia" in *O.H.* and *H;* untitled in *B.* M.W.S. entitled the poem "To Constantia, Singing" in *1824,* probably to avoid confusion with the short lyric "To Constantia" ("The rose that drinks the fountain dew"). "Constantia" is the intellectual, musically gifted heroine of Charles Brockden Brown's *Ormond;* "Pleyel," Shelley's pseudonym in *O.H.,* is the rationalist friend and lover of Clara Wieland in Brown's *Wieland.*

TO CONSTANTIA

Thy voice, slow rising like a Spirit, lingers
O'ershadowing me with soft and lulling wings;
The blood and life within thy snowy fingers
Teach witchcraft to the instrumental strings.
   My brain is wild, my breath comes quick,   5
   The blood is listening in my frame,
   And thronging shadows fast and thick
   Fall on my overflowing eyes,
   My heart is quivering like a flame;
As morning dew, that in the sunbeam dies,   10
I am dissolved in these consuming extacies.

I have no life, Constantia, but in thee;
Whilst, like the world-surrounding air, thy song
Flows on, and fills all things with melody:
Now is thy voice a tempest, swift and strong,   15
   On which, as one in trance upborne,
   Secure o'er woods and waves I sweep
   Rejoicing, like a cloud of morn:
   Now 'tis the breath of summer's night
   Which, where the starry waters sleep   20
Round western isles with incense blossoms bright,
Lingering, suspends my soul in its voluptuous flight.

A deep and breathless awe, like the swift change
Of dreams unseen, but felt in youthful slumbers;

1 Her voice is hovering oer my soul—it lingers *B* 2 *Upon the heart
like loves oershadowing wings B* me] it *B, H* 3 The *eloquent blood
B* thy] those *B* 8 *Wrap me in trance divine Steep my faint
eyes in darkness deep B* 11 *Body & soul dissolves in liquid extacies
B* 12 *I am not body or soul or ought but thee B* but in thee]
now but thee *B* 16 as] like *B* trance, upborne *H* 17 *I tread
nor earth nor sea Secure oer seas & hills I pass B* woods] rocks *B,
H* 20 starry] *purple B* 21 *Around the western odorous isles B*

Wild, sweet, yet incommunicably strange,   25
Thou breathest now, in fast ascending numbers:
    The cope of Heaven seems rent and cloven
    By the inchantment of thy strain,
    And o'er my shoulders wings are woven
    To follow its sublime career,   30
    Beyond the mighty moons that wane
Upon the verge of Nature's utmost sphere,
Till the world's shadowy walls are past, and disappear.

Cease, cease—for such wild lessons madmen learn:
Long thus to sink,—thus to be lost and die   35
Perhaps is death indeed—Constantia turn!
Yes! in thine eyes a power like light doth lie,
    Even tho' the sounds its voice that were
    Between thy lips are laid to sleep—
    Within thy breath and on thy hair   40
    Like odour it is lingering yet—
    And from thy touch like fire doth leap:
Even while I write my burning cheeks are wet—
Such things the heart can feel and learn, but not forget!

34 Cease cease *for of such things do maniacs tell   for thus tis said that madmen feel B*   36 Perhaps is] Perchance were *B*   37 In thy dark eyes *the* a power *is lingering yet B*   38 its voice that were] *which were its voice B*   39 Slumber *within those trembling lips B*
44 Alas, that the torn heart can bleed but not forget. *B*

---

44. *Such things the heart can feel and learn, but not forget!* The line is omitted in *H*. *B* seems more characteristic than the faintly platitudinous conclusion of *O.H.* Shelley may have first omitted, then changed the line to avoid the hint of a romantic attachment in the "torn heart" of *B,* or, alternately, to avoid the suggestion that the singer's power comes from her torn and bleeding heart—a possible reference to Byron's desertion of Claire, and her subsequent misery.
    Additional lines, possibly a first draft for the opening stanza:

My spirit like a charmed *boat* bark doth *float* swim
Upon the *lulling* liquid waves of thy sweet singing
I feel Far far away *amid* into the regions dim
As   Even as Of rapture, as a *rapid* boat with swift sails winging
Its way adown some many winding river
Speeds thro dark forests oer the waters swinging   *B*

Stanzas written in Dejection—
DECEMBER 1818, NEAR NAPLES

First published in *Posthumous Poems* (1824).

HOLOGRAPHS:
> Bodleian MS Shelley adds. e. 11, pp. 73 rev.–67 rev.; draft (B^1)
> ———— e. 5, pp. 7–9; fair copy (B^2)
> Pierpont Morgan MA 406; fair copy (*PM*)

The text is based on B^2, with some punctuation from *PM* and pointing added at the ends of lines. *1824* appears to be drawn from B^2, with some punctuation changes; line 5 is omitted but restored in the errata sheet, and "might," line 4, reads "light" (a slip probably caused by the dropped line). *PM* consists of pages 72–74 torn from Harvard MS Eng. 258.2. Apart from the title, there is only one substantive difference between *PM* and B^2, "stainless" (B^2) for "cloudless" (*PM*), line 44. The draft reading, in B^1, is "cloudless," which suggests that *PM* is earlier than B^2; one other draft reading occurs in *PM*, is there revised, and the revision retained in B^2 ("dead" changed to "cold," line 37). Both *PM* and B^2 are beautifully written out, though B^2 is more fully punctuated.

STANZAS WRITTEN IN DEJECTION—
DECEMBER 1818, NEAR NAPLES

> The Sun is warm, the sky is clear,
> The waves are dancing fast and bright,
> Blue isles and snowy mountains wear
> The purple noon's transparent might,

1 the sky is *bright* clear the sun is warm B^1 2 dancing] leaping bright & fast B^1 4 The purple *atmosphere of light* B^1

---

title: "Naples—December 1818 *Written in a fit of low spirits*" in *PM*.

The breath of the moist earth is light   5
Around its unexpanded buds;
Like many a voice of one delight
The winds, the birds, the Ocean-floods;
    The City's voice itself is soft like Solitude's.

I see the Deep's untrampled floor   10
With green and purple seaweeds strown,
I see the waves upon the shore
Like light dissolved in star-showers, thrown;
I sit upon the sands alone;
The lightning of the noontide Ocean   15
Is flashing round me, and a tone
Arises from its measured motion,
    How sweet! did any heart now share in my emotion.

Alas, I have nor hope nor health
Nor peace within nor calm around,   20
Nor that content surpassing wealth

5 The *Earths moist breath is fresh & light   fragrant B¹*   9 like] as *B¹*
10 *You see the Oceans purple B¹*   12 *You hear* the waves *leap to B¹*
19–20 Alas that I were not alone / *For I have neither B¹*   21 content] within *B¹*

19–27. This stanza precedes Stanza 2 in *B¹*. It is followed by what appears to
be a first draft for a third stanza:

And who feels discord now or sorrow
Or contempt: love is God to day
And these ?dark slaves of dim tomorrow
Follow the path where far away
It stalks
Track that great shade which far away
Beckons, betrayed & to betray
Love

rewritten as:

And who feels discord now or Sorrow
Love is the universe today
These are the slaves of dim tomorrow
Which on lifes labyrinthine way
Beckons betrayed & to betray

And round that cheek once pressed to pain
Health hangs like a fresh atmosphere   *B¹*

The last two lines appear to be still another beginning for a third stanza of *B¹*.

The sage in meditation found,
And walked with inward glory crowned;
Nor fame nor power nor love nor leisure—
Others I see whom these surround,   25
Smiling they live and call life pleasure:
To me that cup has been dealt in another measure.

Yet now despair itself is mild,
Even as the winds and waters are;
I could lie down like a tired child   30
And weep away the life of care
Which I have borne and yet must bear,
Till Death like Sleep might steal on me,
And I might feel in the warm air
My cheek grow cold, and hear the sea   35
Breathe o'er my dying brain its last monotony.

Some might lament that I were cold,
As I, when this sweet day is gone,
Which my lost heart, too soon grown old,
Insults with this untimely moan—   40
They might lament,—for I am one
Whom men love not, and yet regret;
Unlike this Day, which, when the Sun
Shall on its stainless glory set,
Will linger though enjoyed, like joy in Memory yet.   45

23 *Who lived alone & called it pleasure B*¹   24 fame, *B*²   27 in]
with *B*¹   34 might] should *B*¹   35 cold] *pale B*¹   36 Breathe
oer my failing brain its last sound murmuringly *B*¹   37 cold] dead
*B*¹   41 might] may *B*¹   44 stainless] cloudless *B*¹; *PM*

Ode to the West Wind

First published in *Prometheus Unbound* (1820)

HOLOGRAPHS:

Huntington HM 2176, fols. *4r–*6v; draft of Stanzas I–III
Bodleian MS Shelley adds. e. 12, pp. 63–65; revised copy of
Stanzas I–III (B^1)
———— adds. e. 12, p. 155; draft of Stanza IV (B^2)
———— adds. e. 6, pp. 138 rev.–137 rev.; draft of Stanza IV
and lines 66–70 of Stanza V (B^3)

The text is taken from *1820*ᵃ. B^1 is headed "Octr 25," and the stanzas
marked "1," "2," and "3;" it appears to be a copy, with numerous revisions, of the draft of the three stanzas in *Hn*. B^1 includes all the readings in *1820*ᵃ, but in some instances it is not clear which of two versions
is canceled. Both drafts of Stanza IV differ considerably from *1820*ᵃ;
Stanza V is incomplete in the draft. It is clear that copy for *1820*ᵃ must
have been transcribed from an intermediate text, now lost. Punctuation
in *1820*ᵃ, as in all the *1820*ᵃ texts, probably includes some normalization
of the text Shelley sent Ollier; dashes would have been removed, and
probably the whole is more heavily punctuated than the original. But
since the drafts are incomplete and Shelley's punctuation too unsystematic to reconstruct from the holograph hints, I hesitate to emend the
punctuation of *1820*ᵃ. I have, however, restored holograph spelling and
capitalization where it conforms to Shelley's usual practice, particularly
when two drafts agree. Most variants and deletions from *Hn* are cited
from *1911*ᵃ, I, 163–70; the pencil is barely decipherable in microfilm,
though I have checked *1911*ᵃ where possible. I have not been able to
examine the original notebook. B^2 and B^3 are transcribed, with some
errors, in *1934,* pp. 57–58 and 148–49, and one page of B^3 is reproduced
in facsimile facing page 56.

ODE TO THE WEST WIND

I.

O, wild West Wind, thou breath of Autumn's being,
Thou, from whose unseen presence the leaves dead
Are driven, like ghosts from an enchanter fleeing,

Yellow, and black, and pale, and hectic red,
Pestilence-stricken multitudes: O, Thou,   5
Who chariotest to their dark wintry bed

The winged seeds, where they lie cold and low,
Each like a corpse within its grave, until
Thine azure sister of the Spring shall blow

Her clarion o'er the dreaming earth, and fill   10
(Driving sweet buds like flocks to feed in air)
With living hues and odours plain and hill:

Wild Spirit, which art moving everywhere;
Destroyer and Preserver; hear, O, hear!

---

2 *Thou which didst whose swift steps Hn*   3 *Gather & Hn*
4 *Pestilence-stricken nation Hn*   5 *Like famine-stricken multi-*
tudes thou whom Hn   8 Like a dead body in a grave, until *Hn*
11–12 With radiant ?blooms & living leaves / The atmosphere investing
plain & hill *Hn*   13 Wild] O *Hn*

"This poem was conceived and chiefly written in a wood that skirts the Arno,
near Florence, and on a day when that tempestuous wind, whose temperature is
at once mild and animating, was collecting the vapours which pour down the
autumnal rains. They began, as I foresaw, at sunset with a violent tempest of
hail and rain, attended by that magnificent thunder and lightning peculiar to the
Cisalpine regions.
"The phenomenon alluded to at the conclusion of the third stanza is well
known to naturalists. The vegetation at the bottom of the sea, of rivers, and of
lakes, sympathizes with that of the land in the change of seasons, and is con-
sequently influenced by the winds which announce it.—" Shelley's Note, *1820*ᵃ.
11–12. first drafts:

The depth of vacant depth of the inodorous atmosphere
   and all circling air
Cradling in hues & odours
In With softest hues investing plain & hill
In the ?low vacant space of atmosphere   Hn

II.

Thou on whose stream, 'mid the steep sky's commotion,   15
Loose clouds like Earth's decaying leaves are shed,
Shook from the tangled boughs of Heaven and Ocean,

Angels of rain and lightning: there are spread
On the blue surface of thine aery surge,
Like the bright hair uplifted from the head   20

Of some fierce Mænad, even from the dim verge
Of the horizon to the zenith's height,
The locks of the approaching storm. Thou Dirge

Of the dying year, to which this closing night
Will be the dome of a vast sepulchre,   25
Vaulted with all thy congregated might

Of vapours, from whose solid atmosphere
Black rain, and fire, and hail will burst: O, hear!

III.

Thou who didst waken from his summer dreams
The blue Mediterranean, where he lay,   30
Lulled by the coil of his chrystalline streams,

Beside a pumice isle in Baiæ's bay,
And saw in sleep old palaces and towers
Quivering within the wave's intenser day,

15 Thou, upon whom in *Hn; up*on whose *path* stream *B*¹   16 like
the decaying leaves *Hn*   18 Those angels of strong lightning *Hn*
19 aery] aerial *Hn*   20 bright hair] loose locks *Hn*   27 Of clouds
from which lightning *Hn*   28 Floods of black rain are poured hear
O hear *Hn*   29 who hast wakened *Hn*   31 chrystal streams *Hn*
33 old] *dim B*¹   34 *Steeped in the azure waves diviner day* Quiver
within *Hn*

---

18. "thunder" is written above "lightning" in B¹; "is" is written above *"are,"*
to agree with first version of lines 20 and 23, in *B*¹.
22. "height" in *1820*ᵃ, "height," in *B*¹.
23. *"locks"* is written above *"hair"* in *B*¹.

All overgrown with azure moss and flowers   35
So sweet, the sense faints picturing them! Thou
For whose path the Atlantic's level powers

Cleave themselves into chasms, while far below
The sea-blooms and the oozy woods which wear
The sapless foliage of the ocean, know   40

Thy voice, and suddenly grow grey with fear,
And tremble and despoil themselves: O, hear!

IV.

If I were a dead leaf thou mightest bear;
If I were a swift cloud to fly with thee;
A wave to pant beneath thy power, and share   45

The impulse of thy strength, only less free
Than thou, O, Uncontroulable! If even
I were as in my boyhood, and could be

The comrade of thy wanderings over Heaven,
As then, when to outstrip thy skiey speed   50
Scarce seemed a vision; I would ne'er have striven

36 So sweet the sense dies but to imagine *Hn*   43 *And* if I were *B*³
48 I were, *when thou as when my Spirit B*³

48–52. drafts:

> Thy *spirit* had found no early grave in me
> *Which rode with thine in visions* Heaven
> ?As ?And with the splendour of its shadow, wrapt
> The naked world of life, where it had striven
> Whence it escaped victoriously! o now   *B*²

50–52. drafts:

> When to outstrip thee in thy skiey speed
> Scarce seemed a *visionary   dream* vision
>   *then should I not have striven   my soul would not have striven*
>   I should neer have striven
> *Against the load of life,   I should not need*
> In prayer with thy strong Spirit in my need—   *B*³

Additional lines:

> The gentleness of rain is in the Wind
> But all the earth and all the leaves are dry   *Hn*

As thus with thee in prayer in my sore need.
Oh! lift me as a wave, a leaf, a cloud!
I fall upon the thorns of life! I bleed!

A heavy weight of hours has chained and bowed   55
One too like thee: tameless, and swift, and proud.

V.

Make me thy lyre, even as the forest is:
What if my leaves are falling like its own!
The tumult of thy mighty harmonies

Will take from both a deep, autumnal tone,   60
Sweet though in sadness. Be thou, Spirit fierce,
My spirit! Be thou me, impetuous one!

Drive my dead thoughts over the universe
Like withered leaves to quicken a new birth!
And, by the incantation of this verse,   65

Scatter, as from an unextinguished hearth
Ashes and sparks, my words among mankind!
Be through my lips to unawakened Earth

The trumpet of a prophecy! O, Wind,
If Winter comes, can Spring be far behind?   70

---

53 *But* Oh lift me like B^3 56 One too like thee, yet mortal—swift &
proud B^3 66 *Like* Those ashes from an unextinguished hearth B^3
67 *Scatter them* Mingled with sparks; scatter among mankind B^3
68 *Be thy   Be thou in me,* to the *frozen* B^3 70 When Winter comes
Spring lags not far behind B^3

Ode to Liberty

First published in *Prometheus Unbound* (1820)

HOLOGRAPHS:

Bodleian MS Shelley adds. e. 6, pp. 147–42, 135–118, 108–98, all rev.; draft (B^1)

———— adds. c. 4, fols. 84–91; translation into Italian of Stanzas I–XIII and XIX (B^2)

"Ode to Liberty" was sent directly to Peacock for inclusion in *Prometheus Unbound,* with instructions to substitute asterisks, if necessary, for the objectionable expressions in Stanzas XV and XVI, i.e. "Kings" and "Priests" (Letter of July 12, 1820, *Letters of P.B.S.,* II, 213–14). A transcript of lines 1–21 by M.W.S. is in Harvard MS Eng. 258.2, fol. 19v. M.W.S. may have transcribed the copy sent to Peacock, but it is very unlikely that she transcribed the text directly from the draft, which is nearly indecipherable in many places. The numerous changes in the text, as well, suggest that there must have been an intermediate text by Shelley, now lost. The *1820*ᵃ text must therefore serve as copy text, despite some likely errors and normalization of punctuation and spelling. Three corrections are marked in *1820*ᵇ; these are also adopted in *1829* and *1839,* but not consistently in modern editions. The *1820*ᵇ corrections probably do not have independent authority; the inscription on the title page of the volume ("Percy Shelley———to———Leigh Hunt") seems to be in Hunt's hand, and the corrections were probably made by him from the same source used by M.W.S. for *1829* and *1839*. These corrections (in lines 50–51, 249, and 250) are in any case supported by the draft. Shelley's Italian version appears to be a very literal translation of his finished text; I have therefore used it to check possible errors in *1820*ᵃ, notably in lines 80, 116, and 194. The Harvard transcript is reproduced in *1929;* one stanza of B^2 is transcribed in Rogers, *Shelley at Work,* p. 343. *1820*ᵃ is followed in *1926,* which also includes notes to *Tr.* Because of the length of the poem and the necessity of using *1820*ᵃ as copy text, I do not present a complete text but offer instead the following selective list of holograph variants and canceled readings from B^1. Suggested emendations to the *1820*ᵃ text are marked with an asterisk.

206

1. "vibrated" in *1820*ᵃ; *"lifted once again"* in *B*¹.
4. "fire" is written above "flame" in *B*¹, neither canceled.
6. "rapid" in *1820*ᵃ; "radiant" in *B*¹.
7. "Clothed" in *1820*ᵃ; "Arrayed" in *B*¹.
8. "young" in *1820*ᵃ; "bright" in *B*¹.
8–9. "My spirit sprung / Out of the ragged cave of its dismay" in *B*¹.
10–15. first draft:

And then the whirlwind of the Spirit came
    And rapt it like a *vapour* Comet   *cloud   far away*
Beyond the remotest sphere of living flame
    And night & day & time & space, like one
Breathless & blind with speed, 'till there was flung
A ? of harmony   *B*¹

26–27. "And they devoured each other / With mutual war" in *B*¹.
28–29. "Wounding the bosom of their groaning nurse / Beasts war-red on beasts" in *B*¹.
33. "Like worms upon a corpse by the wayside" in *B*¹.
*41. "slaves" in *1820*ᵃ; "slaves;" in *1829, 1839;* an error corrected in all modern editions.
49. "favouring" in *1820*ᵃ; "favourable" in *B*¹.
*50–51. The text should read: "Prophetic echoes flung dim melody / On the unapprehensive wild." *1820*ᵃ has a period after "melody"; no punctuation after "wild." In *1820*ᵇ, the period after "melody" is canceled and a period inserted after "wild"; this correction is made in *1829* and *1839*. *1820*ᵃ is obviously in error, but of modern editions only *1911*ᵇ follows *1839*. *B*¹ reads: "Prophetic echoes flung dim melody / On the unapprehensive wild—."
57. first drafts: *"Those forms of marble   shadows of eternal grace living shapes"* *B*¹.
60. *"lidless"* is canceled, "lynx-like" uncanceled in *B*¹.
70. "Rose oer the Aegean" in *B*¹.
74. "that *sacred* hill" in *B*¹.
79. "cannot pass away" in *1820*ᵃ; "cannot" is written above "never fades" in *B*¹, neither canceled. *B*² reads: "ma mai non puo svanire"—literally, "but can never vanish."
*80. The text should read: "The voices of its bards and sages thunder." *B*¹ reads "its bards;" "thy bards" in *1820*ᵃ. The reference is to "that hill," line 74, whose image lies in Time's fleeting river, and cannot pass away, largely because of the renewed power of "the voices of its bards and sages." The line may have been changed to accord with

line 90: "As Athens doth the world with thy delight renew;" "thy" refers here to Liberty, who is being addressed throughout. But this seems more likely a transcriber's or editor's change than an authorial revision. B^2 confirms the reading of B^1: "Le voci dei suoi poeti e savi" ("The voices of its poets and sages").

81. "earth-awakening" is written above "spirit thrilling" in B^1, neither canceled.

84. "Winged sound of joy" is written above "music of delight" in B^1, neither canceled.

85. "Which spreads its wings where Fancy never flew" in B^1.

89. "life and love" in 1820^a; "love & life" in B^1.

99–100. "But when upon thy feet of vestal whiteness / Tears of blood fell—& gold prophaned thy throne" in B^1.

110. "desert rocks" in 1820^a; "hollow rocks" in B^1. B^2 reads "i solinghi rupi" ("solitary rocks"), which indicates that the meaning of "desert" in 1820^a is "deserted"—as the context also suggests.

*113. Text should read: "Of that sublimest lore;" "love" in 1820^a, "lore" in *1829, 1839,* and B^1, and in all modern editions. B^2 reads: "Di quel sublima dottrina."

114. *"Scythian* wizard" in B^1.

115. "Druid's steep" in B^1; "Druid's sleep" in 1820^a. "sleep" seems like a possible error for "steep;" but B^2 reads "il sonno del Druido" ("Druid's sleep"). Evidently the change was authorial, possibly suggested by the "Scald's dreams" in the same line.

*116. Text should read: "What if the tears rained through thy scattered locks." 1820^a reads "shattered locks;" B^1 reads "streaming" and "scattered" in separate drafts; "scattered" is deleted, but Shelley may have used it for his final text. If so, "shattered" would be a likely transcriber's or printer's error. B^2 reads: "tuoi capelli diradati"—literally, "thinned-out" or "outspread" hair, which seems close enough to "scattered" to support the case for emendation.

118–120. first drafts:

> When from its Jewish den, to kill & burn
> The Galilean serpent crept—

> When Faith did creep
> A hooded *worm to poison & to burn* snake whose breath is poison
> From Sion's bloody cave—like slaughtered sheep
> The Nations lay, *in blood* an indistinguishable heap B^1

123–24. first draft: *"Through the dissolving smoke of blood below* / On Dantes cradle" B^1

127. "tempestuous" in *1820*ᵃ; *"stormy* raging   tumultuous" in *B*¹.

160. "Of its own glorious light" in *1820*ᵃ; "Of his" in *B*¹.

184. "in sunder" in *1820*ᵃ; "asunder" in *B*¹. But "in sunder," though unusual, is precise, i.e., "cloven into parts" rather than "cloven apart."

*194–95. "impress us from a seal, / All ye have thought and done!" in *1820*ᵃ; "impress upon a seal," in *B*¹. The MS suggests that it would have been possible to derive the *1820*ᵃ reading from Shelley's hand, even in a fair copy. *1820*ᵃ may then be a transcriber's error; several editors have struggled with the resulting crux. *B*² reads: "sigillate la [no accent] / Tutto ciò che voi avete pensato e fatto." The meaning would seem to be: "seal there" (i.e. upon the "eternal years" enthroned in the West) "All ye have thought and done!" In both *B*¹ and *B*² the object of "impress" or "seal" is "All ye have thought and done!" not "us." I would emend *1820*ᵃ to read: "impress upon a seal."

*212, 228. "King" and "Priest," in *B*¹ and all modern editions, are omitted in *1820*ᵃ and replaced by asterisks, as authorized by Shelley.

*249. Text should read: "Or what if Art." *1820*ᵃ reads: "O, what if Art." "O" is canceled, and "Or" inserted marginally in *1820*ᵇ. *1829* and *1839* read "Or;" *1904* follows *1839*. *B*¹ reads: "And what if Art."

*250. Text should read: "Diving on fiery wings." *1820*ᵃ reads "Driving." "r" is canceled in *1820*ᵇ; *1829, 1839,* and *B*¹ read "Diving." An error corrected in *1926* but not in *1904*.

253. "If Life can breed" in *1820*ᵃ; "must breed" in *B*¹.

270. "Wept tears, and blood like tears?" in *1820;* "Wept blood, & tears like blood" in *B*¹. The stanza is missing from *B*².

Ode to Naples

First published in the *Military Register and Weekly Gazette . . . for the Army, Navy, Colonies and Fashionable World,* October 1 and 8, 1820 (*M.R.*), signed "P.B.S." Another version was published in *Posthumous Poems* (1824).

HOLOGRAPHS:

>Bodleian MS Shelley adds. e. 8, pp. 4–11; a draft mainly of lines 1–51, 127–76 (B^1)
>——— d. 1, fols. 10–14; fair copy (B^2)
>——— adds. c. 4, fols. 93–95v; fair copy, beginning at line 52 (B^3)

The text of the "Introduction" is taken from B^2; the text of the "Ode" proper is taken from B^3. Punctuation missing from the holographs is adapted from *M.R.* and *1824*. "Ode to Naples" was written on or about August 24, 1820, according to M.W.S. (*Mary Shelley's Journal*, p. 137); Claire Clairmont quotes lines 87–88 in her journal entry for September 2 (*Journals of Claire Clairmont*, p. 173), and H. B. Forman notes the existence of a copy in Claire's hand with corrections by Shelley (*Athenaeum* 4043, 22 April 1905, 497–98), present location unknown. The *M.R.* publication was unknown to Shelley's editors until White recorded it (White, II, 223); it has not, to my knowledge, been previously collated. Shelley seems not to have known that the poem was published in *M.R.* in October, for he sent it to Ollier the following February, for publication "according to your own discretion" (*Letters of P.B.S.*, II, 262). B^2 is a complete fair copy, with numerous revisions that appear to have been made after the copy was fully written out. In its original form it may well have served as the basis for the copy printed in the *Register* (the four *M.R.* variants that do not appear in the unrevised version of B^2, in lines 42, 62, 150, and 162, can be attributed plausibly to transcriber or printer). The revisions made in B^2 affect lines 55, 66–72, 79, 82, 85, 86, 122–23, 134, 135; they are incorporated (with some further changes) in B^3 and *1824*. B^3 is a fair copy, with a few corrections, headed "Ode to Naples" and written out on separate

210

sheets, as if for printer's copy; it appears to represent Shelley's last revisions. The introductory "Epodes" are omitted, as are all stanza headings, and the text includes eleven new readings, in lines 61, 72, 89, 137, 151, 156, 162, 167, 172, 174, and 175. The *1824* text appears to follow the revised version of B^2 closely in its punctuation and form but agrees in several readings with B^3 (i.e., in lines 66–71, 102, 134, 135, 143); it contains no independent readings apart from four apparent errors or editorial emendations, in lines 7, 25, 42, and 45. It would appear to be based, then, on (1) an eclectic text made by M.W.S. from the two holographs in her possession; or (2) a text intermediate between B^2 and B^3, containing revisions subsequently incorporated in B^3. If (2), then the source may have been the MS Shelley sent Ollier in February, 1821, which Ollier may have returned along with the other unpublished texts in his possession, for the preparation of *Posthumous Poems*. One page of a transcript in Mary's hand survives, and corresponds closely to the *1824* text; this may have formed part of an intermediate text. Given the political nature of the poem, and Shelley's evident desire to get it into print, it may be that B^3 represents an alternative text, rather than a definitive final version. In view of the large number of "good" texts, both printed versions and holographs, I have adopted the following compromise: to print the introductory Epodes as an "Introduction," using B^2 as copy text; and to use B^3 as copy text for the "Ode to Naples" proper, with continuous line-numbering. B^2 is described in *1903*, pp. 14–18, and the *1903* readings are adopted by subsequent editors; B^3 has not been previously collated.

INTRODUCTION TO ODE TO NAPLES

I stood within the City* disinterred,
    And heard the autumnal leaves like light footfalls
Of spirits passing through the streets, and heard
    The Mountain's slumberous voice at intervals
        Thrill through those roofless halls: 5
The oracular thunder penetrating shook
    The listening soul in the suspended blood—
I felt that Earth out of her deep heart spoke—
    I felt, but heard not—through white columns glowed
        The isle-sustaining Ocean-flood,   10
A plane of light between two Heavens of azure!
    Around me gleamed many a bright sepulchre,
Of whose pure beauty, Time, as if his pleasure
    Were to spare Death, had never made erasure;
        But every living lineament was clear   15

7 the suspended blood] my suspended blood *1824*   11 plane] line *B*¹

Introductory Note: "The Author has connected many recollections of his visit to Pompeii and Baiæ with the enthusiasm excited by the intelligence of the proclamation of a Constitutional Government at Naples. This has given a tinge of picturesque and descriptive imagery to the introductory Epodes which depicture these scenes, and some of the majestic feelings permanently connected with the scene of this animating event.—*Author's Note.*" This Note appears in *1824,* but not in *M.R.* or the holographs. It suggests that Shelley may have had some question about the propriety of the introductory stanzas, which are, after all, only indirectly related to the Neapolitan crisis. In *B*³ the stanzas are omitted altogether.

    stanza headings: In *M.R.:* Epode I.A.; Epode II.A; Strophe I; Strophe II; Antistrophe I.A; Antistrophe II.A; Antistrophe I.B; Antistrophe II.B; Epode I.B; Epode II.B. Headings in *B*² follow a similar pattern but use Greek letters and Roman numerals. The headings are confused in *1824; 1903* restores a reasonable order, which is followed by later editors. The first two stanzas of *B*³ are headed "1" and "2;" but these numbers are deleted, and the remaining stanzas left unnumbered.

    1. *the City* disinterred:* "*Pompeii." Shelley's note, *M.R., B², 1824.*

    7. *the suspended blood:* "my suspended blood" in *1824* appears to be an editorial emendation by M.W.S.

As in the sculptor's thought, and there
The wreaths of stony myrtle, ivy and pine,
　　Like winter-leaves o'ergrown by moulded snow,
　　Seemed only not to move and grow
Because the chrystal silence of the air   20
　　Weighed on their life, even as the Power divine
　　Which then lulled all things brooded upon mine.

　　　　Then gentle winds arose,
　　　　With many a mingled close
Of wild Æolian sound and mountain odours keen;   25
　　　　And where the Baian Ocean
　　　　Welters with airlike motion,
Within, above, around its bowers of starry green,
　　Moving the sea-flowers in those purple caves,
　　Even as the ever stormless atmosphere   30
　　　　Floats o'er the Elysian realm—
　　It bore me, like an Angel, o'er the waves
　　Of sunlight, whose swift pinnace of dewy air
　　　　No storm can overwhelm—
　　　　I sailed where ever flows   35
　　　　Under the calm Serene
　　　　A spirit of deep emotion
　　　　From the unknown graves
　　Of the dead Kings of Melody*—

28–29 its vales of living green / And bowers of purple moss & emerald
caves B^1　　29 sea-flowers] *moon*-flowers B^2　　30 stormless] cloudless B^1　　32 It bore me] *I floated* Piloted B^1　　37–39 A spirit, &
emotion / Out of the sacred graves / Of the Kings of melody B^1
38 unknown] *distant* B^2

───────────────────

25. "odours" in *M.R.* and B^2; "odour" (*1824*) is corrected in *1903* and later
editions.
32. *It bore me, like an Angel, o'er the waves:* Punctuation from B^2. The meaning appears to be: "It [the Power divine] bore me o'er the waves of sunlight,
like an Angel whose swift pinnace of dewy air no storm can overwhelm." That
is, the poet is rapt above the waters (as in "Ode to Liberty"), from which
vantage point he has the spectacular view described in lines 40–46.
39. *the dead Kings of Melody**: "*Homer and Virgil." Shelley's note, *M.R.*,
B^2, *1824*.

Shadowy Aornos darkened o'er the helm   40
The horizontal æther; Heaven stript bare
Its depth over Elysium, where the prow
Made the invisible water white as snow;
From that Typhæan Mount, Inarime,
There streamed a sunbright vapour, like the standard   45
          Of some ætherial host—
          Whilst from all the coast
Louder and louder gathering round, there wandered
    Over the oracular woods and divine sea
    Prophesyings which grew articulate—   50
They seize me,—I must speak them:—be they fate!

ODE TO NAPLES

Naples! thou Heart of men, which ever pantest
    Naked beneath the lidless eye of Heaven!
Elysian City, which to calm enchantest
    The mutinous air and sea! they round thee, even   55
          As Sleep round Love, are driven;
Metropolis of a ruined Paradise
    Long lost, late won, and yet but half regained;
Bright Altar of the bloodless sacrifice
    Which armed Victory offers up unstained   60
          To Freedom, flower-enchained.—
Thou which wert once, and then didst cease to be,

40–41 Aornos & its desarts oer the helm /
Obscured the purple æther *B*[1]   42 depth] depths *M.R., 1824*
45 sunbright] sunlike *1824*   49 divine] mystic *B*[1]   51 They seize
me & I speak them   they are fate *B*[1]   55 they] which *M.R.*   61
To Love, the flower-enchained!   *M.R., B*[2], *1824*   62 didst] did *M.R.*

---

42. *depth:* Unmistakably "depth" in *B*[1]; less clearly so in *B*[2]. Though *M.R.* and
1824 both read "depths", I doubt a connection between the two.
45. "sunbright" in *M.R.* and *B*[2]; "sunlike" (*1824*) is corrected in *1903* and
later editions.
52. *B*[3] begins here, entitled "Ode to Naples."

Now art, and henceforth ever shalt be free;
  If Hope and Truth and Justice can avail;
    Hail, hail, all hail!   65

    Thou youngest Giant birth
    Which from the groaning Earth
Leap'st, clothed in armour of impenetrable scale;
    Last of the Intercessors
    Who 'gainst the proud Transgressors   70
Pleadest before God's love! Arrayed in Wisdom's mail
    Lift thy lightning-lance in mirth,
    Nor let thy high heart fail
Though from their hundred gates the leagued Oppressors
    With hurried legions move!—   75
    Hail, hail, all hail!

What, though Cimmerian Anarchs dare blaspheme
  Freedom and thee? thy shield is as a mirror
To make their blind slaves see, and with fierce gleam
  To turn his hungry sword upon the wearer: 80
    A new Actæon's error
Shall theirs have been—devoured by their own hounds.
  Be Thou, like the imperial Basilisk,
Killing thy foe with unapparent wounds.
  Gaze on Oppression, till at that dread risk   85
    Aghast, she pass from the Earth's disk.—
Fear not, but gaze—for freemen mightier grow
And slaves more feeble, gazing on their foe.

66 youngest] latest *M.R.*, *B*²   67–68 Which the Titanian Earth /
Clothes as with armour *M.R.*, *B*²   70 proud] Crowned *1824*   70–
71 Against the proud transgressors / Who hide the lamp of love! *M.R.*;
Who cite the crowned Transgressors / Before Love's equal throne *B*²
72 Lift] Wave *M.R.*, *B*², *1824*   79 their] his *M.R.*   82 Shall his
. . . his *M.R.*   85 at] from *M.R.*   86 Aghast, she] She *M.R.*
pass] *shrink B*²

If Hope and Truth and Justice can avail
  Thou shalt be great. All hail!   90

  From Freedom's form divine,
  From Nature's inmost shrine,
Strip every impious gawd; rend Error, veil by veil;
    O'er Ruin desolate,
    O'er Falsehood's fallen state,   95
Sit Thou sublime, unawed; be the Destroyer pale!
    And equal laws be thine,
    And winged words let sail
Freighted with truth, even from the throne of God.
    That wealth, surviving fate,   100
    Be thine. All hail!

Didst thou not start to hear Spain's thrilling Pæan
  From land to land re-echoed solemnly
Till Silence became music? From the Ææan*
  To the cold Alps, eternal Italy   105
    Starts to hear thine! The Sea
Which paves the desart streets of Venice, laughs
  In light and music; widowed Genoa wan
By moonlight spells ancestral epitaphs,
    Murmuring, "where is Doria"; fair Milan,   110
    Within whose veins long ran
The Viper's* palsying venom, lifts her heel
To bruise his head. The signal and the seal,
  If Hope and Truth and Justice can avail,
  Art thou of all these hopes. All hail!   115

  Florence, beneath the Sun,
  Of cities fairest one,

89 can] may *M.R., B²*, *1824*   103 land to land] every heart *M.R., B²*
115 All hail!] O Hail! *M.R., B²*, *1824*

---

   104. *the Ææan**: "*Ææa, the island of Circe." Note, *1824*.
   112. *The Viper's**: "*The device of the Visconti—whose tyranny has been inherited by the German Emperors." Shelley's note, *M.R.* "The viper was the armorial device of the Visconti, tyrants of Milan." Note, *1824*.

Blushes within her bower for Freedom's expectation;
    From eyes of quenchless hope
    Rome tears the priestly cope,   120
As ruling once by power, so now by admiration;
    An athlete stript to run
    From a remoter station
For the high prize lost on Philippi's shore:
    As then Hope, Truth, and Justice did avail,   125
    So now may Fraud and Wrong. All hail!

Hear ye the march as of the Earthborn Forms
    Arrayed against the ever-living Gods?—
The crash and darkness of a thousand storms
    Bursting their inaccessible abodes   130
    Of crags and thunderclouds?
See ye the banners blazoned to the day,
    Inwrought with emblems of barbaric pride?
Dissonant threats kill Silence far away.
    The serene Heaven which wraps our Eden wide   135
    With iron light is dyed!
The Anarchs of the North pour forth their legions
    Like Chaos o'er creation, uncreating;
An hundred tribes nourished on strange religions
    And lawless slaveries. Down the aerial regions   140
    Of the white Alps, desolating,
    Famished wolves that bide no waiting,—
Blotting the glowing footsteps of old glory,

122 Eager again to run *M.R.*   123 remoter] sublimer *M.R.*
126 All hail!] Hail *Naples hail B²*; O hail! *1824*   134 Dissonant] Their
dissonant *M.R., B²*   135 serene] innocent *M.R., B²*   137 pour]
lead *M.R., B², 1824*   138 Like] As *B¹* uncreating] miscreating *B¹*
139 nourished] suckled *B¹*   143 old] lost *M.R., B²*

143. *old glory:* The word "past" is written above "lost" in *B²*. The final reading,
in *B³* and *1824,* is "old."

Trampling our columned cities into dust,
Their dull and savage lust   145
On Beauty's corse to sickness satiating,
   They come; the fields they tread look black and hoary
   With fire: from their red feet the streams run gory.

         Great Spirit! deepest Love,
         Which rulest and dost move   150
All things that live and are within the Italian shore!
         Who spreadest Heaven around it,
         Whose woods, rocks, waves, surround it;
Who sittest in thy star o'er Ocean's western floor;
      Spirit of Beauty, at whose soft command   155
      The sunbeams and the showers distil sweet foizon
         From the Earth's bosom chill!
      O bid those beams be each a blinding brand
      Of lightning! bid those showers be dews of poison!
         Bid the Earth's plenty kill!   160
            Bid thy bright Heaven above,
            While light and darkness bound it,
            Be their tomb, who planned
            To make it ours and thine!
         Or, with thine harmonizing ardours fill   165
And raise thy sons, as o'er the prone horizon
Thy lamp feeds every western wave with fire.
Be Man's high hope and unextinct desire
The instrument to work thy will divine!

---

145 dull] rude *B*[1]   147 The golden fields at once *B*[1]   148 run]
flow B[2]   149 *Thou Eternal Being B*[1]   150 Which] Who *M.R.*
151 that] which *M.R., B*[2], *1824*   156 sweet] its *M.R., B*[2], *1824*
162 While] Whilst *M.R., B*[2], *1824*   light] night *M.R., B*[1]   163
tomb] sepulchre *B*[1]; *grave B*[3]   167 western] twilight *M.R., B*[1], *B*[2],
1824   169 instrument] instruments *M.R.*

168–69. *Be Man's high hope and unextinct desire / The instrument to work thy
will divine!:* Punctuation from *B*[2]. *B*[3] has a comma after "hope," suggesting that
the meaning may be: "Be [Thou] Man's hope, and desire the instrument to work

Then, clouds from sunbeams, antelopes from leopards,   170
      And frowns and fears from Thee,
      Shall not more swiftly flee,
Than Celtic wolves from the Ausonian shepherds.
     Whatever, Spirit, from thy sphered shrine
     Thou yieldest or withholdest, yet let be   175
     This City of thy worship, ever free!—

172 Shall] Would *M.R., B², 1824*   174 sphered] starry *M.R.,
B¹, B², 1824*   175 yet] oh *M.R., B¹, B², 1824*

---

his will." There is no comma after "hope" in *M.R., B²*, or *1824;* the resulting
grammatical ambiguity is corrected in *M.R.* (probably by transcriber or editor)
by making "instruments" plural. But "high hope" and "unextinct desire" are
close enough in meaning to constitute a single "instrument."

Ode to Heaven

First published in *Prometheus Unbound* (1820)

HOLOGRAPHS:
    Huntington HM 2177, *42r–*45r; draft
    Bodleian MS Shelley e. 3, fols. 17–20, recto only; fair copy

The text is taken from *B,* with some punctuation from *1820*ᵃ. In addition to the two holographs, there is a transcript of the poem by M.W.S. in Harvard MS Eng. 258.2, fols. 15–16. Woodberry attributes *H* incorrectly to Shelley. *H* appears to be based directly on *B,* which it follows in punctuation, and to some extent in capitalization; section headings are omitted, though the poem is titled "Ode to Heaven." In line 53, *H* reads "millions" for "million" in *B;* this appears the likely source of the *1820*ᵃ reading. It seems probable that M.W.S. transcribed the printer's copy from *H,* restoring "Chorus of Spirits" from *B,* and supplying punctuation where missing; alternatively, punctuation could have been supplied by Shelley. Punctuation and capitalization of *1820*ᵃ are quite different from both *B* and *Tr,* however; all dashes (which occur in both *B* and *H*) are replaced by colons, semicolons, or periods; and capitals are consistently lowercased. These changes could conceivably have been made by M.W.S., with or without Shelley's approval, or by Ollier or Peacock in his proof revision. But since Shelley retains dashes and capitals in the poems he supervised through the press, like *Laon and Cythna* and *Adonais,* it seems unlikely that he would have made or sanctioned such changes himself. Since *1820*ᵃ appears then to bear the final marks of a hand other than Shelley's, and since *B* is a finished copy, fully revised and ready for transcription, I use *B* as copy text, following *1820*ᵃ only when all punctuation is missing from *H* and *B* (as in the first two lines), and in one or two instances modifying punctuation for consistency. *Hn* is transcribed in *1911*ᵃ, II, 141–51.

ODE TO HEAVEN

CHORUS OF SPIRITS

Palace-roof of cloudless nights!
Paradise of golden lights!
Deep, Immeasurable, Vast,
    Which art now, and which wert then;
Of the present and the past,   5
    Of the eternal Where and When,
        Presence chamber, Temple, Home,
        Ever-canopying Dome
    Of acts and ages yet to come!

Glorious shapes have life in thee,   10
Earth and all Earth's company,
Living globes which ever throng
    Thy deep chasms and wildernesses,
And green worlds that glide along,
    And swift stars with flashing tresses,   15
        And icy moons most cold and bright,
        And mighty suns, beyond the Night,
    Atoms of intensest light!

4 Which was then, & which is now, *Hn*   8 *Calm* *Most inalienable Home Hn*   10 *Thou whose azure wilderness Hn*   11 *Wandering thro eternity Hn*

---

title: "To Heaven" in *Hn*, "Ode to Heaven" in *1820*ᵃ, untitled in *B*.
  subtitles: The poem is subtitled "Chorus of Spirits" in *1820*ᵃ, and the three sections headed "First Spirit" "Second Spirit" and "Third Spirit." *B* is headed "Chorus of Spirits" but the heading appears to refer to the first three stanzas alone; Stanza 4 is headed "a Remoter Voice;" Stanza 5, "a louder & still remoter Voice." *H* omits headings altogether. I retain headings from *B*, which suggest that the three sections are not alternatives (First, Second, and Third), but rather represent progressively distanced perspectives.
  1–2. These lines are reversed in *Hn;* also in *B,* where, however, they are numbered to indicate final order.

Even thy name is as a God,
Heaven! for thou art the abode   20
Of that Power which is the glass
    Wherein man his nature sees;—
Generations as they pass
    Worship thee with bended knees—
        Their unremaining Gods and they   25
        Like a river roll away—
        Thou remainest such—alway!—

                 A REMOTER VOICE
Thou art but the mind's first chamber,
Round which its young fancies clamber
Like weak insects in a cave   30
    Lighted up by stalactites;
But the portal of the grave,
    Where a world of new delights
        Will make thy best glories seem
        But a dim and noonday gleam   35
        From the shadow of a dream.

        A LOUDER AND STILL REMOTER VOICE
Peace! the abyss is wreathed with scorn
At your presumption, Atom-born!

25 *But their fleeting works Hn*   32 *Will it pass beyond the grave Hn*
34 thy best] all thy *Hn*   35 But a] Like some *Hn*   36 From]
Athwart *Hn*   37 *Peace, presumptuous spirit—Hn*

19–27. This stanza precedes Stanza 2 in *Hn*. Earlier drafts for the stanza read:

That of which thou art th'abode
Can its name be God

Below thy depth, *beyond* above thy height
Within thine omnipresent might
What feelest thou? we gaze & see
A power beyond all names of power
Stamped, as on a scroll, on thee—   *Hn*

28–29. draft:

Art thou but *some mighty* chamber
Of the mind which gazes on thee   Hn

What is Heaven? and what are ye
  Who its brief expanse inherit?   40
What are suns and spheres which flee
  With the instinct of that spirit
    Of which ye are but a part?
    Drops which Nature's mighty heart
    Drives through thinnest veins. Depart!   45

What is Heaven? a globe of dew
Filling in the morning new
Some eyed flower whose young leaves waken
  On an unimagined world.
Constellated suns unshaken,   50
  Orbits measureless, are furled
    In that frail and fading sphere,
    With ten million gathered there
    To tremble, gleam, and disappear!

42 the spirit *Hn*   47 Filling] *Trembling Hn*   48 *Within* a half-
awakening awakened flower   On some flower it *seems* to waken *Hn*
53 With a million *Hn;* With ten millions *1820*ᵃ

---

53. "millions" in *H* and in *1820*ᵃ appears to be originally a transcription error;
there is no reason to assume that Shelley approved it.

To a Sky-Lark

First published in *Prometheus Unbound* (1820)

HOLOGRAPHS:
   Bodleian MS Shelley adds. e. 6, p. 97 rev.; draft of lines 1–4, 31–35, 76–77

   Harvard MS Eng. 258.2, fols. 23–25; fair copy, with corrections.

The text is taken from *H*, with some punctuation adapted from *1820*ᵃ. *H* is a fair copy, carefully punctuated for the most part, with several revisions made evidently after the poem was written out; these revisions include a shift of position for the second stanza, originally occurring fifth, and several verbal substitutions. It seems likely that M.W.S. transcribed the poem directly from *H,* along with other poems she transcribed for *1820*ᵃ; two ampersands and two unclear letters are written out above the text, as if for ease of transcription. There are only two substantive differences between *H* and *1820*ᵃ, the shift of "those" to "these" in line 55, and of "should" to "would" in line 104; but there are numerous differences in punctuation and orthography, as with all the *1820*ᵃ texts. Since it appears likely that Peacock regularized the printer's copy for *1820*ᵃ, I have given primacy to the punctuation and orthography of *H*, but have adapted *1820*ᵃ where punctuation is missing from the copy text. *B,* evidently a first draft, is reproduced in facsimile and discussed in Rogers, *Shelley at Work,* pp. 207–10; *H* is reproduced in facsimile in *1929.*

TO A SKY-LARK

Hail to thee, blithe Spirit!
   Bird thou never wert—
That from Heaven, or near it,
   Pourest thy full heart
In profuse strains of unpremeditated art.   5

Higher still and higher
  From the earth thou springest
Like a cloud of fire;
  The blue deep thou wingest,
And singing still dost soar, and soaring ever singest.   10

In the golden lightning
  Of the sunken Sun,
O'er which clouds are brightning,
  Thou dost float and run;
Like an unbodied joy whose race is just begun.   15

The pale purple even
  Melts around thy flight,
Like a star of Heaven
  In the broad day-light
Thou art unseen,—but yet I hear thy shrill delight,   20

Keen as are the arrows
  Of that silver sphere,

12 Sun— *H*   14 Thou dost] *Thy wings H*   20 shrill delight,]
blithe delight *H*   21 Keen as are] *Thy notes, like H*

6–10. This stanza originally occurs fifth, following line 25; it is marked "2"
and insertion indicated after Stanza 1 in *H*. It is written in *H* without punctuation at the end of lines:

Higher still & higher
  From the earth thou springest
Like a cloud of fire
  The blue deep thou wingest
                    and
And singing still dost soar, & soaring ever singest.

If M.W.S. transcribed the poem directly from *H* (the writing out of "and," and
the marking of the stanza for insertion at the proper place argue that she did),
then final punctuation could have been provided by M.W.S., by the printer, or by
Peacock, as well as by Shelley. The unpunctuated MS raises the possibility that
the stop may come after "springest" rather than "fire;" "like a cloud of fire"
could modify "thou wingest" or "thou springest." Shelley uses similar comparisons to suggest either upward or horizontal motion ("thou didst from her bosom,
like a cloud / Of glory, arise, a spirit of keen joy!" *Prometheus Unbound*, I, 157–
58; "As over wide dominions / I sped, like some swift cloud that wings the wide
air's wildernesses," *Prometheus Unbound*, I, 763–64). I retain the punctuation of
*1820*ᵃ, however, in the absence of strong evidence for either reading.

Whose intense lamp narrows
   In the white dawn clear
Until we hardly see—we feel that it is there.   25

   All the earth and air
     With thy voice is loud,
   As when Night is bare
     From one lonely cloud
The moon rains out her beams—and Heaven is overflowed.   30

   What thou art we know not;
     What is most like thee?
   From rainbow clouds there flow not
     Drops so bright to see
As from thy presence showers a rain of melody.   35

   Like a Poet hidden
     In the light of thought,
   Singing hymns unbidden
     Till the world is wrought
To sympathy with hopes and fears it heeded not: 40

   Like a high-born maiden
     In a palace-tower,
   Soothing her love-laden
     Soul in secret hour,
With music sweet as love—which overflows her bower: 45

   Like a glow-worm golden
     In a dell of dew

25 there; *H*   26 air— *H*   33 From *the* rainbows *H*   45 sweet
as] *which is H*   which] *& H*

---

40. *not*: "not—" in *H*. Shelley's dash here and in line 100 has been replaced by
the punctuation of *1820*[a].

Scattering unbeholden
   Its aerial hue
Among the flowers and grass which screen it from the view: 50

Like a rose embowered
   In its own green leaves—
By warm winds deflowered—
   Till the scent it gives
Makes faint with too much sweet those heavy-winged thieves: 55

Sound of vernal showers
   On the twinkling grass,
Rain-awakened flowers,
   All that ever was
Joyous and clear and fresh, thy music doth surpass.   60

Teach us, Sprite or Bird,
   What sweet thoughts are thine;
I have never heard
   Praise of love or wine
That panted forth a flood of rapture so divine: 65

Chorus Hymeneal
   Or triumphal chaunt
Matched with thine, would be all
   But an empty vaunt,
A thing wherein we feel there is some hidden want.   70

What objects are the fountains
   Of thy happy strain?

53 warm] *the H*   55 faint] *sick H*   those] *the H;* these *1820*ᵃ
60 surpass: *1820*ᵃ   65 divine. *1820*ᵃ   72 happy strain] *drunken*
strain*s H*

    55. Modern editions correct what is clearly an error in *1820*ᵃ, "these" for
"those."

What fields or waves or mountains?
   What shapes of sky or plain?
What love of thine own kind? what ignorance of pain?   75

With thy clear keen joyance
   Languor cannot be—
Shadow of annoyance
   Never came near thee;
Thou lovest—but ne'er knew love's sad satiety.   80

Waking or asleep
   Thou of death must deem
Things more true and deep
   Than we mortals dream,
Or how could thy notes flow in such a chrystal stream?   85

We look before and after
   And pine for what is not—
Our sincerest laughter
   With some pain is fraught—
Our sweetest songs are those that tell of saddest thought.   90

Yet if we could scorn
   Hate and pride and fear;
If we were things born
   Not to shed a tear,
I know not how thy joy we ever should come near.   95

Better than all measures
   Of delightful sound—
Better than all treasures
   That in books are found—
Thy skill to poet were, thou Scorner of the ground!   100

---

87. "not:" in *1820ª*; but colon is misleading—probably a replacement for Shelley's dash. No punctuation in *H* after "fraught" (line 89); I add a dash (rather than the semicolon of *1820ª*) to maintain a parallel with line 87.

Teach me half the gladness
   That thy brain must know,
Such harmonious madness
   From my lips should flow,
The world should listen then—as I am listening now.   105

104 should] would *1820*ᵃ

---

104. I retain "should" on the assumption that M.W.S. transcribed the poem
directly from *H*, and on the evidence of similar transcription slips in other poems
(e.g., "The Two Spirits," line 10).
  first draft:

What art thou Hail to thee blithe Spirit
  For bird thou *hardly art* never wert!
That from *blue* Heaven or near
  Dost pour from Pourest thy full heart
Such sweet sounds   In these   art

Ah, what thou art we know not
  But what is like to thee?
From the *morning star   clouds* rainbow flow not
  Clear   Beams so sweet   Dew drops so   silver Drops so bright to see
As from thy presence showers *quick* a rain   melody

Heaven *is all above*

Yet that in thy joyance
?*These* Languor cannot be   *B*

The Cloud

First published in *Prometheus Unbound* (1820)

HOLOGRAPHS:

   Bodleian MS Shelley adds. e. 6, pp. 21, 31; draft of lines 59–66, 71–72, 77–84 (*B¹*)

   ———— adds. e. 6, pp. 35–37; fair copy of lines 35–84 (*B²*)

Lines 1–34 of the text are taken from *1820ᵃ*, with two emendations from ink corrections in *1820ᵇ* ("buds" for "birds," line 6, and "swings" for the misprint "swins," line 36; both confirmed by *1829* and *1839*). Lines 35–84 are based on *B²*, with some punctuation (mainly at the ends of lines) adapted from *1820ᵃ*. *B²* probably served as the basis of a transcript made by M.W.S. for *1820ᵃ*; the missing lines 1–34 may have been on a page subsequently removed from the notebook. *1820ᵃ* agrees with *B²* except for the following substantive variants: "of love" instead of "love," line 40; and three words altered from plural to singular, in lines 42, 71, and 75. Each of these variants seems plausibly ascribed to transcriber or printer. Punctuation and capitalization of *1820ᵃ* are normalized (i.e., no dashes, and no medial capitalization except for "Spirit," line 28); I restore some capitalization in lines 1–34 for consistency. Lines 71–84 of *B²* are reproduced in facsimile in *1934*, xi.

THE CLOUD

I bring fresh showers for the thirsting flowers,
   From the seas and the streams;
I bear light shade for the leaves when laid
   In their noon-day dreams.

---

3. *shade:* "shades" in *1829* and *1839;* but the medial rhyme clearly requires "shade."

From my wings are shaken the dews that waken 5
    The sweet buds every one,
When rocked to rest on their mother's breast,
    As she dances about the sun.
I wield the flail of the lashing hail,
    And whiten the green plains under, 10
And then again I dissolve it in rain,
    And laugh as I pass in thunder.

I sift the snow on the mountains below,
    And their great pines groan aghast;
And all the night 'tis my pillow white, 15
    While I sleep in the arms of the blast.
Sublime on the towers of my skiey bowers,
    Lightning my pilot sits,
In a cavern under is fettered the thunder,
    It struggles and howls at fits; 20
Over earth and ocean, with gentle motion,
    This pilot is guiding me,
Lured by the love of the genii that move
    In the depths of the purple sea;
Over the rills, and the crags, and the hills, 25
    Over the lakes and the plains,
Wherever he dream, under mountain or stream,
    The Spirit he loves remains;
And I all the while bask in Heaven's blue smile,
    Whilst he is dissolving in rains. 30

The sanguine Sunrise, with his meteor eyes,
    And his burning plumes outspread,
Leaps on the back of my sailing rack,
    When the morning star shines dead;
As on the jag of a mountain crag 35
    Which an earthquake rocks and swings,
An eagle alit one moment may sit
    In the light of its golden wings;

6 buds] birds *1820*ᵃ; buds *1820*ᵇ, *1829, 1839*   34 dead. *1820*ᵃ

And when Sunset may breathe, from the lit Sea beneath,
     Its ardours of rest and love,   40
And the crimson pall of eve may fall
     From the depths of Heaven above,
With wings folded I rest, on mine aëry nest,
     As still as a brooding dove.

That orbed maiden with white fire laden   45
     Whom mortals call the moon,
Glides glimmering o'er my fleecelike floor,
     By the midnight breezes strewn;
And wherever the beat of her unseen feet,
     Which only the angels hear,   50
May have broken the woof of my tent's thin roof,
     The stars peep behind her, and peer;
And I laugh to see them whirl and flee
     Like a swarm of golden bees,
When I widen the rent in my wind-built tent,   55
     Till the calm rivers, lakes, and seas,
Like strips of the sky fallen through me on high,
     Are each paved with the moon and these.

I bind the Sun's throne with a burning zone
     And the moon's with a girdle of pearl;   60

---

40 love] of love *1820*ᵃ   42 depths] depth *1820*ᵃ   51 woof, *B*²
55 rent, *B*²   56 Till] *And B*²   60 moon's] moon *B*¹

---

40. *Its ardours of rest and love:* "of love" (*1820*ᵃ) seems more likely a transcriber's or printer's change than an authorial correction, perhaps an unconscious attempt to fill out the anapestic meter. Cf. the change in the *1820*ᵃ text of "The Sensitive Plant," line 49: "And the sinuous paths of lawn and of moss" for "of lawn and moss" in M.W.S.' transcript, Harvard MS Eng. 258.2, fol. 2v.

42. *depths:* Shelley uses "depths" and "depth" almost interchangeably, but loss or addition of a final "s" seems more likely a copying slip than a deliberate alteration. Cf. "depths" for the holograph "depth" in the two printed texts of "Ode to Naples," line 42.

51. In this line and several others (55, 67, 69, et al.), Shelley employs a medial comma in *B*², as if to mark the internal rhyme. I have omitted these, on the grounds that they are inconsistent with Shelley's punctuation elsewhere and would have been edited out in any contemporary printing (as indeed they are in *1820*ᵃ).

The volcanos are dim and the stars reel and swim
    When the Whirlwinds my banner unfurl.
From cape to cape with a bridge-like shape,
    Over a torrent sea,
Sunbeam-proof, I hang like a roof—   65
    The mountains its columns be!
The triumphal arch through which I march
    With hurricane, fire, and snow,
When the Powers of the Air are chained to my chair,
    Is the million-coloured Bow;   70
The sphere-fires above its soft colours wove
    While the moist earth was laughing below.

I am the daughter of Earth and Water,
    And the nursling of the sky;
I pass through the pores of the oceans and shores;   75
    I change, but I cannot die—
For after the rain, when with never a stain
    The pavilion of Heaven is bare,
And the winds and sunbeams, with their convex gleams,
    Build up the blue Dome of Air—   80
I silently laugh at my own cenotaph,
    And out of the caverns of rain,
Like a child from the womb, like a ghost from the tomb,
    I arise, and unbuild it again.

62 When the Whirlwinds] When Whirlwinds B^1 67 arch, B^2
69 Air, B^2 71 *By* the bright sphere B^1 sphere-fires] sphere-fire
1820[a]   73 daughter, B^2 75 pores, B^2 oceans] ocean *1820*[a]
78 *The dome of the skies is spread* B^1 81 laugh, B^2 my own] *that*
B^1 82 And *from* the fountains B^1 83 Like a ghost from the
tomb, like a child from the womb B^1

---

71. *sphere-fires:* Literally, the fires of the sphere (sun), which weave the colors
of the rainbow out of their own light; the plural seems called for. Both the draft
(in its second version) and the fair copy agree; I infer that *1820*[a] is a transcriber's or printer's error.
    75. *oceans:* "Earth" and "Water" are singular (line 73); "the oceans and
shores" plural; one refers to myth, the other to natural fact.

Two Songs for "Midas"
SONG OF APOLLO AND SONG OF PAN

First published in *Posthumous Poems* (1824), entitled "Hymn of Apollo" and "Hymn of Pan." A new text of "Song of Apollo," entitled "Apollo Sings," was published in G. M. Matthews, ed., *Shelley: Selected Poems and Prose* (London, 1964).

HOLOGRAPHS:
> Bodleian MS Shelley adds. e. 6, pp. 22–29

The text is taken from *B;* punctuation is silently added at the ends of lines, and between noun series. M.W.S. transcribed *B* into her copy of "Midas" (Bodleian MS Shelley d. 3, fols. 22–23); discrepancies between *B* and *Tr* seem to be transcription errors, as the following partial list indicates. "Song of Apollo:" "open" omitted, line 3; "power" for "spirit," line 24 (cf. "power," line 22); "wander" (deleted in *B*) for "linger," line 26. "Song of Pan:" "are" (deleted in *B*) for "were," line 4; "cicale" for "cicadae," line 9; "ever" for "even," line 11; "Pelion" for "Olympus," line 15. There are no indications in *B* or *Tr* that Shelley made or approved of any of these changes. *1824* follows *Tr,* and incorporates additional editorial changes (i.e., "Listening to my sweet pipings" for "Listening my sweet pipings," "Song of Pan," line 5). All modern editions except for Matthews follow *1824,* with emendations from *Tr.* Matthews' text is based on *B,* with some changes in punctuation and orthography; no textual annotation is supplied. My text of "Song of Apollo" agrees with Matthews except for some differences in punctuation and orthography. The draft of "Song of Apollo" is transcribed (with some errors) in *1934,* p. 56.

234

SONG OF APOLLO

The sleepless Hours who watch me as I lie
  Curtained with star-enwoven tapestries
From the broad moonlight of the open sky;
  Fanning the busy dreams from my dim eyes,
Waken me when their mother, the grey Dawn,   5
Tells them that Dreams and that the moon is gone.

Then I arise; and climbing Heaven's blue dome,
  I walk over the mountains and the waves,
Leaving my robe upon the ocean foam;
  My footsteps pave the clouds with fire; the caves   10
Are filled with my bright presence, and the air
Leaves the green Earth to my embraces bare.

2 *That from the moonlight on my golden bed B*   7 *Then with my*
countenance to Heaven upturned B   Heaven's blue dome,] *the* blue
dome / *Of Heaven B*   8 mountains] *Earth & sea B*

1–6. drafts:

The Hours, are weaving all the night
The curtains which

The Hours, when from their wings the dews are shaken
Whose silver sounds the dreaming flowers awaken
  Then waken me
With glowing hands they draw the star inwoven
Curtains, which *keep* shield the moonlight from my lids
  And having harnessed my bright steeds

From my soft pillow of clouds dark & golden
Opening the star-inwoven curtain

With golden glowing

Out of my couch of fleecy clouds, surrounded
The gentle hours   *B*

3–4. Matthews, following *1824,* punctuates thus: "From the broad moonlight
of the open sky, / Fanning the busy dreams from my dim eyes,—" But *B* has a
semicolon after "sky;" no punctuation after "eyes;" which suggests that "Fanning
the busy dreams from my dim eyes" modifies the implied subject of "Waken me"
(line 5). That is, the Hours watch Apollo as he lies asleep, then waken him,
fanning the dreams away.
  additional lines:

Bacchus & Ceres & Vertumnus fill
Thier ?bursting grapes   *B*

The sunbeams are my shafts with which I kill
    Deceit, that loves the night and fears the day;
All men who do, or even imagine ill   15
    Fly me; and from the glory of my ray
Good minds and open actions take new might
Until diminished by the reign of night.

I feed the clouds, the rainbows and the flowers
    With their ætherial colours; the moon's globe   20
And the pure stars in their eternal bowers
    Are cinctured with my power as with a robe;
Whatever lamps on Earth or Heaven may shine
Are portions of one spirit; which is mine.

I stand at noon upon the peak of Heaven;   25
    Then with unwilling steps, I linger down
Into the clouds of the Atlantic even;
    For grief that I depart they weep and frown—
What look is more delightful, than the smile
With which I soothe them from the Western isle?   30

I am the eye with which the Universe
    Beholds itself, and knows it is divine;
All harmony of instrument and verse,
    All prophecy and medicine are mine;
All light of art or nature—to my song   35
Victory and praise, in its own right, belong.

SONG OF PAN

From the forests and highlands
    We come, we come,
From the river-girt islands

16 glory] *spirit B*   17 minds, *B*   20 ætherial] *delightful B*   the moon's globe] *and the moon B*   21 *And the comets & the meteors B* 26 linger] *wander B*   27 clouds] *depths B*   Atlantic] *Hesperian B* 28 *Whose Which grieving B*

Where loud waves were dumb
Listening my sweet pipings.   5
   The wind in the reeds and the rushes,
   The bees on the bells of thyme,
   The birds in the myrtle bushes,
   The cicadæ above in the lime,
     And the lizards below in the grass,   10
Were silent as even old Tmolus was,
   Listening my sweet pipings.

Liquid Peneus was flowing—
   And all dark Tempe lay
In Olympus' shadow, outgrowing   15
   The light of the dying day,
   Speeded with my sweet pipings.
   The sileni and sylvans and fauns
   And the nymphs of the woods and the waves,
   To the edge of the moist river-lawns   20
   And the brink of the dewy caves,
     And all that did then attend and follow

4 loud] *the B*   were] *are B*   6 *From Erymanthus B*   12 piping *B*
15 Olympus'] *the Ossa's B*   17 *With its forests & rocks & fountains*
B   18 *And I sang of And the nymphs & the fauns & the B*
19 waves] *waters B*   20 moist] *dewy B*

---

5. "Listening my" is archaic now, and may have been so in Shelley's time; hence M.W.S.' editorial correction: "Listening to my sweet pipings" (*1824*). But Milton uses the transitive form often, and *OED* cites examples from Wordsworth, Byron, and Tennyson.

12. "piping" in *B;* "pipings" in *Tr.* The singular form appears to have no special rationale, and may well be an oversight. I emend on the ground that the rhyming is consistent throughout, and "pipings" therefore required.

15. *Olympus:* The word written above "Ossa's" is hard to decipher but appears to begin with "O" and end with "pus;" I read "Olympus." M.W.S. transcribed it as "Pelion's," which seems unquestionably an error, geographically and on the evidence of the MS. According to the myth, Poseidon split the mountains of Olympus and Ossa apart, enabling the river Peneus to rush to the sea, forming the vale of Tempe. Shelley first wrote "Ossa's shadow" but must have realized his error; since Ossa is to the southeast of the valley and Olympus to the northwest, as the sun sets, the valley lies in the shadow of Olympus.

Were as silent for love, as you now, Apollo,
　　For envy of my sweet pipings.

I sang of the dancing stars,   25
　　I sang of the dædal Earth,
And of Heaven, and the giant wars,
　　And Love and Death and Birth;
　　　And then I changed my pipings,
　　　Singing how, down the vales of Mænalus   30
　　　I pursued a maiden and clasped a reed.
　　　Gods and men, we are all deluded thus!—
　　　It breaks on our bosom and then we bleed;
　　　They wept as, I think, both ye now would,
If envy or age had not frozen your blood,   35
　　　At the sorrow of my sweet pipings.

23 for] *with B*   you now] *thou art B*   24 For] *With B*
30–31 *And sang of Syrinx, the bright maiden / Whom I once loved &
love forever   Singing of Syrinx,   how she became / A reed B*   down
the vales] *in the mountains B*   33 on] *in B*   35 *Were not Apollo
Were both not envious & one rather old B*

The Two Spirits: An Allegory

First published in *Posthumous Poems* (1824)

HOLOGRAPHS:
Bodleian MS Shelley adds. e. 12, pp. 13–17; draft

The text is taken from *B,* with punctuation added at the ends of lines. *1824* is taken from M.W.S.' transcript of *B,* in Bodleian MS Shelley adds. d. 7, pp. 62–65; *Tr* contains several errors incorporated in *1824* and all later editions. The poem is probably earlier than 1820, the date M.W.S. assigns it to, possibly as early as the summer of 1818, when Shelley began Act I of *Prometheus Unbound.* Drafts for lines 752–63 appear in the same notebook, and resemblances suggest a similar date for both.

THE TWO SPIRITS: AN ALLEGORY

FIRST SPIRIT

O Thou who plumed with strong desire
Would float above the Earth—beware!
A shadow tracks thy flight of fire—
  Night is coming!
Bright are the regions of the air   5

---

2 *Floatest B*   5 Bright] *Wide B*

Canceled introduction:

> *Two genii stood before me in a dream*
> *Art thou not the shades of ?*

2. *Tr* and *1824* read "Would," but the errata to *1824* list "Wouldst," evidently an editorial correction by M.W.S. The auxiliary verb agrees with "who" rather than "thou" ("O Thou who plumed with strong desire / Would float"). Cf. "Hymn to Intellectual Beauty," lines 13–14: "Spirit of BEAUTY, that doth consecrate . . . all thou dost shine upon."

And when winds and beams [   ]
It were delight to wander there—
        Night is coming!

SECOND SPIRIT

The deathless stars are bright above;
If I should cross the shade of night   10
Within my heart is the lamp of love
        And that is day—
And the moon will smile with gentle light
On my golden plumes where'er they move;
The meteors will linger around my flight   15
        And make night day.

FIRST SPIRIT

But if the whirlwinds of darkness waken
Hail and Lightning and stormy rain—
See, the bounds of the air are shaken,
        Night is coming!   20
And swift the clouds of the hurricane
Yon declining sun have overtaken,

11 lamp] *light B*   13 gentle] *silver B*   15 *And the lightnings B*
17 darkness waken] *night awaken B*   19 *Even now the bounds of*
Heaven   Behold B   22 *That the sinking B*

---

6. The line is much canceled; presumably Shelley would have completed it to
rhyme with "desire" and "fire." *Tr* and *1824* read: "And among the winds and
beams." I do not find "among" in *B*.
9. drafts:

> *O what   What I   have I to do with*
> *O what   storm & darkness*
> *These are the golden   B*

17. Before line 17 and line 25, the words "First spirit" and "Second spirit" are
missing in *B;* they are supplied in *1824*, and seem clearly implied by the context.
21–22. The lines must first have read: "And swift the clouds of the hurricane / That the sinking sun have overtaken." "swift" appears to be written in a
second time ("And the swift") but is canceled. In *Tr* M.W.S. misreads "And" as
"red:" "The red swift clouds."

The clash of the hail sweeps o'er the plain—
  Night is coming!

SECOND SPIRIT

I see the glare and I hear the sound—   25
I'll sail on the flood of the tempest dark
With the calm within and light around
  Which make night day;
And thou when the gloom is deep and stark,
Look from thy dull earth slumberbound—   30
My moonlike flight thou then mayst mark
  On high, far away.

Some say there is a precipice
Where one vast pine hangs frozen to ruin
O'er piles of snow and chasms of ice   35
  Mid Alpine mountains;
And that the languid storm pursuing
That winged shape forever flies
Round those hoar branches, aye renewing
  Its aery fountains.   40

Some say when the nights are dry [and] clear
And the death dews sleep on the morass,
Sweet whispers are heard by the traveller
  Which make night day—

*23 And   Hark B   25 I see & rejoice B   29 Do thou, when the
night is drear B   33 Tis said B   34 Which a frozen pine oerhanging B   41 And others B   42 And the dews of death sleep on the
grass B   43 A sound   voice   Strange B*

---

34. *Where one vast pine hangs frozen:* "hangs" is written above "is," neither
canceled; I print "hangs" in view of the first version of the line: "Which a frozen
pine oerhanging." *Tr* and *1824* read "is."

 41. *Some say when the nights are dry [and] clear: Tr* reads: "when the nights
are;" *1824* reads "when nights are." In *B,* the "s" on "nights" is canceled, "are" is
canceled, and "is" written above; "is" is canceled as well, and no final preference
indicated. But since "is" must have been canceled after "are," I retain the first
version. "and" is omitted in *B.*

And a shape like his early love doth pass   45
Upborne by her wild and glittering hair,
And when he awakes on the fragrant grass
He finds night day.

45 *And a winged   silver B*

---

45. *Tr* and *1824* read: "And a silver shape like his early love doth pass."
M.W.S. arrived at an extrametrical line by combining the first and second ver-
sions of the line. But "silver" is plainly canceled. The line must first have read:
"And a winged [or "silver"] shape like his early love."

To Night

First published in *Posthumous Poems* (1824)

HOLOGRAPHS:
> Huntington HM 2176, inside cover, fols. 1–2v, 3v; draft
> Harvard MS Eng. 258.2, fols. 12v–13; fair copy

The text is taken from *H*, with some punctuation added. *1824* appears
to be based directly on *H*, with one change ("over" for "o'er," line 1).
H seems drawn directly from *Hn*; there is no reason to assume any
intermediate texts. *H* is reproduced in facsimile in *1929*, where it is
attributed mistakenly to M.W.S.; *Hn* is fully described in *1911*, I, 108–
18.

TO NIGHT

Swiftly walk o'er the western wave,
    Spirit of Night!
Out of the misty eastern cave
Where, all the long and lone daylight
Thou wovest dreams of joy and fear,   5
Which make thee terrible and dear,
    Swift be thy flight!

4 all] thro *Hn*   5 wovest] dreamedst *Hn*

---

1. *o'er:* "over" in *1824, 1839;* "o'er" in *H, Hn.* Corrected in modern editions.
4–6. drafts:

> *Where all the day, thou didst dream   sleep*
> Thou dreamedst *of thy ghosts   shades*

> Where with the shadow of thy night
> Thou coveredst as with joy & fear
> An how much envied hemisphere   *Hn*

Wrap thy form in a mantle grey,
    Star-inwrought!
Blind with thine hair the eyes of day,   10
Kiss her until she be wearied out—
Then wander o'er city and sea and land,
Touching all with thine opiate wand—
    Come, long-sought!

When I arose and saw the dawn   15
    I sighed for thee;
When Light rode high, and the dew was gone,
And noon lay heavy on flower and tree,
And the weary Day turned to his rest,
Lingering like an unloved guest,   20
    I sighed for thee.

Thy brother Death came, and cried,
    Wouldst thou me?
Thy sweet child Sleep, the filmy-eyed,
Murmured like a noontide bee,   25
Shall I nestle near thy side?

11 Kiss her *asleep Hn*   12 And wander *Hn*   17 When the sun *Hn*
18 When noon lay bright *Hn*   25 Murmured thus enchantingly *Hn*
26 Let me nestle by thy side, *Hn*

---

10. Both *H* and *Hn* show uncertainty about capitalization of "day." But in *H* "day" is clearly lowercased in line 10, capitalized in line 19. It may be that Shelley intended to differentiate between the two personifications, one of whom is female ("Kiss her until she be wearied out"), and one of whom is male ("And the weary Day turned to his rest").

19. first version: *"When the Day turned him to his rest" Hn*

22–25. drafts:

As   Once I called on Death, or Sleep—
    Never on for thee   Mother of dreams
I thought they *had* what thou dost keep

Thou who makest darkness Day,

Thy brother Death came, at my door and he cried
    Seekest *Wantest* thou me?
That sweet child Sleep, *just kissed whom Love & thou*
    Whom Love to thy embraces bore Hn

Wouldst thou me? and I replied,
    No, not thee!

Death will come when thou art dead,
    Soon, too soon—   30
Sleep will come when thou art fled;
Of neither would I ask the boon
I ask of thee, beloved Night—
Swift be thine approaching flight,
    Come soon, soon!   35

27 Wouldst] Seekest *Hn*   30 Far too soon *Hn*   32 would] *will*
Hn   34 *Swift as* be thy flight *Hn*

29–31. Lines 29 and 31 are reversed in *Hn,* in an order which reads more
smoothly, perhaps, than *H:*

    Sleep will come when thou art fled
        Far too soon—
    Death will come when thou art dead

additional lines:

    Come sweet Night
    Some do   *Others seek thee, for thou art*
    Some call thee, because thou *seemest*
        Deaths calm ghost—
    Others because think the things

    Charm to sleep the *Argus eye* envious eyes
        Of *this false* the Suns slaves   *Hn*

"O World, O Life, O Time"

First published in *Posthumous Poems* (1824)

HOLOGRAPHS:
Bodleian MS Shelley adds. e. 8, p. 123 rev.; draft (B^1)
———— adds. e. 18, p. 164 rev.; fair copy (B^2)

The text is taken from B^2, with some punctuation from B^1. Both holographs are discussed in J. Carter and J. Sparrow, "Shelley, Swinburne, and Housman," *TLS* (November 21, 1968), 1318–19.

O World, O Life, O Time,
On whose last steps I climb,
Trembling at that where I had stood before—
When will return the glory of your prime?
No more, O never more!   5

Out of the day and night
A joy has taken flight—
Fresh spring and summer [   ] and winter hoar
Move my faint heart with grief, but with delight
No more, O never more!   10

---

3 Trembling at those which I have trod before B^1 4 your] thy B^1
8 Green spring, and *summer   gr*   autumn & winter hoar B^1
9 Move] Fill B^1

---

8. In both the revised version of the draft and the fair copy, a space is left after "summer."

"My dearest M. wherefore hast thou gone"

First published in *Poetical Works* (1840)

HOLOGRAPH:

Bodleian MS Shelley adds. e. 12, p. 179 rev.

The text is a literal transcription of *B*. Since the lines are incomplete, I do not attempt to provide a critical text. *1840* is based on a transcript of *B* by M.W.S. in Bodleian MS Shelley adds. d. 7, p. 44, recopied with slight changes in Bodleian MS Shelley adds. d. 9, p. 33 (recorded in Irving Massey, *Posthumous Poems of Shelley,* Montreal, 1969, p. 88).

My dearest M. wherefore hast thou gone
And left me in this dreary world alone
Thy form is here indeed, a lovely . . .

But thou art fled,—gone down the dreary road
Which leads to Sorrow's most obscure abode   5
Thou sittest on the hearth of pale despair
It   where
For thine own sake I cannot follow thee
Do thou return for mine—

2 world] *place B*   4 road] *path B*

---

3. *Tr* and *1840* supply "one" after "lovely"; an editorial addition by M.W.S.

6. *hearth:* "heath" in *Tr* (a plausible misreading of *B*), corrected to "hearth" in *1840*.

7. The first and last words of a new line were written in darker ink here, evidently after the lines that follow. *1840* omits "It" and prints "Where" as a 7th line—a reasonable editorial compromise.

9. *Do thou return for mine—:* This line was missed by M.W.S. and subsequent editors.

The Indian Girl's Song

First published in the *Liberal: Verse and Prose from the South,* I (London, 1822), p. 397 (*Lib.*), entitled "Song, written for an Indian Air;" reprinted with some changes in *Posthumous Poems* (1824), entitled "Lines to an Indian Air."

HOLOGRAPHS:

Bodleian MS Shelley adds. e. 7, pp. 144–53, draft (B^1); and fair copy of Stanzas 1 and 2 (B^2)

—————— adds. e. 17, pp. 199–200 rev.; fragment (B^3)

A fair copy described in Sotheby's Catalogue, Lot No. 473, for April, 1962, entitled "The Indian girls song," present owner unknown.

The text is taken from a photostat of the holograph sold at Sotheby's (*S*). Since *S* is scrupulously punctuated, I transcribe it literally except for one emendation: commas are inserted to mark the series in line 18. Two transcripts by M.W.S. have usually been ascribed by editors to Shelley, one in Harvard MS Eng. 258.2, fol. 20; another in the Pierpont Morgan Library MA 814 (*M*) (a water-stained copy presumably found on Shelley's body after his death and described by Browning); both transcripts are entitled "The Indian Serenade." *M* appears to be the source of the *Liberal* text, and perhaps of *1824* as well. Since these transcripts were both made during Shelley's lifetime, they may conceivably have independent authority. But five readings of *M* (in lines 3, 4, 7, 11, 15) are canceled or corrected in *H;* and the other variant readings, which have no support in any of the holographs, are probably suspect as well. The transcripts have nonetheless formed the basis of all subsequent texts. One stanza of the Bodleian draft is reproduced in facsimile and transcribed in *1934*, p. 55.

248

THE INDIAN GIRL'S SONG

I arise from dreams of thee
In the first sleep of night—
The winds are breathing low
And the stars are burning bright.
I arise from dreams of thee—   5
And a spirit in my feet
Has borne me—Who knows how?
To thy chamber window, sweet!—

The wandering airs they faint
On the dark silent stream—   10

1–2 *From dreams of thee beloved, I have risen wild & joyous* B¹
8 window] *lattice* B¹   10 On the dark & silent stream B²

1.–2. In the first draft all lines are written out as hexameters.

2. *In the first sleep of night:* Thus in B¹, B², B³, and S. Both transcripts (M
and H), *Lib.*, and *1824* read "In the first sweet sleep of night" as do all subsequent editions. The introduction of "sweet" appears to be a transcription error
by M.W.S.; possibly the word slipped in from line 8 or 12.

3. *The winds are breathing low:* Thus in B¹, B², and S. M reads "When the
winds are breathing low" as do *Lib.* and *1824;* "When" is written but deleted
in H.

4. *burning:* Thus in B¹, B², S, M, H, and *Lib.* "shining" in *1824, 1839,* and
most subsequent editions. "shining" appears to be a late editorial change or slip
by M.W.S.

7. *Has borne me—Who knows how?:* Thus in B¹, B², and S. The line undergoes the following mutations: "Hath led me, oh! who knows how?" (*M*); "Has
borne me, *oh!* who knows how?" (*H*); "Hath led me, Who knows how?" (*Lib.*);
"Has led me—who knows how?" (*1824*). "oh!" is clearly an error, corrected in
H and both printed texts; agreement of all holographs suggests that "Hath led"
is an error as well (and certainly tamer and less characteristic than "Has borne").

9–14. drafts:

> *The wind of night expires on the bosom of the stream*
> *The winds around me die,*
> The airs around me faint on the flowers & the stream
> The *dewy* odours die away on the dewy dying breeze
> The nightingales complaint, grows weak *in her wild dream*
> The wandering airs—they faint—upon the silent stream
> The champac odours *die   fail*, like thoughts of a *sad* sweet dream   B¹

10. Both transcripts, *Lib.*, and *1824* read "On the dark, the silent stream."
Shelley made changes in the line ("Upon the silent stream;" "On the dark &
silent stream;" "On the dark silent stream"), but the holographs offer no support
for the transcript reading, and I would therefore ascribe the rather awkward
locution to M.W.S.

The champak odours fail
Like sweet thoughts in a dream;
The nightingale's complaint—
It dies upon her heart—
As I must die on thine   15
O beloved as thou art!

O lift me from the grass!
I die, I faint, I fail!
Let thy love in kisses rain
On my lips and eyelids pale.   20
My cheek is cold and white, alas!
My heart beats loud and fast.
Oh press it close to thine again
Where it will break at last.

11 The odours of my chaplet fail B^2 17 grass] *earth* B^1 19 *Let
thy kisses fall like dew* B^1 21 *My breath is ebbing and my heart* B^1
23–24 O press it against thine again—there let it break at last B^1

11. "And the champak" in *M*.
15. *As I must die on thine:* "die" is omitted in *M, Lib.*, and *1824*, but restored
in *1839*.
16. *O beloved as thou art:* "O" is omitted in *Lib.* and *1824*, but restored in
1839.
23. *Oh press it close to thine again:* Thus in *S, H,* and *1824*. In *S* the draft
reading: "press it against thine" was followed, but "against" is deleted and "close
to" substituted. *M* reads "Oh press it to thine own again;" *Lib.* reads: "O! press
me to thine own again" (clearly an error, in view of the pronoun left dangling
in line 24).
additional lines; possibly intended for a second stanza:
   I faint   I fail   I die away
   Open I faint   I die
   Come forth, look forth—I die away

   Come sisters of the dance
   Weave the splendours of the dance
   As the wind leads forth the clouds through the Heavens wild & wide
   As the moon leads forth her stars in the purple eventide
   I lead ye—to the dance
   To the dance B^1
another fragment:
   I arise from dreams of thee
   In the first sleep of night
   O pillow cold & wet with tears
   Thou breathest sleep no more B^2

"When passion's trance is overpast"

First published in *Posthumous Poems* (1824)

HOLOGRAPHS:

Bodleian MS Shelley adds. e. 12, pp. 6–7

The text is taken from *B*.

> When passion's trance is overpast,
> If tenderness and truth could last
> Or live, whilst all wild feelings keep
> Some mortal slumber, dark and deep,
> I should not weep, I should not weep!　　　　5
>
> It were enough to feel, to see
> Thy soft eyes gazing tenderly . . .
> And dream the rest—and burn and be
> The secret food of fires unseen,
> Could thou but be what thou hast been.　　　10
>
> After the slumber of the year
> The woodland violets reappear;
> All things revive in field or grove
> And sky and sea, but two, which move
> And form all others—life and love.　　　　15

1 trance] *storm B*　　3 all wild feelings keep] *passion　sleep B*　　6 It were enough *for mine B*　　7 gazing] *looking B*　　8 be] *die B*　9 *As one consumed with B*

---

10. *Could thou but be what thou hast been.: 1824* and all later editions read: "Couldst thou but be as thou hast been." There is no transcript in the two notebooks M.W.S. used for the poems published in *1824,* which raises the possibility that she had access to another text, now lost. But the line is clearly written out in *B,* and there seems no reason, without further evidence, to prefer *1824.*

"The flower that smiles today"

First published in *Posthumous Poems* (1824), entitled "Mutability"

HOLOGRAPHS:

> Bodleian MS Shelley adds. e. 7, p. 2 and front endpaper; draft (*B*¹)
> ——— adds. e. 7, p. 154; fair copy (*B*²)

The text is taken from *B*²; I have added a comma after "night," line 6, but otherwise follow the holograph punctuation exactly. *1824* is based on a transcript of *B*² by M.W.S. in Bodleian MS Shelley adds. d. 7, pp. **18–19**.

> The flower that smiles today
> 　　Tomorrow dies;
> All that we wish to stay
> 　　Tempts and then flies;
> What is this world's delight? 　　　　　　　　5
> Lightning, that mocks the night,
> 　　Brief even as bright.—
>
> Virtue, how frail it is!—
> 　　Friendship, how rare!—
> Love, how it sells poor bliss 　　　　　　　　10
> 　　For proud despair!
> But these though soon they fall,
> Survive their joy, and all
> 　　Which ours we call.—

1 smiles] *blooms B*¹　　　7 even as] *although B*²　　　11 proud] *rich B*²
13 their] *its B*¹

---

9. "Friendship too rare!" in *1824* and *1839,* corrected in modern editions.

12. *But these though soon they fall:* "these" in *B*¹ and *B*²; "we" in *1824* and all later editions. *Tr* reads "these." *1824* evidently represents an editorial change, an attempt to clarify a difficult thought. But "these" refers to "Virtue," "Friendship," "Love," which, unhappily, outlive their fall, or betrayal.

252

Whilst skies are blue and bright, 15
   Whilst flowers are gay,
Whilst eyes that change ere night
   Make glad the day;
Whilst yet the calm hours creep
Dream thou—and from thy sleep 20
   Then wake to weep.

21 to] and B^1

"When the lamp is shattered"

First published in part in [T. Medwin], *Ahasuerus the Wanderer* (London 1823), pp. 96–97; published in a complete version in *Posthumous Poems* (1824), entitled "Lines."

Holographs:
    Bodleian MS Shelley adds. e. 18, pp. 159–57, 155, all rev.; draft
    Glasgow University Library MS Gen. 505/34; fair copy, first three
    stanzas only (*G*)
    British Museum Add. MS 37232.f.75; fair copy (*BM*)

The text is taken from *BM*. *G* appears to be based on the final draft in *B;* it includes corrections which agree with the version in *BM* (possibly added by someone other than Shelley). *BM* is beautifully written out and punctuated; I have added or altered punctuation only in lines 22 and 24. *1824* appears to be based on *BM,* which it reproduces accurately, with minor changes in punctuation. I have not seen a copy of the extremely rare *Ahasuerus* (there is a copy in the British Museum), but H. B. Forman transcribes the text in his edition of Medwin's *Life of Shelley* (London, 1913), pp. 491–92. Forman accepts Medwin's text as a genuine variant, but it seems far more likely to be an inaccurate version of the text used for *1824*.

> When the lamp is shattered
> The light in the dust lies dead—
> When the cloud is scattered
> The rainbow's glory is shed—
> When the lute is broken   5

5–8, 17–20. drafts:

> The harp,—*it* is broken
>   The *music is* tones are dead;
> *The lips—they have spoken*
>   *The breath is now fled*
> The lips *would* which have spoken—
>   Their accents are soon forgot.

254

Sweet tones are remembered not—
  When the lips have spoken
Loved accents are soon forgot.

  As music and splendour
Survive not the lamp and the lute,   10
  The heart's echoes render
No song when the spirit is mute—
  No song—but sad dirges
Like the wind through a ruined cell
  Or the mournful surges   15
That ring the dead seaman's knell.

  When hearts have once mingled
Love first leaves the well-built nest—
  The weak one is singled

6 Sweet *music is soon forgot G*   tones] notes *G*   14 through] in *G*
16 dead] lost *G*   17 Where *G*

5–8, 17–20. drafts (continued):

> *The heart would have which had bounded*
>   *To greet him again*
> *When the heart is cold grows heavy*
>   *As the clay where it soon will rest*

> When the *harp* lute is broken
>   *The* Sweet tones are remembered not—
> When the lips have spoken
>   *Their* Loved accents are *soon* quite forgot—
> *When from hearts once mingled*
>   *The wild bird flies from the fixst nest—*
>   *The wild bird of that weak nest*
>   *Love first leaves that soft nest*
> The weak one is singled
>   To endure   *B*

9–10. drafts:

> Light music & splendour
> In the rainbow the lamp & the lute   *B*
> additional lines, possibly for a first stanza:
> The rude wind is singing
>   The dirge of the music dead
> The cold worms are clinging
>   Where kisses even lately fed—   *B*

17–24. This stanza is preceded by the words "second part" in *G*. Lines 25–32 presumably were written on a second page, now lost.

To endure what it once possest.   20
  O Love! who bewailest
The frailty of all things here,
  Why choose you the frailest
For your cradle, your home and your bier?

  Its passions will rock thee   25
As the storms rock the ravens on high—
  Bright Reason will mock thee
Like the Sun from a wintry sky—
  From thy nest every rafter
Will rot, and thine eagle home   30
  Leave thee naked to laughter
When leaves fall and cold winds come.

23 choose] chose *G*   24 bier. *BM*   25 passions] tempests *B*
26 *And thy heaven must be still despair—B*   28 Like the *frost* of
the *B*   32 *When the day of thy destiny come B*

The Magnetic Lady to her Patient

First published in the *Athenaeum,* August 11, 1832, and in Medwin, *The Shelley Papers;* reprinted in *Poetical Works* (1839); a corrected text published in *Poetical Works* (1840).

HOLOGRAPH:
University Library, King's College, Aberdeen, MS 937; fair copy *(K)*

The text is taken from the holograph. *K* seems to be the source both of Medwin's printing and *1840;* but there are several errors in both, and those in *1840* are perpetuated in all later editions. There are two verbal errors in *1840:* one "sleep" is omitted in line 10, and "But" is substituted for "Yet" in line 11. The repunctuation is significant, too, and is compounded by the repunctuation of later editors. Several lines are thus garbled in all modern editions: the ellipsis is omitted after "unborn," line 20; punctuation is omitted after "wake," line 22; and the comma placed before "yet," line 44, instead of after it. Like all the Trelawny MSS, the holograph is beautifully written out, and I print it unchanged, except for the addition of commas at the ends of lines 2, 3, 40, 42. Stanza indention is irregular, however; I have used what seems the most consistent pattern.

THE MAGNETIC LADY TO HER PATIENT

"Sleep, sleep on, forget thy pain—
My hand is on thy brow,
My spirit on thy brain,
My pity on thy heart, poor friend;
And from my fingers flow   5

At the top of the page is written "For Jane & Williams alone to see." The outer wrapping of the poem reads: "To Jane. Not to be opened unless you are alone, or with Williams." The person Jane would be likely to be with, of course, was Mary.

257

The powers of life, and like a sign
Seal thee from thine hour of woe,
And brood on thee, but may not blend
    With thine.

"Sleep, sleep, sleep on,—I love thee not—   10
    Yet when I think that *he*
    Who made and makes my lot
As full of flowers, as thine of weeds,
    Might have been lost like thee,—
And that a hand which was not mine   15
Might then have charmed his agony
As I another's—my heart bleeds
    For thine.

"Sleep, sleep, and with the slumber of
    The dead and the unborn . . .   20
    Forget thy life and love;
Forget that thou must wake,—forever
    Forget the world's dull scorn.—
Forget lost health, and the divine
Feelings which died in youth's brief morn;   25
And forget me, for I can never
    Be thine.—

"Like a cloud big with a May shower
    My soul weeps healing rain
    On thee, thou withered flower.—   30
It breathes mute music on thy sleep,
    Its odour calms thy brain—
Its light within thy gloomy breast
Spreads, like a second youth again—
By mine thy being is to its deep   35
    Possest.—

25 died] *fell K*

"The spell is done—how feel you now?"
   "Better, quite well" replied
   The sleeper—"What would do
You good when suffering and awake,   40
   What cure your head and side?"
"What would cure that would kill me, Jane,
And as I must on earth abide
Awhile yet, tempt me not to break
   My chain."   45

To Jane
("THE KEEN STARS WERE TWINKLING")

First published in part by Medwin, in the *Athenaeum,* November 17, 1832, entitled "An Ariette for Music. To a Lady singing to her Accompaniment on the Guitar;" reprinted in *Poetical Works* (1839); a complete corrected text published in *Poetical Works* (1840).

HOLOGRAPHS:

Bodleian MS Shelley adds. c. 4, fols. 56, 33v, 38v rev.; draft (*B*)
University of Manchester Library, fair copy (*M*)

The text is taken from *M*. Punctuation is followed exactly except for a comma added at the end of line 2. *M,* one of the Trelawny MSS, appears to be based on *B* and is in turn the basis of *1840*. The Bodleian draft readings are noted in Reiman, *Shelley's "The Triumph of Life,"* pp. 245–46.

TO JANE

The keen stars were twinkling
And the fair moon was rising among them,
Dear Jane.
The guitar was tinkling
But the notes were not sweet till you sung them   5

1 were] *are B*   2 And the moon *is* rising among them, *bright B*

---

written across the page of *M:* "I sate down to write some words for an ariette which might be profane—but it was in vain to struggle with the ruling spirit, who compelled me to speak of things sacred to yours & Wilhelmeister's indulgence—I commit them to your secrecy & your mercy & will try & do better another time."

5. *But the notes were not sweet till you sung them:* Reiman reads "sang" for "sung" in *B*. The word could conceivably be either (though it looks like "sung" to me), but the rhyme with "among," line 2, suggests "sung," and *M* is unambiguous.

Again.—
As the moon's soft splendour
O'er the faint cold starlight of Heaven
　　　　Is thrown—
So your voice most tender　　　　　　　　　　10
To the strings without soul had then given
　　　　Its own.

The stars will awaken,
Though the moon sleep a full hour later,
　　　　Tonight;　　　　　　　　　　　　15
No leaf will be shaken
While the dews of your melody scatter
　　　　Delight.
Though the sound overpowers
Sing again, with your dear voice revealing　　20
　　　　A tone
Of some world far from ours,
Where music and moonlight and feeling
　　　　Are one.

8 faint] *dim B*　　9 thrown] *spread M*　　10 So *thy* voice sweet &
tender *B*　　13 *If the stars should still tremble B*　　14–15 Though
the moon *will not rise from the mountain / So soon. — an hour more in
the Ocean / Will sleep B*　　16 *Do not seek to resemble B*
17 While] Whilst *B*　　20 Sing again, for thy voice is revealing *B*
22 ours] this one *B*　　23–24 Where moonlight & music & feeling /
Are won *B*

10. *So your voice most tender:* Reiman reads "one" for "your" in *B;* the word
written above "*thy*" could be "your" with a blotted "y," or "one" with a blot
preceding it.
16. Reiman reads "Not a leaf will *be* shaken" in *B;* the line is almost indecipherable. Shelley may have written "Not a leaf," then changed it to "No leaf"
for the rhythmic pattern (as Reiman suggests).

With a Guitar

TO JANE

First published by Medwin, in the *Athenaeum,* October 20, 1832, and *The Shelley Papers* (lines 43–90 only); lines 1–42 were published in *Fraser's Magazine,* January, 1833. Medwin's text is reprinted in *Poetical Works* (1839); a complete corrected text is published in *Poetical Works* (1840), entitled "To a Lady with a Guitar."

HOLOGRAPHS:

> Bodleian MS Shelley adds. e, 18, p. 105; draft of lines 1–12 (B^1)
> ————adds. e. 3; fair copy (B^2)

The text is taken from B^2, the Trelawny MS, which is the source of *1840;* there are no substantive differences between the two, except for the substitution of "friend" for "Jane" in line 90. But it still seems useful to present Shelley's text as he punctuated it in this beautifully written holograph, and I have accordingly made no emendations in punctuation. *1904* follows *1840,* but restores "Jane" to line 90 from B^2.

WITH A GUITAR
TO JANE

Ariel to Miranda;—Take
This slave of music for the sake
Of him who is the slave of thee;
And teach it all the harmony,
In which thou canst, and only thou,   5
Make the delighted spirit glow,
Till joy denies itself again

2 This *child* *of* B^1 4 And of the *hidden* antient harmony B^1
6 Make his delighted B^1 7 Till pleasures *hide* B^1

262

And too intense is turned to pain;
For by permission and command
Of thine own prince Ferdinand   10
Poor Ariel sends this silent token
Of more than ever can be spoken;
Your guardian spirit Ariel, who
From life to life must still pursue
Your happiness, for thus alone   15
Can Ariel ever find his own;
From Prospero's enchanted cell,
As the mighty verses tell,
To the throne of Naples he
Lit you o'er the trackless sea,   20
Flitting on, your prow before,
Like a living meteor.
When you die, the silent Moon
In her interlunar swoon
Is not sadder in her cell   25
Than deserted Ariel;
When you live again on Earth
Like an unseen Star of birth
Ariel guides you o'er the sea
Of life from your nativity;   30
Many changes have been run
Since Ferdinand and you begun
Your course of love, and Ariel still
Has tracked your steps and served your will;
Now, in humbler, happier lot   35
This is all remembered not;
And now, alas! the poor sprite is
Imprisoned for some fault of his
In a body like a grave:—
From you, he only dares to crave   40
For his service and his sorrow
A smile today, a song tomorrow.

25 sadder] *darker B²*

The artist who this idol wrought
To echo all harmonious thought
Felled a tree, while on the steep   45
The woods were in their winter sleep
Rocked in that repose divine
On the wind-swept Apennine;
And dreaming, some of autumn past
And some of spring approaching fast,   50
And some of April buds and showers
And some of songs in July bowers
And all of love,—and so this tree—
O that such our death may be—
Died in sleep, and felt no pain,   55
To live in happier form again,
From which, beneath Heaven's fairest star,
The artist wrought this loved guitar,
And taught it justly to reply
To all who question skilfully   60
In language gentle as thine own;
Whispering in enamoured tone
Sweet oracles of woods and dells
And summer winds in sylvan cells
For it had learnt all harmonies   65
Of the plains and of the skies,
Of the forests and the mountains,
And the many-voiced fountains,
The clearest echoes of the hills,
The softest notes of falling rills,   70
The melodies of birds and bees,
The murmuring of summer seas,
And pattering rain and breathing dew
And airs of evening;— and it knew
That seldom heard mysterious sound,   75
Which, driven on its diurnal round
As it floats through boundless day
Our world enkindles on its way—

54 may] *should* B²

All this it knows, but will not tell
To those who cannot question well   80
The spirit that inhabits it:
It talks according to the wit
Of its companions; and no more
Is heard than has been felt before
By those who tempt it to betray   85
These secrets of an elder day.—
But, sweetly as its answers will
Flatter hands of perfect skill,
It keeps its highest holiest tone
For our beloved Jane alone.—   90

To Jane
THE INVITATION; THE RECOLLECTION

First published in *Posthumous Poems* (1824) as one poem, entitled "The Pine Forest in the Cascine." Published as two separate poems in *Poetical Works* (1840). Lines 41–52 of "The Recollection" were first published in [T. Medwin], *Ahasuerus the Wanderer* (London, 1823), pp. 89–90. "The Invitation" is newly edited in Matthews, ed. *Shelley: Selected Poems and Prose.*

HOLOGRAPHS:

> Bodleian MS Shelley adds. c. 4, fol. 64; draft of lines 29–32 of "The Recollection"
> University Library, Cambridge, add. MS 4444; fair copy of "The Invitation" (*C*)
> British Museum add. MS 37538, fols. 40–41v; fair copy of "The Recollection" (*BM*)

The text for "The Invitation" is taken from *C;* for "The Recollection" from *BM* with one emendation from *1824.* Both holographs are exquisitely written out, and I follow their punctuation closely, though commas are added between series and at line-endings. *1840* is based on *C* and *BM* with a half-dozen variants, erratically corrected in modern editions. *1824* is based on a transcript by M.W.S. in Bodleian MS Shelley adds. d. 7, pp. 53–62, of an earlier draft. If all passages from *Tr* are included, it appears that M.W.S. was working from an essentially complete draft of the final version. The draft must have been much-canceled, however, and *Tr* is so obviously faulty that there seems no point in providing a full collation. I am indebted to G. M. Matthews for information about the extract in *Ahasuerus the Wanderer.*

THE INVITATION

Best and brightest, come away—
Fairer far than this fair day
Which like thee to those in sorrow

Comes to bid a sweet good-morrow
To the rough year just awake   5
In its cradle on the brake.—
The brightest hour of unborn spring
Through the winter wandering
Found, it seems, the halcyon morn
To hoar February born;   10
Bending from Heaven in azure mirth
It kissed the forehead of the earth
And smiled upon the silent sea,
And bade the frozen streams be free
And waked to music all their fountains   15
And breathed upon the frozen mountains
And like a prophetess of May
Strewed flowers upon the barren way,
Making the wintry world appear
Like one on whom thou smilest, dear.   20

Away, away from men and towns
To the wild wood and the downs,
To the silent wilderness
Where the soul need not repress
Its music lest it should not find   25
An echo in another's mind,
While the touch of Nature's art
Harmonizes heart to heart.—
I leave this notice on my door
For each accustomed visitor—   30
"I am gone into the fields
To take what this sweet hour yields.
Reflexion, you may come tomorrow,
Sit by the fireside with Sorrow—
You, with the unpaid bill, Despair,   35
You, tiresome verse-reciter Care,

9. *Found, it seems, the halcyon morn:* "this halcyon morn" in *1824* and *Tr;* evidently Shelley's draft reading was "this." It may be that "the halcyon morn" is a slip. Matthews emends to "this."

I will pay you in the grave,
Death will listen to your stave—
Expectation too, be off!
To-day is for itself enough—   40
Hope, in pity mock not woe
With smiles, nor follow where I go;
Long having lived on thy sweet food,
At length I find one moment's good
After long pain—with all your love   45
This you never told me of."

Radiant Sister of the day,
Awake, arise and come away
To the wild woods and the plains
And the pools where winter-rains   50
Image all their roof of leaves,
Where the pine its garland weaves
Of sapless green and ivy dun
Round stems that never kiss the Sun—
Where the lawns and pastures be   55
And the sandhills of the sea—
Where the melting hoar-frost wets
The daisy-star that never sets,
And wind-flowers, and violets
Which yet join not scent to hue   60
Crown the pale year weak and new,
When the night is left behind
In the deep east dun and blind
And the blue noon is over us,
And the multitudinous   65
Billows murmur at our feet

60 yet] *now* C   62 When] *Now* C   64–65 *The blue   And the*
noon like Heaven's love / Is built around & roofed above C

---

57. "Where" in *1840* and modern editions; "When" in Matthews. The MS looks
to me like "Where," though Shelley's "n" and "re" are not always clearly differentiated.

Where the earth and ocean meet,
And all things seem only one
In the universal Sun.—

THE RECOLLECTION
Feb. 2, 1822

Now the last day of many days,
All beautiful and bright as thou,
The loveliest and the last, is dead.
Rise Memory, and write its praise!
Up to thy wonted work! come, trace   5
The epitaph of glory fled;
For now the Earth has changed its face,
A frown is on the Heaven's brow.

1.
We wandered to the pine forest
    That skirts the ocean foam;   10
The lightest wind was in its nest,
    The Tempest in its home;
The whispering waves were half asleep,
    The clouds were gone to play,
And on the bosom of the deep   15
    The smile of Heaven lay;
It seemed as if the hour were one
    Sent from beyond the skies,
Which scattered from above the sun
    A light of Paradise.   20

1 days; *BM*   6 fled] dead *BM*

---

6. *Tr* and *1824* read: "The epitaph of glory fled;" (presumably Shelley's draft reading). I follow modern editors in emending *BM*, which seems a likely authorial slip.

2.

We paused amid the pines that stood
    The giants of the waste,
Tortured by storms to shapes as rude
    As serpents interlaced,
And soothed by every azure breath   25
    That under Heaven is blown
To harmonies and hues beneath,
    As tender as its own;
Now all the tree-tops lay asleep
    Like green waves on the sea,   30
As still as in the silent deep
    The Ocean woods may be.

3.

How calm it was! the silence there
    By such a chain was bound
That even the busy woodpecker   35
    Made stiller with her sound
The inviolable quietness;
    The breath of peace we drew
With its soft motion made not less
    The calm that round us grew.—   40
There seemed from the remotest seat
    Of the white mountain-waste,
To the soft flower beneath our feet
    A magic circle traced,
A spirit interfused around   45
    A thrilling silent life,
To momentary peace it bound
    Our mortal nature's strife;—
And still I felt the centre of
    The magic circle there   50
Was one fair form that filled with love
    The lifeless atmosphere.

29 Now] *And* *BM*   52 lifeless] *breath*less *BM*

4.

We paused beside the pools that lie
  Under the forest bough—
Each seemed as 'twere, a little sky   55
  Gulfed in a world below;
A firmament of purple light
  Which in the dark earth lay
More boundless than the depth of night
  And purer than the day,   60
In which the lovely forests grew
  As in the upper air,
More perfect, both in shape and hue,
  Than any spreading there;
There lay the glade, the neighboring lawn,   65
  And through the dark green wood
The white sun twinkling like the dawn
  Out of a speckled cloud.

5.

Sweet views, which in our world above
  Can never well be seen,   70
Were imaged in the water's love
  Of that fair forest green;
And all was interfused beneath
  With an Elysian glow,
An atmosphere without a breath,   75
  A softer day below—
Like one beloved, the scene had lent
  To the dark water's breast,
Its every leaf and lineament
  With more than truth exprest;   80
Until an envious wind crept by,
  Like an unwelcome thought

77–80. These lines follow line 64, in *Tr* and *1824,* an order which seems clearer than that of *BM* (and which presumably reflects the original order of Shelley's draft). But it is clear from the stanza break in *BM* that Shelley intended the change.

Which from the mind's too faithful eye
    Blots one dear image out.—
Though thou art ever fair and kind   85
    And forests ever green,
Less oft is peace in ——'s mind
    Than calm in water seen.

---

87. "S——'s" in *1824* and *1840;* most editors fill in "Shelley's."
additional stanza:

Were not the crocuses that grew
    Under that ilex-tree
As beautiful in scent and hue
    As ever fed the bee?   *1824*

In *Tr* these lines occur separately; M.W.S. places them arbitrarily before line 81
of *1824*. It seems to me they must have been intended to follow lines 57–60 of
"The Recollection," and were probably canceled in favor of lines 61–64, which
repeat the rhyme and the sentiment.

Lines written in the Bay of Lerici

First published by Richard Garnett in *Macmillan's Magazine,* 6 (June, 1862), 122–23, and in *Relics of Shelley;* a new text was published in G. M. Matthews, "Shelley and Jane Williams," *Review of English Studies,* n.s. 12 (1961), 40–48; additional readings are offered in Reiman, *Shelley's "The Triumph of Life,"* pp. 244–45.

HOLOGRAPH:
 Bodleian MS Shelley adds. c. 4, fols. 35–36v

The text is taken from *B,* with some punctuation silently added. The poem appears essentially complete, though one line has been left unfinished. I must record particular indebtedness to Matthews' rendering of the text; he also lists Garnett's readings and some deletions in *B.* Deletions are also discussed in Donald H. Reiman, "Shelley's 'The Triumph of Life:' The Biographical Problem," *PMLA,* 78 (1963), 536–50.

LINES WRITTEN IN THE BAY OF LERICI

Bright wanderer, fair coquette of Heaven,
To whom alone it has been given
To change and be adored for ever. . . .
Envy not this dim world, for never
But once within its shadow grew   5
One fair as [thou], but far more true.

---

title: *B* is untitled; Garnett provides the title given.
6. *One fair as [thou], but far more true.:* The fourth word is almost indecipherable; Matthews reads "you," but I do not see these letters in *B.* Shelley would probably have used "thou" in any case, and the internal rhyme would be uncharacteristic. The last four words are equally difficult to read; "but far more true" is by no means certain.

273

She left me at the silent time
When the moon had ceased to climb
The azure dome of Heaven's steep,
And like an albatross asleep,   10
Balanced on her wings of light,
Hovered in the purple night,
Ere she sought her Ocean nest
In the chambers of the west.—
She left me, and I staid alone   15
Thinking over every tone,
Which though now silent to the ear
The enchanted heart could hear
Like notes which die when born, but still
Haunt the echoes of the hill: 20
And feeling ever—O too much—
The soft vibrations of her touch
As if her gentle hand even now
Lightly trembled on my brow;
And thus although she absent were   25
Memory gave me all of her
That even fancy dares to claim.—
Her presence had made weak and tame
All passions, and I lived alone,
In the time which is our own;   30

9 dome] *path B*   steep] *deep B*   12 night—*B*   13 *And I, who
sate beside her feet*   Ere she *flew to seek her B*   15 staid] *sate B*
19 *Like music past which B*   24 trembled] *placed B*   25–26 *And
thus contented with a lot / Which others, who have suffered not, B*
26 Memory] *Fancy B*   27 *I dare to   That fate B*   28–29 *Thus
was I happy,   if the name / Of happiness   Charmed by her presence,
meek & tame / The demon of my spirit lay B*   29–30 *Desire & fear:
I thought no more / Of pleasure lost or sorrows B*   30 is] *was B*

---

7. The poem probably began with this line, which is written in an earlier form
on fol. 36v rev. (underneath the last lines of the draft), evidently a discarded
opening: "She left me when the moon was." Lines 1–6 look as if they were
written in after the poem was completed, and Garnett prints them as a separate
fragment.

The past and future were forgot
As they had been, and would be, not.—
But soon, the guardian angel gone,
The demon reassumed his throne
In my faint heart . . . I dare not speak   35
My thoughts; but thus disturbed and weak
I sate and watched the vessels glide
Along the ocean bright and wide,
Like spirit-winged chariots sent
O'er some serenest element   40
For ministrations strange and far;
As if to some Elysian star
They sailed for drink to medicine
Such sweet and bitter pain as mine—
And the wind that winged their flight   45
From the land came fresh and light,
And the scent of sleeping flowers
And the coolness of the hours
Of dew, and the sweet warmth of day
Was scattered o'er the twinkling bay;   50
And the fisher with his lamp
And spear, about the low rocks damp
Crept, and struck the fish who came
To worship the delusive flame:

33 *But now I desired,—I dare not* B   35 faint] *weak* B   speak]
tell B   39 *Like chariots of   oer an element* B   40 serenest]
divinest B   43 sailed] *went for some clear* B   45 *I saw   watched
the dark rocks* B   51 fisher*men* B   his] *their* B   52 *In the dark
rocks* B   53 *Watching to destroy the* B

---

41. Matthews reads "To ministrations;" Reiman reads "For."
47–50. early drafts:

So that on the sifted sand
  Which divided sea & land
Like   Only a thread of moonlight lay
  Upon   On the disentangled spray

And the warmth the day had left
And the breath of night

> Too happy, they whose pleasure sought   55
> Extinguishes all sense and thought
> Of the regret that pleasure [   ]
> Seeking life not peace.

58 Seeking] *Destroy*ing *B*   not peace] alone *B*

---

57. *Of the regret that pleasure:* The line is incomplete in *B;* Garnett added
"leaves," possibly on the analogy of "The Witch of Atlas," lines 159–60.

58. *Seeking life not peace.:* The line was first written: "Destroying life not
peace." "Destroy" is canceled, and "Seeking" is written underneath. "alone" is
written above "not peace," and "not peace" is underlined, Shelley's usual method
of indicating his final preference. Line 57 was probably left incomplete pending
the choice of the rhyme word in line 58. The order of composition appears to
have been: "Destroying life not peace;" "Seeking life alone;" "Seeking life not
peace." Matthews renders the line: "Seeking Life alone *not peace;*" but it seems
to me that Shelley's underlining here indicates "stet," not "italics." Reiman reads
a colon after peace, which would suggest that the poem is unfinished. But the
colon looks to me like a period; I read the last four lines as an unmistakable
final quatrain, similar in its aphoristic tone to the final quatrain of "The Recollection."

TWO TEXTUAL PUZZLES

Two LYRICS that Mary Shelley published for the first time in *Posthumous Poems* (1824), "I fear thy kisses, gentle maiden" and "Music, when soft voices die," present special textual difficulties. Both lyrics have been loved for generations (they were both anthologized in Palgrave's *Golden Treasury*), but their sole manuscript sources appear to be incomplete drafts substantially longer and more chaotic than the versions printed by Mary Shelley. It is possible that the poems as Mary printed them are Shelley's in substance but not in form, so to speak; that is, they may represent an attempt either by Mary or one of the friends she consulted to extract a finished poem from an incomplete draft. In neither case, I believe, are literary considerations alone decisive, and in default of new textual evidence, both puzzles are likely to remain unsolved.

I. "I fear thy kisses, gentle maiden"

The poem as Mary printed it in *Posthumous Poems* reads as follows:

TO ——

> I fear thy kisses, gentle maiden,
>   Thou needest not fear mine;
> My spirit is too deeply laden
>   Ever to burthen thine.
>
> I fear thy mien, thy tones, thy motion,
>   Thou needest not fear mine;
> Innocent is the heart's devotion
>   With which I worship thine.

Unlike most of the lyrics printed for the first time in *Posthumous Poems,* there is no copy of the poem in Mary's notebooks. The only other record of the poem is the holograph draft (Bodleian MS Shelley adds. e. 12, pp. 115–16).[1] The text occurs on two facing pages, and there is no clear indication which of the two precedes the other. But it seems more likely to me that Shelley began, as he often does in the notebooks, on the right-hand page (p. 116), and continued on the left-hand page (p. 115), and I print the stanzas in that order. (Deletions are in italic type.)

p. 116   I fear thy *singing* sweet voice   child of *sweetness* Beauty
           It is too sweet for me
     Thy sweet voice makes   song dissolves   It binds more
           tight the chain of Duty
           Heavy & tight for

---

1. Lines from the holograph are published in *Works,* IV, 45.

278

Whilst thou remainest free
And lingerest

I fear thy *look* mein thy *mein* tones thy motion
    Thou needest not fear mine
What is there in
Innocent is the hearts devotion
    With which I worship thine

Yet kiss me,

p. 115   *I kiss*
     Fear not my kisses, fairest maiden

    I fear thy kisses gentle maiden—
    Thou needest not fear mine
My spirit is too deeply laden
    Ever to burthen thine;
How wouldst thou walk beneath the load
    Which I bear smiling.

From the holograph I would conjecture that Shelley began to draft the poem on page 116, with the stanza beginning "I fear thy sweet voice child of Beauty;" wrote a second stanza beginning "I fear thy mein thy tones thy motion;" moved from the half-line "Yet kiss me," to the page opposite, and began again: "Fear not my kisses, fairest maiden;" then wrote the stanza beginning: "I fear thy kisses gentle maiden—." This stanza, possibly the last in order of composition, may have been intended as a new beginning for the lyric. It is the only stanza that appears to have been fully revised; the pencil of the draft is written over in ink, in the form in which it appears above, and despite the uncharacteristic irregularity of form in the last two lines, the stanza appears complete. Hence the puzzle; for if we had Mary's version alone, and no holograph (as is the case, for instance, with "One word is too often profaned"), we would probably accept the charming eight-line poem published in *Posthumous Poems* as a completed lyric.

The most attractive possibility is that Shelley extrapolated the eight lines himself, in a copy that has since disappeared (given perhaps to Sophia Stacey, the presumptive maiden). The fact that

Mary *could* have derived the poem directly from the draft, however, makes it somewhat more likely that she did so; for if she was in fact working from a copy now missing, there is a good chance that some additional change would have been made. On literary grounds, I must confess some reluctance to accept the printed text as a finished poem; Shelley's short lyrics, whether two or three stanzas (and three seems the preferred length) make more emphatic use of balance and contrast; the rhetorical organization is usually more pointed. On the other hand, Mary has presented the reader with a more satisfactory lyric than we can probably extract unaided from the draft, and it may be that she had Shelley's authority for doing so. Since Shelley undoubtedly wrote the lines of which the poem is composed, I would be unwilling to jettison Mary's text. But I would also be hesitant to subject it to extensive literary analysis. In printing the text, I would recommend some indication of doubt as to its authority.

II. "Music, when soft voices die"

"Music, when soft voices die" presents the same kind of textual puzzle as "I fear thy kisses;" every line in it was written by Shelley, but its final shape is problematic.[2] The text as Mary Shelley printed it in *Posthumous Poems* reads as follows:

TO ——

Music, when soft voices die,
Vibrates in the memory—
Odours, when sweet violets sicken,
Live within the sense they quicken.

Rose leaves, when the rose is dead,
Are heaped for the beloved's bed;
And so thy thoughts, when thou art gone,
Love itself shall slumber on.

There seems little doubt that Mary took these lines directly from her notebook copy, in which, however, the two stanzas are reversed, and the whole is entitled "Memory," as follows:[3]

MEMORY

Rose leaves, when the rose is dead
Are heaped for the beloved's bed,

2. See Irving Massey, "Shelley's 'Music, When Soft Voices Die:' Text and Meaning," *JEGP*, 59 (1960), 430–38; and E. D. Hirsch, Jr., "Further Comment on 'Music, When Soft Voices Die,'" *JEGP*, 60 (1961), 296–98. Massey was the first critic, as far as I know, to challenge the *1824* text. Both the holograph and Mary Shelley's notebook copy are transcribed in Massey, *Posthumous Poems*, pp. 92, 257.
3. I omit some canceled letters and words; for a complete transcription, see Massey, *Posthumous Poems*, p. 92.

And so thy thoughts, when thou art gone,
Love itself shall slumber on

Spirit sweet—when soft voice
Music, when soft voices die,
Vibrates in the memory,—
Odours, when sweet violets sicken
Live within the sense they quicken—

Mary's notebook transcript is an attempt to disentangle the holograph draft of the poem, printed below (Bodleian MS Shelley adds. e. 8, p. 154 rev.). Some of the corrections and additions are written in a darker ink than the rest, which I indicate by boldface type.

A roseleaf when
Rose leaves, when the rose is dead,
Are heaped for *a Sultana's* the beloveds bed—
Poets   When   When a Poet   gone
The thoughts
And so thy thoughts, when thou art gone,
Love itself shall slumber on . . .

Spirit sweet! from th
Melodies even when they die,   Music when *sweet* **soft** voices die,
Linger   **Vibrates** in the memory.—
Odours,   *though*   **when sweet violets sicken**
Live within the sense **they quicken**

As desire within
As without hope
As desire when hope is dead   cold
As passion

Mary was correct in assuming that her transcript did not represent a finished poem of two quatrains, in the order in which she had copied them. The holograph does not offer any conclusive evidence as to the final shape of the lyric (if indeed it was finished), but the stages of revision, as indicated by the two kinds of ink, suggest that Shelley did not mean lines 3–4 of the second stanza on the page to be the final couplet. Presumably they were to be followed either by the lines written in darker ink, below, or by the final version of the stanza written above (as in Mary's printed version). On the basis of the ink changes and spacing, I would (very tentatively) reconstruct the process of composition as follows. Shelley first writes two parallel couplets, which he leaves incomplete:

> Rose leaves, when the rose is dead,
> Are heaped for a Sultana's bed—
> When a Poet   gone
> The thoughts

He then tries a new tack (more likely a new beginning than a second stanza, though either would be possible):

> Spirit sweet! from th——

(The unfinished word might perhaps be "thy".) He then writes two new couplets; meant perhaps to precede the couplets already written:

> Melodies even when they die,
> Linger in the memory.—
> Odours though
> Live within the sense

He leaves the second couplet unfinished, and returns to the lines first written, changes "a Sultana's" to "the beloveds," and completes a final couplet:

> And so thy thoughts, when thou art gone,
> Love itself shall slumber on . . .

At this time he also changes "Melodies even when they die," to "Music when sweet voices die." He then makes the changes in darker ink, experimenting with still another line ("As desire when hope is cold"), which is presumably discarded.

Obviously this reconstruction of the process of composition must remain conjectural. If correct, it would support Mary's final rendering of the lyric, though her decision to reverse the two stanzas

of her transcription may have been based on literary grounds, rather
than on an analysis of the holograph.

The poem as she finally printed it requires some hint of a context, to suggest that the lines are addressed to a particular person,
and that the "thoughts" which Love shall slumber on (as the "beloved" sleeps on a bed of rose leaves) are poetic thoughts, or poems,
like the poet's "dead thoughts" in "Ode to the West Wind." That
context could be provided by *Epipsychidion,* drafts of which appear in the same notebook as "Music, when soft voices die." The
images of the short lyric appear in the opening sections of the
longer poem: music, sweet melody, dead rose petals, faded blossoms. Emilia is apotheosized as "A cradle of young thoughts of
wingless pleasure" (line 68), and one of her "thoughts" about Love
graces the title of the poem. It seems reasonable to take Emilia,
addressed as "Sweet Spirit!" in the opening line of *Epipsychidion,*
as the "Spirit sweet!" of the line canceled in the short lyric, and to
read the lyric as a compliment to Emilia's poetry,[4] an affirmation
that it shall survive as a nest for Love, as music and odors survive
in the memory of those whose spirit they have once quickened.

In the case of "Music, when soft voices die," then, it seems to me
that there is strong literary support for the 1824 text, and possibly
textual support. But there is also strong evidence that the printed
version was the result of guesswork on Mary's part—inspired guesswork, perhaps. Therefore in printing the text I would include some
indication of doubt as to whether the poem is a fragment or a finished lyric.

4. Two of Emilia's sonnets are quoted in Enrico Viviani Della Robbia, *Vita
   di una Donna* (Florence, 1936), pp. 94–95; her essay on Love, "Il Vero
   Amore" (from which Shelley takes the inscription to *Epipsychidion*) is
   quoted and translated in Medwin, *Life of Shelley,* ed. Forman, pp. 281–
   84.

TWO DRAFTS
I. Draft of "Hymn to Intellectual Beauty"

Bodleian MS Shelley adds. e. 16, pp. 57–60 (line numbers to *Examiner* text (*1817*) are supplied in square brackets)

The awful shadow of some unseen power
Walks tho unseen amongst us—visiting
All human hearts with as inconstant wing
As summer winds that creep from flower to flower—
Like moonbeams that behind some piny mountain shower   5
    It visits with inconstant glance
    Each human mind & countenance
Like hues & harmonies of evening
    Like clouds in starlight wildly spread
    Like memory of music fled   10
That aught that for its grace may be
Dear & yet dearer for its mystery

Spirit of beauty, that doth consecrate
With thine hues all thou dost shine upon
Of human mind or form, where art thou gone   15
Why dost thou pass away   leave our state

---

3. "human hearts" is deleted but underlined, indicating that it is the preferred reading; alternate versions are: "All *living* hearts" and "All that has thought." *1817* reads "This various world."

7. "mind" is written above "*heart*," which Shelley restores in *1817*, having removed "hearts" in line 3.

11. "That aught" may be a slip; corrected to "Like aught" in *1817*.

15. "mind" is written above "*heart.*"

A dim vast vale of tears vacant & desolate
    Ask why the sunbeams not forever
    Weave rainbows oer yon mountain river
Why does aught pass away that once is shewn   20
    Why, care & pain & death & birth
    Cast on the daylight of this earth
Such gloom—why man has such a scope
For love & hate, despondency & hope

No voice from some sublimer world hath ever   25
To wisest poets these responses given
Therefore the names of Ghosts & God & Heaven
Remain the records of their vain endeavour
Frail spells—whose uttered charm might not avail to sever
    From what we hear &   we see   30
    Doubt chance & mutability
Thy light alone like mist oer mountains driven
    Or music by the night wind sent
    Thro some unconscious instrument
Or daylight on a   stream   35
Give light & truth to lifes tumultuous dream

When yet a boy, I sought for ghosts, & sped   [49]
Thro many a lonely chamber vault & ruin
And starlight wood with frantic   pursuing
Hopes of high talk with the departed dead   40[52]
I called on the false name with which our youth is fed

---

18. Orig. *"Why do the sunbeams."*
20. Parallelism would require: "Why aught does pass away."
21. "Why fear and dream and death and birth" in *1817*. I suspect that "dream" may be an error; the term is not immediately clear in context.
24. "For *joy* & hate" originally.
27. See note to line 27, in text.
36. Orig. *"Sheds light."*
37–48, 49–60. In the draft these two stanzas are reversed, but marked to signify their final order. *1817* includes still another stanza missing from the draft, and presumably written later.
41–42 [53–54]. *I called on the false name with which our youth is fed / He heard me not—* : In *1817*: "I called on poisonous names with which our youth is fed; / I was not heard—." I suspect that this change may have been made along with the change in line 27, possibly at Hunt's request. "poisonous names" refers euphemistically to "the names of Demon, Ghost and Heaven;" but "the false name" is specifically "the name of God;" a much stronger attack. Shelley does not revise the line in the corrected *1817* text in the Harvard notebook, however.

He heard me not—I saw them not—
When musing deeply on the lot
Of life—at that sweet time when winds are wooing
    All vital things to wake & bring   45[57]
    News of buds & blossoming
Sudden thy shadow fell on me
I shrieked & clasped my hands in extacy

I vowed that I would dedicate my powers
To thee & thine!—have I not kept the vow   50[62]
With beating heart & streaming eyes even now
I call the phantoms of a thousand hours
Each from his voiceless grave, that have in visioned hours
    Of studious zeal or loves delight
    Outwatched with me the envious night   55[67]
To tell that never joy illumed my brow
    Unlinked with hope that thou shdst free
    This world from its dark slavery
That thou O awful Loveliness
Wouldst give, whatever words cannot express   60[72]

The day becomes more solemn & serene
When noon is past—there is a harmony
In autumn & a lustre in its sky
Which thro' the summer is not heard or seen
As if it cd not be—as if it had not been.   65[77]
        like the truth
    Of nature on my passive youth
Descended to my onward life supply
    Thy calm, to one that worships thee
    And every form containing thee   70[82]
Whom, awful Power—thy spells did bind
To fear himself & love all human kind.

---

46. *buds:* The draft confirms Shelley's correction of "birds" to "buds" in the Harvard clipping.

II. Draft of "Mont Blanc"

Bodleian MS Shelley adds. e. 16, pp. 3–13 (line numbers to *1817* text are supplied in square brackets)

MONT BLANC, AT THE EXTREMITY OF THE VALE OF SERVOZ

     the stream of   various things
Flows thro the mind & rolls its rapid waves
Now dark—now glittering—now reflecting gloom—
Now lending splendour, where from secret caves
The source of human thought its tribute brings   5
Of waters—with a sound but half its own—
Such as a feeble brook will oft assume
In the wild woods among the mountains lone
Where waterfalls around it leap forever
Where woods & winds contend, & a loud river   10
Over its rocks ceaselessly bursts & raves—

Thus thou ravine of Arve, dark deep ravine—
Thou many colored, many voiced vale—

The draft is faint in places and much-canceled; I have tried to decipher text and punctuation as best I can, but punctuation in particular is often doubtful. The following list of deletions and corrections is selective.

title: M.W.S. records in "Note on Poems of 1816" that the scene was observed from the Bridge of Arve, in the vale of Chamouni. But compare Shelley's letter of July 22 to Byron: "The Valley of the Arve (strictly speaking it extends to that of Chamouni) gradually increases in magnificence and beauty, until, at a place called Servoz, where Mont Blanc and its connected mountains limit one side of the valley, it exceeds and renders insignificant all that I had before seen, or imagined" (*Letters of P.B.S.*, I, 494).

4. "caves" changed to "springs" in *1817*. The interwoven rhymes of *B* are more regular (abcbadcd); Shelley may have been consciously striving in *1817* for the more irregular rhyme effects of *Lycidas*.

10. *loud:* Orig. *"vast;"* "vast" in *1817*.

Over whose rocks & pines & caverns sail
Fast cloud shadows & sunbeams   awful scene   15
Where Power, in likeness of the Arve comes down
From the ice gulphs that gird his secret throne—
Bursting thro these dark mountains like the flame
Of lightning thro the tempest, thou dost lie—
Thy giant brood of pines around thee clinging   20
Children of elder time—in whose devotion
The chainless winds still come & ever came
To drink their odours & their solemn swinging
To hear, an old and awful harmony:
Thy caverns echoing to the Arves commotion   25[30]
A loud lone sound no other sound can tame
Thou art pervaded with that ceaseless motion
Thou art the path of that unresting sound
Mighty Ravine—& when I gaze on thee   [34]
Thine earthly rainbows stretched across the sweep   30[25]
Of the aerial waterfall whose veil
Robes some unsculptured image and the sleep
The sudden pause which does inhabit thee
Which when the voices of the desart fail
And its hues wane, doth blend them all & steep   35
Their tumult in its own eternity,   [29]
I seem as in a vision deep & strange   [35]
To muse on my own separate phantasy
My own my human mind which passively
Now renders & receives fast influencings—   40
Holding an unremitted interchange
With the clear universe of things around   [40]
One legion of wild thoughts, whose wandering wings

---

23. *solemn:* Orig. *"mighty;"* "mighty" in *1817.*

30–36. These lines precede line 25 in *1817,* and lines 35–36 are condensed into
one line: "Wraps all in its own deep eternity." There are markings in *B* which
may indicate reversal. But the original order of *B* is probably clearer than the
revised version: the "ceaseless motion" and "unresting sound" of lines 27–28
summarize the coming and going of the winds, the swinging of the pines, and the
commotion of the Arve, the "awful harmony" of one and the "loud lone sound"
of the other; whereas the "rainbows" stretched across the waterfall and the "sudden pause" are what the poet observes when he gazes on the ravine.

31. *Of the aerial waterfall:* Orig. *"Of the white torrent which with its strange
viel."*

33. *The sudden pause:* Orig. *"The momentary death."*

Now float above thy darkness—& now rest
Near the still cave of the witch Poesy   45
Seeking among the shadows that pass by   [45]
Ghosts of all things that are, some shade of thee
Some likeness—some faint image—till the breast
From which they fled recalls them—thou art there.

Some say that gleams of a remoter world   50
Visit the soul in sleep—that death is slumber   [50]
And that its shapes the busy thoughts outnumber
Of those who wake & live—. . . I look on high—
Has some unknown omnipotence unfurled
The veil of life & death—or do I lie   55
In dream, & does the mightier world of sleep   [55]
Spread far around & inaccessibly
Its circles—for the very spirit fails
Driven like a homeless cloud from steep to steep
Which vanishes among the viewless gales   60
Far far above, piercing the infinite sky   [60]
Mont Blanc appears, still, snowy & serene
Its subject mountains their unearthly forms
Pile round it, ice & rock, broad vales between
Of frozen waves unfathomable deeps   65
Blue as the overhanging Heaven that spread   [65]
And wind among the accumulated steeps
A desart peopled by the storms alone
Save where the eagle brings some hunters bone
And the wolf watches her   how hideously   70
Its rocks are heaped around   rude bare & high   [70]
Ghastly & scarred & riven—is this the scene
Where the old Earthquake demon taught her young
Ruin—were these their toys? or did a sea
Of fire envelope once this silent snow—   75
None can reply—all seems eternal now—   [75]
This wilderness has a mysterious tongue

45[43]. The *1817* reading, "Where that or thou art no unwelcome guest," is
deleted in *B*.
58. *for the very spirit fails:* Orig. *"for the very mind is faint / With aspiration."*
70. *watches her:* See note to line 69, in text.

Which teaches awful doubt,—or faith so mild
So solemn, so serene, that man may be
In such a faith with Nature reconciled—   80
Ye have a voice great Mountains—to repeal   [80]
Large codes of fraud & woe—not understood
By all—but which the wise & great & good
Interpret, or make felt, or deeply feel.—

The fields, the lakes, the forests & the streams,   85
Ocean, & all the living things that dwell   [85]
Within the dædal Earth   lightning & rain
Earthquake & fiery floods & hurricane
The torpor of the year when feeble dreams
Visit the hidden buds, or dreamless sleep   90
Holds every future leaf & flower   the bound   [90]
With which from that detested trance they leap—
The works & ways of man—thier death & birth
And that of him & all that his may be
All things that move & breathe, with toil & sound   95
Are born & die, revolve—subside & swell—   [95]
Power dwells apart in its tranquillity
Remote serene & inaccessible:—
And this—the naked countenance of Earth
On which I gaze—even these primæval mountains   100
Teach the adverting mind.—The glaciers creep   [100]
Like snakes that watch thier prey, from thier far fountains

---

80. *In such a faith:* Shelley clearly had difficulty with lines 77–84 [76–83], which are rewritten several times. Intermediate stages in composition appear to read as follows:

This wilderness has a mysterious tongue
And teaches doubt,—*not understood   a voice that to the wise a voice not understood*

By all nor known
Which teaches awful doubt,—or *a belief* faith so mild
So solemn, so serene, that man *again* may be
To such high thoughts of   With such a faith
In such wise faith with Nature reconciled!—

"But for" is written underneath "In such." The line is rewritten completely, thus: "In such a faith with Nature reconciled—." The *1817* text, to the confusion of critics, reads "But for such faith."
85. Orig. *"The powers that rule the world."*

Slow rolling on—there many a precipice
Frost & the Sun in scorn of human power
Have piled, dome pyramid & pinnacle   105
A city of death, distinct with many a tower   [105]
And wall impregnable of beaming ice.
Yet not a city, but a flood of ruin
Is there—that from the boundaries of the sky
Rolls its perpetual stream—vast pines are strewing   110
Its destined path, or in the mangled soil   [110]
Branchless & shattered stand, the rocks drawn down
From yon remotest waste have overthrown
The limits of the dead & living world
Never to be reclaimed—the dwelling place   115
Of insects beasts & birds becomes its spoil   [115]
Their food & their retreat forever gone—
So much of life & joy is lost—the race
Of man flies far in dread, his work & dwelling
Vanish as smoke before the tempests stream   120
And their place is not known.—Below, vast caves   [120]
Shine in the gushing torrents restless gleam
Which from those secret chasms in tumult dwelling
Meet in one vale & one majestic river
The breath & blood of distant lands, forever   125
Bears its loud waters to the Ocean waves   [125]
Breathes its soft vapours to the circling air.

Mont Blanc yet gleams on high—the Power is there—
The still & solemn power of many sights
And many sounds, & much of life and death: 130
In the calm darkness of the moonless nights   [130]
Or the lone light of day the snows descend
Upon that Mountain—none beholds them then
Nor when the flakes burn in the sinking sun
Or the starbeams dart thro them—winds contend   135
Silently there, & heap the snow—their breath   [135]
Rapid & strong but   its home
The voiceless lightning in these solitudes

130. Orig. "much of *good & ill*."
136–37. Orig. *"The glare / Of the clear sun strikes the white waste."*

Keeps innocently, & like vapour broods
Over the snow—the secret strength of things   140
Which governs thought and to the infinite dome   [140]
Of Heaven is as a law—inhabits thee
And what were thou & Earth & stars & sea
If to the human minds imaginings
Silence & solitude were vacancy   145

---

140. *the secret strength of things:* "things" appears to be deleted. Uncanceled lines immediately preceding read: "The unpolluted dome / Of Heaven is not more silent.—;" lines 140–41 may have read: "the secret strength / Which governs thought."

141. Orig. *"rules the starry dome / Which overhangs."*

143. New line begins *"Pause Poet."*

SELECTED BIBLIOGRAPHY
OF TEXTUAL SOURCES

FIRST EDITIONS OF SHELLEY'S POEMS

Alastor; or, The Spirit of Solitude: and Other Poems. London: Baldwin, Cradock, and Joy; and Carpenter and Son, 1816.

History of a Six Weeks' Tour through a Part of France, Switzerland, Germany, and Holland: with Letters Descriptive of a Sail Round the Lake of Geneva, and of the Glaciers of Chamouni. London: T. Hookham, Jr., and C. and J. Ollier, 1817.

Laon and Cythna; or, The Revolution of the Golden City: A Vision of the Nineteenth Century. London: Sherwood, Neely, & Jones; and C. and J. Ollier, 1818.

The Revolt of Islam; A Poem, in Twelve Cantos. London: C. and J. Ollier, 1818.

Rosalind and Helen, A Modern Eclogue; with other Poems. London: C. and J. Ollier, 1819.

The Cenci: A Tragedy, in Five Acts. London: C. and J. Ollier, 1819 [1820].

Prometheus Unbound: A Lyrical Drama in Four Acts, with Other Poems. London: C. and J. Ollier, 1820.

Epipsychidion: Verses Addressed to the Noble and Unfortunate Lady Emilia V—— Now Imprisoned in the Convent of ———. London: C. and J. Ollier, 1821.

Adonais: An Elegy on the Death of John Keats, Author of Endymion, Hyperion etc. Pisa, 1821.

Hellas: A Lyrical Drama. London: Charles and James Ollier, 1822.

Posthumous Poems of Percy Bysshe Shelley [ed. Mary Shelley]. London: John and Henry L. Hunt, 1824.

The Poetical Works of Coleridge, Shelley, and Keats. Paris: A. and W. Galignani, 1829.

The Masque of Anarchy. A Poem, ed. Leigh Hunt. London: Edward Moxon, 1832.

The Shelley Papers. Memoir of Percy Bysshe Shelley, by T. Medwin, and Original Poems and Papers by Percy Bysshe Shelley. Now first collected. London: Whittaker, Treacher, & Co., 1833.

The Poetical Works of Percy Bysshe Shelley, ed. Mrs. Shelley. 4 vols. London: Edward Moxon, 1839; one-volume edition, 1839 [1840].

Essays, Letters from Abroad, Translations and Fragments, ed. Mrs. Shelley. 2 vols. London: Edward Moxon, 1840.

Shelley Memorials, from Authentic Sources, ed. Lady Shelley. London: Smith, Elder & Co., 1859.

Relics of Shelley, ed. Richard Garnett. London: Edward Moxon, 1862.

Verse and Prose from the Manuscripts of Percy Bysshe Shelley, ed. Sir John C. E. Shelley-Rolls and Roger Ingpen. London: privately printed, 1934.

CRITICAL EDITIONS AND TEXTUAL STUDIES

Cameron, Kenneth Neill, ed. *Shelley and His Circle: 1773–1822.* Cambridge, Mass.: Harvard University Press; vols I–II, 1961, vols. III–IV, 1970.

———— ed. *The Esdaile Notebook: A Volume of Early Poems, by Percy Bysshe Shelley.* New York: Alfred A. Knopf, 1964.

Carter, J., and J. Sparrow. "Shelley, Swinburne and Housman," *Times Literary Supplement* (November 21, 1968), 1318–19.

Chernaik, Judith. "Shelley's 'To Constantia': A Contemporary Printing Examined," *Times Literary Supplement* (February 6, 1969), 140.

———— "Textual Emendations for Three Poems by Shelley," *Keats-Shelley Journal,* 19 (1970), 41–48.

Curran, Stuart. "Shelley's Emendations to the *Hymn to Intellectual Beauty,*" *English Language Notes,* 7 (1970), 269–72.

Forman, H. Buxton, ed. *The Poetical Works of Percy Bysshe Shelley*. 4 vols. London: Reeves and Turner, 1876.

—— *The Shelley Library: An Essay in Bibliography*. London: published for the Shelley Society by Reeves and Turner, 1886.

—— ed. *Note Books of Percy Bysshe Shelley, from the Originals in the Library of W. K. Bixby*. 3 vols. Boston: printed for members of the Bibliophile Society, 1911.

—— ed. *The Life of Percy Bysshe Shelley, by Thomas Medwin*. London: Oxford University Press, 1913.

Hutchinson, Thomas, ed. *The Complete Poetical Works of Shelley*. Oxford: Clarendon Press, 1904. London: Oxford University Press, 1905, 1934 (Oxford Standard Authors edition).

Ingpen, Roger, and Walter E. Peck, eds. *The Complete Works of Percy Bysshe Shelley*. 10 vols. London: Ernest Benn, 1926–30 (Julian Edition).

Locock, C. D. *An Examination of the Shelley Manuscripts in the Bodleian Library*. Oxford: Clarendon Press, 1903.

—— ed. *The Poems of Percy Bysshe Shelley, with an Introduction by A. Clutton-Brock*. 2 vols. London: Methuen, 1911.

Massey, Irving. *Posthumous Poems of Shelley: Mary Shelley's Fair Copy Book*. Montreal: McGill-Queen's University Press, 1969.

Matthews, G. M. " 'The Triumph of Life:' A New Text," *Studia Neophilologica*, 32 (1960), 271–309.

—— "A New Text of Shelley's Scene for *Tasso*," *Keats-Shelley Memorial Bulletin*, 11 (1960), 39–47.

—— "Shelley and Jane Williams," *Review of English Studies*, n.s. 12 (1961), 40–48.

—— ed. *Shelley: Selected Poems and Prose*. London: Oxford University Press, 1964.

Notopolous, James A. *The Platonism of Shelley: A Study of Platonism and the Poetic Mind*. Durham: Duke University Press, 1949.

Raben, Joseph A. "Shelley's 'Invocation to Misery:' An Expanded Text," *Journal of English and Germanic Philology*, 65 (1966), 65–74.

—— "Shelley's 'The Boat on the Serchio:' The Evidence of the Manuscript," *Philological Quarterly*, 46 (1967), 58–68.

Reiman, Donald H. *Shelley's "The Triumph of Life:" A Critical Study, Based on a Text Newly Edited from the Bodleian Manuscript.* Urbana: University of Illinois Press, 1965.

Rogers, Neville. *Shelley at Work: A Critical Inquiry.* Oxford: Clarendon Press, 1956. 2nd edition, 1967.

———— ed. *Percy Bysshe Shelley: The Esdaile Poems.* Oxford: Clarendon Press, 1966.

Rossetti, William Michael, ed. *The Poetical Works of Percy Bysshe Shelley.* Revised ed. 3 vols. London: Moxon, 1878.

Taylor, Charles H., Jr. *The Early Collected Editions of Shelley's Poems: A Study in the History and Transmission of the Printed Text.* New Haven: Yale University Press, 1958.

Webb, Timothy. "Shelley's 'Hymn to Venus:' A New Text," *Review of English Studies,* n.s. 21 (1970), 315–24.

Woodberry, George, ed. *The Complete Poetical Works of Percy Bysshe Shelley.* 4 vols. Boston and New York: Houghton Mifflin Co., 1892. One-volume edition, 1901.

———— ed. *The Shelley Notebook in the Harvard College Library.* Cambridge, Mass.: John Barnard Associates, 1929.

Woodings, R. B. "Shelley's widow bird," *Review of English Studies,* n.s. 19 (1968), 411–14.

Zillman, Lawrence John, ed. *Shelley's Prometheus Unbound: A Variorum Edition.* Seattle: University of Washington Press, 1959.

———— *Shelley's Prometheus Unbound: The Text and the Drafts. Towards a Modern Definitive Edition.* New Haven and London: Yale University Press, 1968.

INDEX

Abrams, M. H., 118n
Aeschylus, 22, 73, 89, 100
Angeli, Helen Rossetti, 161n
Arnold, Matthew, 10

Baudelaire, Charles, 80, 82n
Beccaria, Giovanni Battista, 133
Berkeley, George, 139n
Bible, 22, 30n, 77, 91–94 passim, 99, 101, 118n
Blake, William, 27, 84, 121
Bloom, Harold, 59n, 118n, 159n
Bradley, A. C., 81n
Brooks, Cleanth, 160n
Brown, Charles Brockden, 53
Browning, Robert, 5
Byron, Lord, 26, 66, 161n, 164, 179n; *Childe Harold's Pilgrimage,* 118n; "Prophecy of Dante," 120n

Calderon de la Barca, Pedro, 155
Castlereagh, Lord, 83
Catty, C. S., 150
Cavalcanti, Guido, 161n
Clairmont, Claire, 52, 161n, 179n
Coleridge, Samuel Taylor, 5, 28, 29, 38, 48, 81n, 90, 95, 125, 128, 139n; "Dejection: An Ode," 49, 75; "The Eolian Harp," 47; "Fears in Solitude," 61; "France: An Ode," 98, 118n; "Kubla Khan," 41, 122, 129–30; "Lewti," 151; "Ode to the Departing Year," 98, 108, 120n; "Rime of the Ancient Mariner," 64; "To William Wordsworth," 48
Collins, William, 92, 97

Dante, 9, 10, 12, 13, 22, 30n, 67, 147
Della Robbia, Enrico Viviani, 284n
Drummond, Sir William, 58n

Eliot, T. S., 6
Ellis, F. S., 82n

Genesis, 22, 30n, 94
Gisborne, John, 136, 147, 150, 163–64
Gisborne, Maria, 28, 150
Godwin, William, 44
Grabo, Carl, 139n–140n
"Grongar Hill" (Dyer), 61
Guinicelli, Guido, 161n

Havens, R. D., 160n
Hesiod, 101, 113
Hirsch, E. D., Jr., 281n

299

Hunt, Leigh, 75, 83, 148, 161n
Hutchinson, Thomas, 119n

Indicator, 160n

James, Henry, 10, 52

Keats, John, 21, 29, 126, 143, 169–70
King-Hele, Desmond, 140n

Lawrence, D. H., 84
Leavis, F. R., 139n
Liberal, 160n
Literary Pocket-Book, 160n
Locock, C. D., 52, 119n, 139n, 179n
Lucretius, 59n
Luke, Gospel of, 94

Massey, Irving, 281n
Matthews, G. M., 160n, 161n, 178n
Medwin, Thomas, 150, 178n
Milton, John, 4, 9, 10, 21, 86, 100, 115, 119n
Moore, Thomas, 152, 153, 161n

Naples, Revolution of July 1820, 108, 113, 117
Napoleon, 89
Nitchie, Elizabeth, 58n

Ovid, 101, 135–36, 140n
Oxford University and City Herald, 52

Park, B. A., 160n
Peacock, Thomas Love, 30n, 49, 50, 51, 53
"Peterloo" massacre, 7n, 30n, 83, 88
Plato, 22, 30n, 36, 108, 116
"Pleyel," pseud. for Shelley, 52–53

Pottle, Frederick A., 118n, 139n, 161n
Psalms, Book of, 77, 91–93

Radcliffe, Ann, 11
Reiman, Donald H., 80n, 178n
Revelation of St. John, 99, 118n
Rogers, Neville, 161n
Rossetti, W. M., 160n
Rousseau, Jean-Jacques, 35, 44

Scott, Sir Walter, 11
Shakespeare, William, 4, 15, 63, 72, 158
Shelley, Clara, 82n
Shelley, Harriet, 10
Shelley, Mary W., 10, 19, 37, 52, 78–79, 81n, 126, 135, 139n, 141–61 passim, 162–64, 179n; "The Choice," 150, 160n; "Midas," 135
Shelley, Percy Bysshe
—letters, 30n–31n, 42, 45, 49–51, 75, 81n, 82n, 83–84, 89, 102, 109–10, 118n, 127, 136, 147, 149, 160n, 163, 164, 179n
—works, poetical
  Adonais, 5, 8–30 passim, 46, 55, 57, 143, 147, 177
  Alastor, 8–30 passim, 32, 80n, 95, 154
  "Arethusa," 135
  "Buona Notte," 148
  Cenci, The, 30n, 87–88
  "Charles the First," 141
  "Cloud, The," 137, 141; commentary, 130–35; text, 230–33
  "Daemon of the World, The," 58n
  Epipsychidion, 8–30 passim, 55, 128, 154, 160n, 167, 177
  "Epithalamium," 144–45

This book
was set in eleven
point Times Roman;
it was composed, printed
and bound by Kingsport Press, Inc.,
Kingsport, Tenn.; the paper is sixty pound
Warren's Olde Style Wove, manufactured by the
S. D. Warren Company. The design is by Edgar J. Frank.